Tercentenary Essays

in Honor of

ANDREW MARVELL

MISCELLANEOUS
P O E M S.

BY
ANDREW MARVELL, Esq;

Late Member of the Honourable House of Commons.

LONDON,

Printed for *Robert Boulter*, at the *Turks-Head*
in *Cornhill.* M. DC. LXXXI.

Title page, 1681. Reproduced by permission of The Huntington
Library, San Marino, California.

TERCENTENARY ESSAYS
in Honor of
ANDREW MARVELL

edited by

KENNETH FRIEDENREICH

ARCHON BOOKS

1977

Library of Congress Cataloging in Publication Data

Main entry under title:

Tercentenary essays in honor of Andrew Marvell.

    Includes bibliographical references
    1. Marvell, Andrew, 1621–1678—Criticism and
interpretation—Addresses, essays, lectures. I. Friedenreich,
Kenneth, 1947–
PR3546.T4   821'.4   77-21741
ISBN 0-208-01567-1

Filmset in eleven point on twelve point Bembo by
Asco Trade Typesetting Ltd., Hong Kong

For my sister, Eileen Friedenreich
and for
Elliot Ravetz,
John Halperin, and Dewey Faulkner,
colleagues and friends

CONTENTS

ILLUSTRATIONS

PREFACE

PLANS FOR THIS COLLECTION of essays in honor of Andrew Marvell began in late 1974, and owing primarily to the interest and support of James Thorpe III of The Shoe String Press, I have been able to see my plans materialize. I have benefited from the advice of Professors John Halperin of the University of Southern California and Thomas Kranidas of the State University of New York at Stony Brook, both of whom gladly related their experiences in organizing collections of essays by various hands. Certainly, too, I wish to thank my colleagues at the University of Texas at San Antonio, Professors Alan Craven and Peter Morrison, with whom I have discussed various aspects of this anthology, and who have perused portions of the manuscript. To all my contributors I owe a special debt of thanks for politely enduring my collective correspondence, but mostly for their continuing and percipient interest in the life and work of the man we together honor. Finally, I owe to Donna Williams a debt beyond words for her help with this work and with so much more.

For the sake of unity, and in an effort to minimize notes, references to Marvell's poems are taken throughout from the third edition of H.M. Margoliouth's *The Poems and Letters of Andrew Marvell* prepared by the late Pierre Legouis with E.E. Duncan-Jones, and published by the Oxford University Press in two volumes in 1971. As poems are discussed in the essays, I have inserted references to Margoliouth in parentheses when appropriate.

San Antonio, Texas   K.F.

9

INTRODUCTION

The First Marvell Tercentenary, 1921

KENNETH FRIEDENREICH

THE PUBLIC CELEBRATION of the three-hundredth anniversary of Andrew Marvell's birth occurred in an important year generally for the reputation of seventeenth-century poets.[1] Also in 1921, Herbert J.C. Grierson published his anthology, *Metaphysical Lyrics & Poems of the Seventeenth Century: Donne to Butler*. This book vindicated the efforts of those men in the previous century—like William Campbell, Edward Farr, H.F. Lyte, Alexander B. Grosart, H.C. Beeching, to mention a few—who, for a variety of reasons, sought to revive the poetry of Marvell and his contemporaries. A most influential review of Grierson was written by T.S. Eliot; it has become a minor classic. In it, Eliot proposes his theory of "dissociation of sensibility" and uses the occasion of Grierson's collection to advance his vendetta against Marvell's great friend, John Milton.[2] Notwithstanding the controversies he raised, Eliot's essay is a masterful selling job, commending the writers of one epoch to the readers of another. With Eliot's essay, criticism of seventeenth-century English poetry entered the modern age.

Elsewhere in that same year Eliot wrote a paper dealing exclusively with Marvell on the anniversary of poet's birth. Along with the appreciations of other writers and a record of the public observances of the anniversary, Eliot's essay was collected by the Librarian for the City of Hull, William H. Bagguley, and published in a commemorative volume in the following year.[3] Taken together, the accounts of the public observances and the criticism written in

1921 provide us today with a measure of the course of Marvell's reputation and Marvell studies since.

On that particular March 31st the weather was excellent. The Hull city fathers, led by the Lord Mayor and other dignitaries, assembled in the morning sun at the Guildhall and then marched to Holy Trinity Church where, at noon, they were met by the clergy, including the Right Reverend Herbert Hensley Henson, D.D., Lord Bishop of Durham, the Venerable Archdeacon Lambert, and Canon George Buchanan. Soon after services began inside Holy Trinity with the singing of a hymn, text by Milton, "Let us with a gladsome mind." A sermon called "Puritan Citizenship," exemplified, naturally, by the career of Andrew Marvell, was given by the Lord Bishop. After services, the whole procession was resumed and moved into the public square where a statue of the man they honored that day stands. The group looked on as four hundred fifty boys representing the Hull Grammar School placed a laurel wreath at the base of the effigy, a likeness of the school's most famous alumnus, whose father, the Reverend Andrew Marvell, Sr., had become its headmaster in 1624. Next was lunch at the City Hotel, in which over two hundred guests participated. Meanwhile, down in London, where Marvell had represented Hull in Parliament for so many years (1659–78), delegates of the Society of Yorkshiremen laid a wreath on the tablet in the church of St. Giles-in-the-Fields, the poet's final resting place following his sudden (and suspicious?) death on 16 August 1678. He supposedly died of an ague, which was to the seventeenth-century poet what consumption was to the nineteenth-century poet. The exact whereabouts of Marvell's remains in the church are unknown.

The principal attraction of the day in Hull was the public meeting which commenced at three in the afternoon. The featured speaker was the Right Honourable Augustine Birrell, author and statesman, who had written a slight biography of Marvell in 1905 in the English Men of Letters series. He characterized Marvell as "a powerful trenchant thinker, an honest incorruptible man" (p. 58). This was no startling revelation to be sure but, as Elizabeth Donno shows below, an expression of a belief nurtured throughout the eighteenth century—Marvell was a model politician.[4] It was on the strength of this belief that Captain Thompson undertook to edit Marvell's works in 1776.

On the other hand in 1921 Marvell's esteem as a poet rested on those lyrics published in 1681 as *Miscellaneous Poems*, a reflection of critical taste and opinion nurtured throughout the nineteenth century, a view with which Birrell wholeheartedly concurred: "His satires, though interesting and full of history, are too rough, too coarse, to entitle him to a high place in our literature; while his prose writings, though they contain striking passages, are now seldom read except by a biographer or an inveterate controversialist" (pp. 60–61).

In the discussion following Birrell's talk, the Lord Mayor recognized the Lord Bishop. He reiterated the example of Marvell's career—purposeful, earnest, sensible—suggesting that others would do well to emulate it: "Andrew Marvell represents a blend which is but rarely found today in the strenuous and vulgar business of modern life, the combination of fine culture with practical politics which redeems culture from becoming mere dilettantism and lifts practical politics out of mere business. That precious blend of the best gift of education with the best gift of life's experience is now all too rare" (p. 25). The heavy didactic theme was sounded again in the meeting by Alderman F. Askew, Chairman of the Hull Education Committee, who declared that young people "especially those who in the hands of our teachers, will profit very largely by the prominence given to the worthy character of Andrew Marvell" (p. 27).

The literary opinions Bagguley collected complement the civic-minded and patriotic approbation that Marvell garnered from the scions of church and state. Invariably the critics agree with Birrell about basing Marvell's reputation solely on his lyrics, most of which were probably composed at Nunappleton between 1650–52. In particular, they revere the poems about nature, and English nature at that. This, they believe, is "the real Marvell, the great Marvell":

> His love for the countryside is purer, less complicated by tradition, comes straighter from the heart, than than of Thomson, Shenstone, and the early nature-poets of the following century.
>
> (Cyril Falls, p. 88)

> The poems which Marvell wrote during these two heavenly years are unique in our literature. Nothing in the least like them was produced before them, nor for a century and a half after them.
>
> (Edmund Gosse, p. 103)

There is very little passion in his poetry; but much affection; no majesty, but much grace. Innocence and Quiet were his Muses; looking both at fields and at people he reaped "the harvest of the eye." His is pastoral poetry before it hardens into conventionalism.

(J. C. Squire, p. 117)

[Marvell] has a finer range of natural ecstasy.... In the small world of the Fairfax estate—garden, park, and river leas—he expressed into poetry a philosophy as large as that which Coleridge could not reduce into prose.

(Edward Wright, pp. 125–26)

J.H. Massingham declares that with the exception of his contemporary Henry Vaughan, Marvell "was the only seventeenth-century poet to bespeak Nature to her face" (p. 109). He also declares that "His poetry accurately reflects the transition between the metaphysical and the Augustan schools, and yet holds these incompatibles as perfectly as he reconciled the Puritan and the Cavalier as a man, and Republicanism and Monarchism as a public servant, because he was both and neither, but a personal third into which they melted in harmony." Even in a more sophisticated discussion of Marvell's wit, possessed of "a kind of toughness," the product of an "educated mind," Eliot sounds the themes of probity and good sense that are pervasive in the Hull celebration and in the various appreciations of Marvell in Bagguley's volume (pp. 76–77). However, when Eliot says that Marvell's wit "involves, probably, a recognition, implicit in the expression of every experience, of other kinds of experience which are possible," we are moving, I think, into a new phase of Marvellian interpretation, one more familiar to us now— Marvell's verse is not easily written about because the responses he elicits from readers are multiple and prolix. It is to this question that Thomas Clayton and French Fogle address themselves in their essays below.

The only place the critics in 1921 apparently differ from the public servants who honored Marvell is in their wish that he had not so fervently pursued politics that he ceased writing lyric poems. Falls compares Marvell's decision to the premature death of Keats (p. 98); Squire is even more specific in calculating our loss: "Marvell did not hold high office, and he seldom spoke in the House; few, probably, took the slightest notice of his admirable example of incorruptibility; and if, through his entrance into politics, we lost a few lyric poems equal to his best, we have, I imagine, lost more than his contemporaries gained" (p. 120). Squire's calculation belies a feeling of dismay, even of betrayal. How could so gifted a poet abandon his muse to take up the mundane business of politics? Of course a complaint (or lament) like this can only be made if one is prepared to dismiss everything that Marvell wrote after the retirement at Nunappleton. Celebrants at the first tercentenary believed that Marvell wrote his greatest verse before he was thirty and that it was precious, to be cherished; the poetry ceased when he went into public life. To the civil authorities who honored him, Marvell's poems were an admirable preface to that departure.

The tenor of the first tercentenary was public and ceremonial, enough so as to merit speculation that if Marvell had enjoyed only his literary reputation in 1921, and had not faithfully served the citizens of Hull for many years, his "day" would have been far less elaborate. He was to the men of that time an outstanding and honest public servant who happened to write poetry, and whose best work appropriately glorified English nature, "a cultivated nature, a nature of parklands and gardens" (Falls, p. 88). This is not to denigrate the desire of the citizens of Hull to honor one of their own; after all, when will Hailey, Idaho, honor Ezra Pound or Rutherford, New Jersey, do as much for William Carlos Williams? The first Andrew Marvell tercentenary honored the poet and the patriot according to the traditions and tastes of the eighteenth and nineteenth centuries. Owing to this established bias, it did not break new ground about the poet and his work. Writing after the event Legouis praised the impulse that led to the celebration, but notes "the somewhat naïve, even clumsy worship of Marvell's memory in the town he represented in Parliament for twenty years."[5] Surveying the criticism collected by Bagguley, Carey dismisses the work of all but Eliot and Wright as "negligible."[6] The view may be as accurate as it is severe. While it is fair to say that no one would disagree with Birrell and the others about the greatness of Marvell's lyrics and of their unanimous recognition of his worth as a nature poet, there is something very precious about their response to Marvell's work that even the few excerpts quoted above bear out. Their interpretations are casual and impressionistic; they confirm old saws rather than stimulating new responses to the poems. They but scratch the polished surface of Marvell's writing.

Now in another time and place, we have come the full span of Marvell's years since that sunny morning in March 1921. Our world is very different, but politicians still seem to try their hands at writing albeit as novelists of intrigue rather than as satirists or pugnacious pamphleteers. We surely do not "celebrate" the anniversary of Marvell's death, but we honor him nonetheless in our own way. Nor are we alone—the University of York is planning a lecture series in 1977—78, as is the University of Hull.

Our opinion of Marvell today is better informed because we possess numerous distinct advantages over the participants in the first tercentenary. These readily come to mind. Bagguley included as the last item in his collection, perhaps as a promise of things to come, a letter written by the poet to Lord Wharton, dated 2 April 1667 (pp. 128–31). It was supplied to Bagguley by H.M. Margoliouth, then at work on his edition of *Marvell's Poems & Letters*, which appeared in two volumes in 1927. Margoliouth revised the edition himself in 1953, and in 1972 it was revised again, with a much expanded *Commentary*, by Pierre Legouis and E.E. Duncan-Jones. We possess the Marvell canon in an edition of copious detail that our forebears did not. In 1928, Legouis published his exhaustive biographical and critical study, *Andre Marvell, poetè, puritain, patriotè* (see note 1), organizing the facts of Marvell's life and career more fully than had every previously been done. Our knowledge of Marvell as a polemicist has benefited from George deF. Lord's edition in the series *Poems on Affairs of State* (1963). We possess at the second tercentenary certainly better organized information about Marvell's life and work. We have benefited as well from the labors of literary historians and critics, who have produced in the interim a number of books whose impact has forced the readers of many different poets, Marvell included, to rethink outdated and comfortable notions, to reassess impressions made by poems, sharpened responses, and solutions to long-standing puzzles of interpretation. Among these are Douglas Bush's *Mythology and the Renaissance Tradition in English Poetry* (1932; revised 1963), Rosemund Tuve's *Elizabethan & Metaphysical Imagery* (1947), Rosemary Freeman's *English Emblem Books* (1948), Ruth Wallerstein's *Studies in Seventeenth-Century Poetic* (1950), Maren-Sofie Røstvig's *The Happy Man*

(1954–58), and Earl Miner's three studies of the seventeenth-century modes, Metaphysical, Cavalier, and Restoration, published between 1969 and 1975. Within Marvell studies particularly we have benefited from the 1940 study of the poet by Muriel C. Bradbrook, who contributes to this volume, writing then in collaboration with M.G. Lloyd Thomas; from perceptive essays, such as those on "The Garden" by Frank Kermode (1952), or Renato Poggioli (1959); and certainly from Rosalie Colie's *"My Ecchoing Song"*: *Andrew Marvell's Poetry of Criticism* (1970), a work whose influence is manifest in no small way in the succeeding pages. Marvell's reputation is secure as ever—only now it can truly be said to rest on his poetry and prose tracts. He has had many perceptive readers.

How far attitudes towards Marvell have changed since the 1921 celebration is shown dramatically by the case of *Upon Appleton House*. Many of the early celebrants ignored it. Others believed it had its great moments, but thought it an incomprehensible and sprawling exercise. Eliot goes to it himself to illustrate one of Marvell's "undesirable images" (pp. 69–70). "The longest of the lyrical poems," Falls writes, *"Upon Appleton House*, is not among the best. It contains a tedious history of how the estate came into the hands of the Fairfaxes" (p. 91). A few years later, F.L. Lucas complains that the poem is full of "intellectual abortions."[7] In her quirky little book about Marvell, V. Sackville-West turns to *Upon Appleton House* to display one of the poet's mistakes, "opening as it does with a string of grotesque exaggerations which must be endured before the poem flows out into the simple and splendid verses that rank with Marvell at his best."[8] For George Williamson, the poem contains "a fairly large number of figures which miscarry."[9] As Professor Kermode has pointed out more recently, *Upon Appleton House* has had a recent history of mishandling.[10] There is in the following pages considerable work on this poem. Professor Bradbrook, for instance, suggests that in *Upon Appleton House* Marvell has drawn freely from the traditions of picture and performance intrinsic to the Jacobean court masque. In "Some Apocalyptic Strains in Marvell's Poetry" Professor Summers deals with the poem as an expression of millennial change which Marvell, in his retirement, sees about him. Two very different essays deal with the poem almost exclusively —Isabel G. MacCaffrey argues that the power of the imagination is the unifying theme and process behind the peregrinations in

Upon Appleton House, whereas Professor Røstvig deals with its "Silent Structure" in numerology and circular symbols. These lucid papers attest to a greater appreciation for and understanding of Marvell's long poem than in 1921.

While we would not disagree with the earlier critics' ragard for Marvell as a "nature-poet," our attitudes towards his accomplishment have certainly matured: Falls wrote that Marvell's love for the countryside was "less complicated by tradition"[!] than later poets, and Squire asserted that Marvell's "is pastoral poetry before it hardens into conventionalism." But the whole point we have since learned is that in a period when conceptions of pastoral were being shifted and adapted, Marvell was among the most ingenious. One hates to dispel Falls's quaint suggestion that Marvell's love of nature comes straight from the heart, but we have come to recognize through the years the intelligent, literate, paradoxical, and often humorous perception through which such feeling is strained. Consider, for example, Colie's discussion of the Mower poems: "Pastoral is cruelly intellectualized in these poems—and to intellectualize is radically to invert pastoral values in any case, which frankly relinquish intellectual burdens for the embrace of comfortable natural passivity. In his expose of the *naif*, the poet manages to make us love man's innocence; he manages then at once to play devil's advocate and to canonize withal the beauty and the inadequacy of the pastoral program."[11] The caliber of this criticism does not diminish in any sense our apprehension of beauty in Marvell's poems on nature, but it would suggest that he probably did not loll about in it, waiting for the muses of Innocence and Quiet to set his fancy to flight. The complexity of perspective in his "nature-poems" makes our impression of his greatness as a pastoralist that much more convincing, as I think Harold Toliver shows below in his handling of "The Gallery" in "Marvell's Songs and Pictorial Exhibits."

Where this collection differs further from the first is in the space it devotes to Marvell's political verse and pamphlets. Birrell, we saw, dismissed the writings of the later period as coarse and of little interest except to the "inveterate controversialist." Interest in this later prose and verse has really been a development of the past twenty years; D.I.B. Smith's edition of the two parts of *The Rehearsal Transpos'd* (1971) is the first work published in a project to at last supercede Grosart's edition of the prose works (1872–75).[12] We no longer jettison the work of the parliamentary period—Marvell's political writing reveals qualities of observation and wit which earlier critics believed to be exclusively the property of his Nunappleton lyrics. But this work can stand on its own terms, as is seen in the importance it has to Professor Summers's apocalyptic thesis. Moreover, Warren Chernaik tells us in "Marvell's Satires: The Artist as Puritan" that Marvell was actually rethinking his aesthetic positions in his later work, and that he came to see the function of the artist in society in terms completely different from that in his lyrics. In Joseph Messina's essay following Chernaik's, this new attitude is shown operating in the depiction of heroism in *The Last Instructions to a Painter*.

In spite of the changes in Marvell studies since the 1921 tercentenary, one issue in particular remains to challenge us, one that Eliot identified: "The quality which Marvell had, this modest and impersonal virtue—whether we call it wit or reason or even urbanity—we have patently failed to define" (p. 78). What is, after all, that quality of Marvell's work that seems to create simultaneous sensations of tension and release, impressions of sophistication and innocence, the reflex action of ideas that turn in on themselves—all beneath the seamless surface of smooth lines? Joseph Pequigney takes up this challenge in his discussion of "A Dialogue between the Resolved Soul and Created Pleasure," "A Dialogue between the Soul and Body," and "Eyes and Tears"; it is the focus of the essays by Fogle and Clayton, and of John Hackett's acute analysis of "To His Coy Mistress," although certainly all of the contributors address themselves indirectly to Eliot's query. Perhaps when all is said, we will find ourselves without an answer, which is what Donno means when she terms Marvell "unhoopable."

There is much new and trenchant thinking about Marvell's writing in the succeeding pages, and I have felt much excitement as the essays began to catch up to me through the mails over the past months. If, however, someone were to ask me, "Why another Marvell tercentenary?" I would not go to the excellent materials we now possess for study of his life, or even the lucid criticism his poems have engendered. I would go to my edition of his poems and turn to "The Garden" or "To His Coy Mistress" and say that this verse or continues to delight me in the study and, moreover, delights in the act of teaching poetry in the classroom. Marvell "teaches" very well, I think. And in a time when poetry is too often an after-thought, that is reason enough to honor his memory.

Notes

1. By discussing the "first" tercentenary, it is not my intention to recount the full history of Marvell's reputation since 1678 to the present. In addition to Professor Donno's essay below, the reader is referred to the following: Pierre Legouis, *Andrew Marvell: Poet, Puritan, Patriot* (1928; revised and translated, Oxford: Clarendon Press, 1965), especially pp. 224–44; George deF. Lord, "Introduction," in *Andrew Marvell: A Collection of Critical Views* (Englewood Cliffs, N.J.: Prentice Hall, 1968), pp. 1–17; John Carey, "Introduction," in *Andrew Marvell*, Penguin Critical Anthologies (Baltimore: Penguin Books, 1969), pp. 17–33; 61–71; Michael Wilding, "Marvell's Reputation for Patriotism and Probity," *N&Q*, ns 17 (1970): 252–54; and also Gillian Szanto, "Recent Studies in Marvell," *ELR* 5 (1975): 273–86.

2. Reprinted in T.S. Eliot, *Selected Essays* (1932; New York: Harcourt Brace & World, 1964), pp. 241–50.

3. William H. Bagguley, ed., *Andrew Marvell, 1621–1678, Tercentenary Tributes* (London: Oxford University Press, 1922). Page references to essays and speeches quoted above appear in parentheses.

4. Also see Carey's "Introduction," pp. 23–24.

5. Legouis, *Andrew Marvell*, p. 238.

6. Carey, "Introduction," p. 32.

7. F.L. Lucas, *The New Statesman*, August 1923.

8. V. Sackville-West, *Andrew Marvell* (London: Faber & Faber, 1929), p. 39.

9. George Williamson, *The Donne Tradition* (1930; reprint ed., New York: Noonday Press, 1958), p. 154.

10. Frank Kermode, ed., *The Selected Poetry of Andrew Marvell* (New York: New American Library, 1967), p. xxii.

11. Rosalie Colie, *"My Ecchoing Song": Andrew Marvell's Poetry of Criticism* (Princeton: Princeton University Press, 1970), pp. 40–41.

12. Some notable recent work on the pamphlets and satires includes Raymond L. Anselment, "'Betwixt Jest and Earnest': Ironic Reversal in Andrew Marvell's *The Rehearsal Transpos'd*," *MLR* 66 (1971): 282–93; also his "Satiric Strategy in *The Rehearsal Transpos'd*," *MP* 68 (1970): 137–50; John M. Wallace, *Destiny His Choice: The Loyalism of Andrew Marvell* (Cambridge: Cambridge University Press, 1968); and D.I.B. Smith, "The Political Beliefs of Andrew Marvell," *UTQ* 36 (1966): 55–67.

THE UNHOOPABLE MARVELL

ELIZABETH STORY DONNO

MARVELL'S REPUTATION as a lyric poet has been extremely high in recent years, as the flood of exegetical publications sweeping him into one or another literary, religious, or philosophical eddy attests. Whether these exegetical approaches reveal more about the critical tactics of his twentieth-century proponents than about the poetry is a moot question. In this essay, therefore, I propose to place the poet and prose writer in a historical context, recovering (so far as possible) the ways in which his contemporaries viewed his writings and then glancing at the ways in which subsequent generations came to perceive them.[1] In and of itself such a procedure offers an insight into changing literary sensibilities: the poetry and prose of one seventeenth-century writer serving as litmus paper to detect attitudes that became dominant in later periods. Having established this overview, I shall then consider four of the "early" lyrics in an attempt to demonstrate the hazards of classifying Marvell as representative of any one literary, religious, or philosophic category.

In contrast to his prose writings, the several kinds of difficulties that Marvell's poetry presents should be acknowledged at the outset. Excluding for the moment those that may be termed "intrinsic" since they relate to points of interpretation, one is faced with extrinsic difficulties not only in ascertaining where to place individual poems within the canon but also in ascertaining the canon itself. The hard evidence of publication indicates that only ten selections (one of them in part) were published during the poet's lifetime, and of these only half carried his name or initials. Of the five he chose to lay claim to, all were occasional in nature: the Greek and Latin verses on the birth of Charles I's fifth child, written while he was still a student at Cambridge; the commendatory poems to Lovelace's *Lucasta*, to Dr. Witty's translation of the *Popular Errors* (in Latin and English), to Milton's *Paradise Lost* (the latest in date); and the elegy on the death of Lord Hastings. Though seventeenth-century manuscript copies of a few of the poems are extant, indication of their circulation among his private friends is scant. Such small evidence of publication of circulation affords the critic a slender basis for working out any scheme of poetic development.

Evidence from genre also affords little help. Do the "Dialogue between the Resolved Soul and Created Pleasure" and the "Dialogue between the Soul and the Body", presenting contrary points of view, reflect proximity of composition or a consequent treatment of countering ideas or even a resolution of them (and, if so, which is which)? A predilection for the dialogue form, whether in poems designed as literary *débats* or for musical accompaniment as J.B. Leishman has suggested (*The Art of Marvell's Poetry*, pp. 203–18), might well prompt one to place all of them early in Marvell's career; yet his poetic practice may as easily have been recurrent as developmental. Finally, evidence from style, difficult to rely on with any Renaissance poet but particularly so with a markedly varied lyricist, is equally of scant help.

Still the bits and pieces of factual data provide at least presumptive evidence for chronological groupings and convey some sense of his early reputation and literary associations. One instance is the publishers' handling of two of the texts that Marvell acknowledged. The commendatory poem, written before 1648, for the publication in the following year of his "noble friend" Richard Lovelace's *Lucasta*, was shifted in some copies from its position in the middle of the commendatory group to pride of place as the first of fourteen contributions. Again, the elegy on the death of Lord Hastings, which Marvell contributed in 1649 to the collection entitled *Lachrymae Musarum*, was also shifted in the second issue (dated 1650 but almost certainly following immediately on the first),[2] in accord with the publisher's notion of the degree and quality of the writers. In conjunction, the two instances suggest that by 1649–50 Marvell was known as a poet in Cavalier circles and that his publishers felt his name one to be reckoned with.

The occasional nature of so many of the poems, coupled with internal allusions, affords other clues. Whether composition of the satire on Flecknoe coincided with a period when both the subject and the poet were in Rome or derived from subsequent tranquil recollection is problematical, but the occasions for the *Horatian Ode*, the *First Anniversary*, *Tom May's Death*, etc., provide their own specificity. Published nearly four years after the poet's death (under the direction of his *quondam* housekeeper), the Folio of 1681 remains the most certain guide to attribution, though not to chronology, even if the major poems on Cromwell were cancelled from most copies. As is well known, these three poems were first given general circulation in 1776 in Captain Edward Thompson's three-volume edition, a valuable, if at times misguided, effort, elicited not so much by its editor's admiration for the poetry he printed, including the odd eighteenth-century hymn or ballad, as by his conviction that Marvell was a political figure worthy of attention. (As late as 1861, Herman Merivale could still question whether the *Horatian Ode* was really from the pen of Marvell.)

Taking the evidence then, scanty as it is, one can reasonably assign the lyrics relating to topics used by courtly poets to a period some time between 1637 and 1650 (a date somewhat earlier than most commentators allow), the so-called nature poems and those with a Yorkshire milieu to 1650–52, and the rest to a period subsequent to these dates, with internal allusions or the occasion of writing providing the best indication of time of composition.

In contrast to the poetry, the prose offers few extrinsic problems even though of the five polemical works (counting the two parts of the *Rehearsal Transpros'd*, 1672, 1673, as two publications), only one of them appeared initially with Marvell's name on the title page. Each of them is dated, and contemporaneous references (including those of Marvell himself) solve the problems of their attribution.[3] In a period of prolific anonymous pamphleteering, how were contemporaries so confidently able to assign authorship?

These five pieces, each dealing with some aspect of religious controversy—scarcely subject matter that would be expected to outlive the specific occasions that initiated them—were crammed into five and a half years in a literary career that spanned some forty years. What is of most interest is that they largely, but by no means totally, determined Marvell's reputation for nearly two centuries.[4] And what primarily obtained was the image of a witty

satirist and an incorruptible patriot. This special allocation of attributes is itself noteworthy in that Marvell's age produced satiric wits
aplenty—Rochester, Buckingham, Butler, Dryden—as well as
patriots aplenty, if not all incorruptible.

Though endorsing Cromwellian policies somewhat tardily,
Marvell—at least overtly—seems never to have wavered in his
allegiance after 1654–65 (or, as he would have it, 1657). While one
may have cause to regret much about his *Poem upon the Death of
O.C.*, it is the last of several tributes to the engineer of the Commonwealth. Nonetheless at the Restoration shifts in allegiance on the
part of literary figures did indeed take place, signified by their public
protestations—panegyrics on the death of one ruler offset by paeans
on the return of another—with Waller and Dryden coming conspicuously to mind. By the 1670's the religious and political turbu-
lence leading up to the Popish Plot inevitably induced others even
more pronounced. The alterations in the social, religious, and
political order characterizing the era must, admittedly, have been
provocative of extreme and complex responses—witness the introduction of the word "trimmer"; yet it was the image not of the
poet but of the M.P. from Hull, the fearless opponent of religious
and political tyranny, that emerged as one untouched by corruption
(justifiably or not). The seemingly ephemeral controversial works
were to cast a long shadow.

The earliest, and the most useful for my purpose since it generated the most immediate popular reaction, was undertaken to
confront Samuel Parker, archdeacon and prebendary of Canterbury
and chaplain to Archbishop Sheldon. Born and bred a Puritan
(specifically a Grueller), Parker first met Marvell (who later takes
occasion to remind him of it), at the home of their common acquaintance John Milton. After taking Anglican orders, he became a staunch
royalist and apologist for the establishment, publishing his *Ecclesiastical Polity* in 1670, which was to be answered by the dissenting
minister John Owen, and then following this up with a counter-
attack on Owen. These two works supplied Marvell with a certain
amount of ammunition, but it was nominally a preface (contributed
to Bishop Bramhall's *Vindication of Himself*) that triggered his entry
into ecclesiastical controversy.

Latching on to a technique that was to serve him in good stead
in his second controversy as well, resulting in *Mr. Smirke: Or the*

Divine in Mode, Marvell drew on a current dramatic production to provide a topical correlative. First performed on 7 December 1671, *The Rehearsal* by the Duke of Buckingham (and others) mocked literary *hubris* in general and that of Dryden's heroic drama in particular, singling out that author's propensity for "transprosing" or turning prose into verse and verse into prose "alternativè," as a contemporary put it. Marvell, in turn, was to mock ecclesiastical *hubris* in particular, by applying the pseudonym of the literary "Mr. Bays" to his opponent (in an example of "equivocal generation") and reinforcing the allusion by entitling his work *The Rehearsal Transpros'd*. In choosing to relate elements of the amusing world of London theatrical activity to the (somewhat duller) elements of religious controversy, he adopted an apt strategy, one offering in journalistic fashion a combination that cut across social and religious divisions. Upon its anonymous publication in the fall of 1672, Part I was to elicit half a dozen replies—in themselves a measure of his success.

Like Marvell's own contributions, all of the replies, depending as they do on extensive quotation from the work under defense or attack, have their excessive *langeurs* for a twentieth-century non-involved reader, but most of them also have their moments of vigor. Most usefully, they indicate the ways in which contemporaries responded to the Marvellian prose style, sufficiently distinctive, it seems, to account for their attribution to him of four anonymous or pseudonymous publications.

It is well to consider initially how and where Marvell is seen to fit into the post-Reformation tradition of religious-political controversy, particularly since it has recently been alleged that he identified himself as a "latter-day Martin Marprelate." Does the evidence support this view? One of the earliest replies was that of the London player Richard Leigh, who links Marvell *and* Milton to the tradition of Martin at least by their stellar qualities if not by their style: "Every age," he announces, "is not constellated for heroes; such prodigies are as rarely seen as a new star or a phoenix. Once, perhaps in a century of years, there may arise a Martin Marprelate, a Milton or such a brave as our present author."[5] Leigh's pamphlet was shortly followed by the ecclesiastical Mr. Bays's *Reproof*, a work which Marvell, having seen some three hundred of its more than five hundred pages before publication, adjudged "the *rudest* book . . . that ever was published (I may say), since the first invention of printing" (my italics).[6] Calling his opponent "a true whelp of old Martin's," Parker attempts in it to fix the charge of Martinism; "in one page," Marvell plaintively says in the *Rehearsal Transpros'd*, Part 2, "you do it four times," but in an assumed "lucky hit." Apart from such a lucky hit, it seems dubious, however, that Parker intended anything more than a general identification with the (heretofore) most notorious anti-episcopal polemicist. Rather, it is Parker himself who best exemplifies a development of the vituperative style that had its origin in Martinism. While, admittedly, any single excerpt from a work of controversy is an inadequate index to the whole, one may nonetheless note the different character of the following two quotations:

> Is it any marvel that we have so many swine, dumb dogs, non-residents with their journeymen the hedge priests, so many lewd livers, as thieves, murderers, adulterers, drunkards, cormorants, rascals, so many ignorant and atheistical dolts, so many covetous popish bishops in our ministry; and so many and so monstrous corruptions in our Church, and yet likely to have no redress? Seeing our impudent, shameless, and wainscot-faced bishops, like beasts, contrary to the knowledge of all men and against their own consciences, dare . . . affirm all to be well where there is nothing but sores and blisters, yea where the grief is even deadly at the heart.

> But yet, however, you may assure yourself that he will never take any notice of such a despicable yelper as you, unless with a dog whip. Thou prevaricator of all the laws of buffoonery, thou dastard craven, thou swad, thou mushroom, thou coward in heart, word, and deed, thou Judas, thou crocodile, thus (though it were in thy greatest necessity) after having professed wit and rhythm these fifty years, to snivel out such a whining submission in public is past all precedent of cowardice from the Trojan War to this day. . . .

The first quotation is an example of Elizabethan railing by Martin, soon to become a fugitive; the second is an example of Caroline railing by Parker, a stalwart of the religious establishment. Here the vituperative language is directed very much *ad hominem*.

Marvell, on the other hand, opts for a quite different technique, one based on his recognition that in a street "argument," the auditory, as he avers, concludes that the greatest railer has the least reason.[7] While he directs a sufficiency of piercing gibes at Parker, they represent, in sum, a scattering of shot, so much so that in order to illustrate Marvell's railing "in the common scurrilous way," Richard Leigh is forced to juxtapose two references almost a hundred pages apart in the original text, and the examples he refers to are to his use of the (scarcely shocking) terms "Buffoons"—on p. 207—and "Brokers"—on p. 106, plus a useful "etc." It is precisely his considered civility that Marvell's opponents found so irritating. Commenting on the word "argument" rather than "brawl" in the quotation mentioned above, Leigh snorts, "How civil that is . . . so modest, so gent." Commenting on how this "virtuoso" wounds and cuts, Edmund Hickeringill, the rector of All Saints, Colchester, notes that Marvell keeps a plaster at hand to make all whole again, "crying, O Lord! Sir, I beg your pardon; and then, as you were. All is well again."

Marvell's technique in Part 1 is to punctuate his serious treatment with bursts of levity in a farrago of colloquial and learned anecdote (e.g., "the incorrigible scold . . . with her two thumb-nails in the nit-cracking posture," from Montaigne's *Essays*), pieces of doggerel, obscure historical allusions, and, as his contemporaries invariably point out, farfetched and chimerical conceits. In his own words, it is to be both "merry and angry" but without profaning "those things which are and ought to be most sacred." No friend to Marvell's views, Anthony Wood acknowledged the novelty of his approach, recording Parker's disinclination, following the publication of Part 2, to re-enter the fray "with an untowardly combatant so hugely well versed and experienced in the then but newly refined art (though much in mode and fashion ever since) of sportive and jeering buffoonery." Nonetheless, Dryden, also no friend to Marvell's views by this date, echoes Parker in calling him (1681) a "deceased Judas," and, on one occasion, in speaking of the Elizabethan Martin, he inverts the charge by terming *him* "the *Marvel* of those times . . . who sanctified libels and scurrility to the use of the Good Old Cause."[8]

If then the charge of being a latter-day Martin does not altogether fit (though, one might add, that of being "a coffee-house virtuoso" does), what stylistic elements did his contemporaries remark on? In general, their focus is, first of all, on his use of extravagant rhetoric and, secondly, on his addiction to the proverbial, the latter technique apparently predicated (as Marvell put it in *Mr. Smirke*) on the homely Scotch proverb that an ounce of wit is worth a pound of clergy.

Richard Leigh notes that, in addition to knowing "all the moods and figures" of railing derived from his "scolding commonplace book," Marvell raises and orders his "martial phantoms" in order to set them fighting "through all the tropes and figures of rhetoric."[9] Such a device or "politic fetch" works, it is said, on the assumption that no answerer would have the courage to engage "such a rhetorical soldier" unless he too were able "to give battle in all the metaphors of war." Thus it is that Marvell indulges "in the love of his chimerical conceits, struck blind with his own dazzling Ideas of the Sun, and admiring those imaginary heights which his fancy has raised."[10] A second respondent comments that "sure his rhetoric was born in a time when metaphors were cheap; for though they be farfetched, yet sure they were not dear bought, he is so prodigal of them." Parker himself observes that Marvell achieves his "professed fooling" either by way of "similitude or rhythm [rime] or story [history]," including the techniques of playing on single words, of confusing his introductions and transitions, and of injecting his "smutty" imaginings. Even an admirer, penning a tribute c. 1689, likewise admits that when it came to reproaching a prince's folly or a prelate's pride, "poetic fury" might indeed misguide his pen.

It is, however, an unidentified antagonist who in 1674 sums up most specifically and *in extenso* this particular aspect of Marvell's style:

> Your similitudes are most apposite and unparalleled.... Your examples are without example; for quibbles you are the very wordpecker of wordpeckers, and for rhetorical flourishes (like a whistler before a morris dance), you carry it away from them all with flying colors, your works being most artificially set forth and beautified with choice pieces of poetry, like a cowturd stuck with gillyflowers; most dextrously interwoven with natural experiments; most richly embroidered with theological notions, most magnificently tapestried with reasons of state, hanging down in clusters like bunches of grapes; and most prodigiously stuffed with

28

witty conceits, thicker than cloves in a gammon of bacon at Easter. Your style is for the most part smooth and insinuating, yet happily diversified here and there with jerks and short girds as if you had a piece of the string-halt [the blind spavin incident to horses], although in your clauses and parentheses you are as unhoopable as if you stood with one leg at Dover and the other at Calais.

Again Richard Leigh (called by Marvell, along with the other respondents, a "ghost" of Parker) underscores Marvell's addiction to the proverbial: "For I cannot but remark this admirable way he has of embellishing his writings [with] proverbial: wit . . . which (to express them proverbially) are all out as much to the purpose as any of Sancho Panza's proverbs. For the truth of this comparison, I shall only appeal to the leaf-turners of *Don Quixote*. Some there are below the quality of the squire's wit and would have better become the mouth of his Lady Joan or any old gammer that drops sentences and teeth together."

Parker too remarks on Marvell's proverbial style, as well as on some aspects of his biography, in explaining to his readers by contrast what his own intention in writing is. It is to demonstrate that "it is not reading histories or plays or gazettes, nor going apilgrimage to Geneva, nor learning French and Italian, nor passing the Alps, nor being a cunning gamester" that qualifies a writer to discourse on ecclesiastical policy; nor is it in "capping an argument with a story that will answer it," nor in "clapping an apothegm upon an assertion that will prove it," nor in "stringing up proverbs and similitudes upon one another." Such techniques, he declares, will not produce a "coherent discourse"—an evaluation sufficiently valid for the *RT*, Part i, but one discounting its popular appeal. Apparently, even in the ill-consorted area of polemics, the conceited Marvellian prose style as his contemporaries viewed it is notably seen to accord with the (then) little recognized poetic style as later generations have come to view it.

And the controversialists occasionally do acknowledge that Marvell indeed was a poet. Parker, in fact, asserts that it was largely on the basis of making use of his "juvenile essays of ballads, poesies, anagrams, and acrostics," lying about useless, that he was able to fill up the pages of the first part of *RT*. Still rankled years later by the memory of being worsted, he refers to Marvell by name—as "a

vagabond, ragged, hungry poetaster" who made himself agreeable
to Milton by his "ill-natured wit" and so became undersecretary to
Cromwell's secretary—and provides a specific gloss to the opening
lines of *The First Anniversary*:

> Pleased with which honor, he published a congratulatory poem
> in praise of the tyrant, but when he had labored to squeeze out a
> panegyric, he brought forth a satire upon all rightful kings, saying
> that Cromwell was the sun but other monarchs were slow bodies,
> slower than Saturn in their revolutions and darting more hurtful
> rays upon the earth; that if each of their reigns were to be continued
> to the Platonic age, yet no king would ever do any good to the
> world. . . .[11]

One of the qualities that later generations of readers have come
to admire in the poetry is the counterpoise sustained between conflicting attitudes, with the *Horation Ode* perhaps its most conspicuous
example. Such recognition of ambivalent response was also conceded
in his own day but with something less than admiration in the heady
world of partisan opinion. To his contemporaries, he was, in an apt
appropriation of Marvell's own language, "unhoopable," standing,
as it were, with one leg at Dover and the other at Calais; and it is a
term appropriated again in 1680 by a "plain old Englishman" in
order to characterize Marvell's wit and policy.

Alluding to Marvell as "the headsman Father Greybeard,"
Edmund Hickeringill rhetorically queries:

> Was not this Gregory begot by some Proteus of a chameleon?
> An Oedipus cannot riddle him: he fights backward and forward,
> sometimes for the king and sometimes for modern orth[od]oxy;
> he slashes with a two-edged sword and cuts both ways; brandishes
> against the enemy and then falls foul on his own party and the
> Good Old Cause, but it is with pickerings [skirmishes] and flourishes
> rather than close fight and good earnest; and therefore he gives
> the Good Old Cause a good new name, and because the old one
> is odious, he calls it sometimes primitive simplicity, sometimes
> modern orthodoxy, and [Smith, p. 135] the Cause too good.

In 1678 an anonymous commentator, writing primarily on
The Growth of Poetry but also recalling the earlier controversy,

comments in the same vien: "Therefore make sure of Andrew. He's a shrewd man against Popery, though for his religion you may place him, as Pasquin at Rome placed Henry VIII, betwixt Moses, the Messiah, and Mahomet with the motto in his mouth, *quo me vertam nescio*. 'Tis well he is now *Transprosed* into politics; they say he had much ado to live upon poetry." And, finally, Roger L'Estrange, the "yerker, firker, whipster, scribbler-general of Tory-land," as he is called in an anonymous pamphlet of 1682, who attacked Marvell both alive and dead in a series of virulent pieces, makes a similar point: "The man, I confess, is a great master of words, but then his talent is that which the Lord St. Albans calls 'mother of wonder without worthiness,' being rather the suppleness and address of a tumbler than the force and vigor of a man of business."

Thus in despite of, or perhaps more accurately because of, his religious and political opponents, Marvell's image following his death—not without its suspicion of foul play—tends to become more and more weighted toward that of the incorruptible patriot rather than that of the witty satirist (though this aspect is never lost). While still paying tribute to his wit and eloquence, an anonymous admirer hails him, sometime after 1678, in extravagant terms:

> Athens may boast of virtuous Socrates,
> The chief among the Greeks for moral good,
> Rome of her orator, whose famed harangues
> Foiled the debauched Antony's designs,
> We him, and with deep sorrow wail his loss;
> But whether fate or art unturned his thread
> Remains in doubt; fame's lasting register
> Shall leave his name enrolled as great as theirs
> Who in Phillipi for their country fell.

It is not surprising then that when the second edition of Marvell's poems was published in the early years of the eighteenth century, the motive of its editor was largely political. Prefacing his two-volume edition in 1726 with a biographical account that was to be frequently pilfered, Thomas, alias Hesiod, Cooke makes his intent quite clear: "My design in this is to draw a pattern for all freeborn Englishmen in the life of a worthy patriot, whose every action has truly merited to him, with Aristides, the surname of 'the Just.'" (Elsewhere he calls him a "true Roman spirit.") When Captain

Thompson published his three-volume edition in 1776—notable date—he too makes his political motive clear: "One of my first and strongest reasons for publishing the works of Marvell was the pleasing hopes of adding a number of strenuous and sincere friends to our Constitution."[12] Later, in stressing Marvell's "patriot and parliamentary character," he ascribes to him "more dignity, honor, sense, genius, fortitude, virtue, and religion that ever mixed up [sic] in one man, ancient or modern." And to the meritorious figures earlier invoked, he adds that of the Roman general, Curius Dentatus, content with a plate of turnips for his supper, a comparison that was also to be invoked in the nineteenth century by Disraeli the Elder (whence the general becomes Curtius), to be followed by John Dove in the first single biography of the poet, by Hartley Coleridge, and by E.P. Hood.

A further index to Marvell's posthumous stature is the appropriation either of his manes or his name in order to add significance to political statements. Beginning shortly after his death with the tribute by John Ayloff entitled *Marvell's Ghost*, it was followed in 1688–89 by a second poem with the same title, resulting in Defoe's easy calling up of "old Marvell's Ghost" in 1703, and in the following year, according to a title listed in the *Poems on Affairs of State*, John Toland's addressing a letter to him "at his Mansion House in Elysium." In 1710 and again in 1740, the sobriquet "Andrew Marvell, Jr." was adopted by two unknown writers; and in 1773, a controversy over the building of a marketplace in Philadelphia occasioned a pamphlet and a broadside by plain "Andrew Marvell," directed, this time, against the local tyranny of mayor and aldermen. Later appropriations of the soubriquet "junior" or "younger" occur in 1829, 1838, and 1855.

Other scattered allusions attest to the ease with which later generations called up the image of Marvell's character in order to contrast it with the corrupt nature of contemporary politicians. For example, in Caleb D'Anvers's *Craftsman* for 8 February 1735, Mr. Bay's depiction in the *RT* is brought up to date by a comparison with "the Walsinghams and Osbornes of these days"—a comparison that received wide circulation by its being almost immediately reprinted in the *Gentleman's Magazine*. In 1794 in an account of his "excursion" to the United States, the entrepreneur Henry Wansey pointedly commends "honest Andrew Marvell" rather than (the less than) "honest" Edmund Burke, "ruminating (but not in trope and figure)" on his £3,700 pension. In the next century, James Russell Lowell refuses to compare Marvell with John Quincy Adams because of the "vast deal of humbug" implicated in the latter's reputation (though he compares Marvell to Milton to the advantage of the former because of his possessing an even "purer mind" than the "great poet" did).

Akin to this image of Marvell as the champion of political and civil liberties is one curiously revelatory of his stature vis à vis Milton, who is identified in 1738 as "the famous apologist" for the beheading of Charles I. Marvell's own poetic merit may have been scanted but his ability to champion it in others was not. In 1720, Giles Jacob (in the two-volume *Historical Account of the Lives and Writings of Our Most Considerable English Poets*) devotes seven lines to the biography and identifies some of the poems—four lyrics (with a misprint of *Tubal* for *Jubal* in the citation from "Music's Empire") and nine of the attributed satires. Conceding that as a person of wit and learning, Marvell had given the world "several performances" of his poetical studies, he notes that what most redounded to his honor, however, was that he was the first to have found out "the beauties of Milton." In commenting the next year on Dryden's tagging of Milton's epic that resulted in *The State of Innocence* (1677), John Dennis acknowledges that Dryden's public discovery of its merit had been anticipated by "those Gentlemen" whose commendatory verses prefaced the 1674 edition, that is, by Marvell and Dr. Barrow, though they are not identified by name. Marvell's second editor also observes that when *Paradise Lost* was first published, it was valued "no more than a lifeless piece" until publicly espoused by Marvell and Dr. Barrow. Captain Thompson likewise asserts that it would have lain "in lifeless rust and obscurity longer" had not these two "unveiled its beauties to the undiscerning eyes of the heedless world." The notion seeps into the next century with an anonymous writer in 1824–25 repeating it and with John Dove reporting in 1832 that it was a belief held by many. The following year Hartley Coleridge was to comment tartly on the "truly absurd surmise that either Marvell's English couplets or Dr. Barrow's Latin elegiacs preserved the production of Milton from obscurity," a situation "as probable," he adds, "as that a sealed and unopened epistle should reach its destination if directed only on the inside." Nonetheless, Dove's statement is repeated in the two issues of the *Life of Marvell* appearing in 1835 with different imprints and so to give continued currency to the notion; it is a notion which is to be repeated as late as 1874 in England in a civil service handbook and as late as 1877 in the United States.

Though occasional allusions to the poetry in eighteenth-century encyclopedias and dictionaries are to poems like "Bellipotens virgo" (praised in 1699 by John Toland), to the verses on Joseph de Maniban, on Blood's stealing the crown, on *Paradise Lost*, and on Flecknoe, there were exceptions. In 1720 Giles Jacob termed "Music's Empire" one of the best of the lyrics; in 1747 Dr. James Parsons publicly extolled "Eyes and Tears", a view receiving circulation by its being reprinted in the *Gentleman's Magazine* the following year; in 1753 Robert Shiels printed the "Dialogue between the Resolved Soul and Created Pleasure" and in 1793–94 Josph Ritson "The Nymph Complaining for the Death of her Fawn". As early as 1716, in fact, nine of the lyrics (and none of the satires) were included in Tonson's (or Dryden's) popular *Miscellany*, which was to be reprinted in 1727. More importantly, it should be recognized that despite the primary political motives of his eighteenth-century editors, three editions of the poetry had appeared in a little more than fifty years, Cooke's edition having been reprinted in 1772. With the posthumous Folio, the resultant total of four editions of the poems in less than a century is a conspicuous record in comparison with any number of sixteenth- and seventeenth-century literary figures (and one in marked contrast to the record of public circulation in his own day).

Evaluated according to Whiggish or Tory predilections, the essentially political image of Marvell continues into the nineteenth century, though in line with altering sensibilities, the focus begins to shift. In 1802 Wordsworth still hails him as the republican friend of Milton but copies the *Horatian Ode* into his notebook W, and others of his contemporaries turn to the poet of nature and "exquisite hyperbole."

It is William Lisle Bowles, the now maligned inciter of the "Pope and Bowles" controversy, who first acclaims him (1806) "an accurate descriptive rural poet," citing "the hatching throstle's shining eye" from *Upon Appleton House* (which Mark Pattison was later to counter with the sour observation that it proved only that both Bowles and Marvell had been schoolboys and addicted to birds' nesting). Nonetheless, the notes Bowles appended to his

edition of *Windsor Forest* were to be incorporated into the introductory essay of Whitwell Elwin's 1871 edition of Pope's work.
Throughout the nineteenth (and the twentieth) century derivative
judgments were to secure an amazing amount of currency. Just as
the comment in John Aikin's *General Biography* (10 volumes, 1799–
1815)—"His early poems express a fondness for the charms of rural
nature and much delicacy of sentiment; they were ingenious and full
of fancy, after the manner of Cowley and his contemporaries"—
was frequently repeated, so Charles Lamb's descriptive phrase "witty
delicacy" (1821) was frequently echoed, giving rise to the (surely
mistaken) notion that Marvell's poetic recovery was owing to the
endorsement of the author of *Essays of Elia*.

The several brief expositions of Hazlitt in public lectures and
the lengthier examples of Leigh Hunt in a half-dozen journalistic
pieces did much to familiarize the name of Marvell as a lyric and
humorous writer. And in 1824 and 1825, the years in which eight
of the lyrics appeared in Hazlitt's *Select British Poets*, reprinted as
Select Poets of Great Britain, a two-part essay appeared in the *Retrospective Review* consisting of a biographical account and a discussion
of the published works with "copious" extracts from thirteen of
the poems. Reluctantly closing his citations, the anonymous critic
forecasts that the works under consideration will one day attract
the attention they "so justly merit" and confidently asserts that it
is a day not very far distant. The influence of this essay was far-
reaching. When Dove compiled his biography (1832), he pillaged
material from it as well as from Captain Thompson's edition and
from Disraeli's engaging account in 1814 of Marvell's quarrel with
Parker, the last source, however, duly acknowledged. More importantly, he printed seventeen of the lyrics, while Hartley Coleridge,
who, in turn, was to cop most of his material from Dove, appended
seven of them in one of the two derivatives of his multiply issued
account of Andrew Marvell, worthy of Yorkshire. Publication of the
Dove-Coleridge volumes inevitably helped to direct attention to
the poetry.

As the poetry came to be better known, an image of the romantic
writer of the love lyrics begins to merge with that of the patriot.
We learn "that he was threatened, he was flattered, he was thwarted,
he was caressed, he was beset with spies, and, if all tales be true, he
was waylaid by ruffians and courted by beauties" (1832); that

"among all the rich and costly luxuries of that time, all the over flowing wealth surrounding the throne and the court, probably there was not one rich thing that might not have been ... at his command. How many of those voluptuous houries who surrounded the court of the king might have been his slaves?" (1853); that what the opposition dared not compass by persecution, they endeavored by temptation: "The king complimented him, Rochester praised him; the frail beauties of the courts offered him their blandest smiles and their most honied flatteries," but, this anonymous writer declares, also in 1853, "'Aristides' was proof against all."

Thus by mid-century there was a sufficiency of biographical, critical, and textual material to allow for an evaluation of Marvell on several counts.[13] The household anthologies of the 1860's (Gilfillan, Palgrave, Macdonald, and Trench) made at least ten of the lyrics exceedingly well known, so that by the time of Grosart's edition of the poetry and prose (1872–75), W.D. Christie could observe that though now the prose pieces are little read, "the poetry has found its way to men's hearts." With certain exceptions, there is in general a catholicity of taste up to the last decade of the nineteenth century and the opening decades of the next when it solidifies into a pronounced subjectivity of likes and dislikes. The *fortuna* of two markedly different poems illustrates this movement. "Eyes and Tears," publicly extolled in 1747, considered one of the four most beautiful of the lyrics in 1853, is judged little more than a string of conceits in 1892; "The Character of Holland," which induced "uncontrollable laughter" in Lamb and Hunt and later in Carlyle who laughed for half an hour on hearing Tennyson's reading of *one* line, had become no more than a heavy-handed squib by 1897. Furthermore, these years show the replacement of the image of the patriot—with Alice Meynell commenting on the portly dullness of the individual who could call Marvell "the British Aristides"—and of the witty prose writer by that of the poet; the recent rise into fame of the lyrical verse of Marvell, H.C. Beeching writes in 1901, perhaps being sufficient proof of the marked superiority in "poetical taste" of his own generation. By the time of the tercentenary tributes, a very mixed bag of goods edited by the Hull city librarian, the seventeenth-century estimate of Marvell had been quite reversed. Or had it?

Ascriptions of literary affinity in the nineteenth and in the early years of this century suggest that the seventeenth-century designation of Marvell as the offspring of a chameleon begot by a Proteus was not altogether inappropriate. As a prose writer, we learn that in his "playful exuberance of figure," he resembles Burke (1819), that he is the originator not only of the style of Junius (1832) but also of the stream of wit that issued in the writings of Swift, Addison, Steele (1836, 1844), and, ultimately, of Sidney Smith (1869). As a poet, he not only reflects the conceits of Cowley and his contemporaries Cleveland, Herbert, and Crashaw, but he is also a synthesis of Donne and Butler even as his models are said to include Jonson and Milton. At different points he is said to touch Lovelace, Suckling, Wither, Herrick, Habingdon, Waller, Vaughan, and Dryden. In his personal sympathy with nature he anticipates not only Crabbe, Cowper (1897), and Wordsworth (1885), but also Meredith (1892). In his "imaginative intensity" he is allied both to Coleridge and Shelley (1861, 1913) and in his "sensuousness" to Keats (1912). Though he founded "no school of verse" (1905), he influenced Clare (who in 1825 palmed off a lyric of his own as Marvell's), Emerson, and Hopkins "both in measure and music." Of lesser figures, he can be compared with Barron Field (this by Charles Lamb, the "recoverer" of Marvell's poetical reputation, 1820) or Ralph Hodgson because of "the hatching throstle's shining eye" (1921).

With such a plethora of avowed literary affinities, it is perhaps not surprising that recent ingenious critics are able to find in Marvell elements of St. Bonaventura, Plotinus, Ficino, Hermes Trismegistus, and other recondite authors. Perhaps, as the writers in the seventeenth century declared and as subsequent critics imply, the quintessential Marvell—prose writer, poet, and even patriot—is to be found in his "unhoopable" quality: *le style est l'homme même*.

In contrast to recent commentators who find the clue to Marvell's enigmatic lyrics in abstruse areas of philosophy or in sectarian religion, others find it in his exploitation of popular traditions, which, for a Renaissance poet, seems the sounder approach. One can scarcely doubt that Marvell was pointedly aware of generic forms, pointedly aware of the ways in which other poets had employed them, as his frequent echoes indicate (though his appropriation of others' phrases may indeed have a function ulterior to that of unacknowledged recollection), and pointedly aware of their potential for subtle twists simply because of their common currency. His simplicity of diction with its marked use of monosyllables and dissyllables (the occasional hard words—amphibium, deodands, planisphere—sticking out conspicuously if not exactly like gillyflowers in a cowturd), his often contorted syntax that in its functional complexity jolts the reader into admitting intellectual complexity, and the informing ideas that move irresistibly to their logical conclusions make for complicated results. While the enigmatic quality partly derives from his avoiding visual appeal in order to stress the cerebral, he counters this at the same time with a kind of lulling metrical appeal that, in effect, teases the reader out of thought. While a kind of compelling logic seems to inhere in individual poems, it is a logic that shifts according to context, with the (happy) result that there is no necessary sum of received ideas but rather glancing instances from multiple perspectives. Some instances of variable thematic stress will perhaps serve to illustrate one aspect of his "unhoopable" quality.

"A Dialogue between Thyrsis and Dorinda," if by Marvell and the only reason to doubt it is its omission from the Popple manuscript, is perhaps his earliest lyric in the vernacular. The considerable problems of determining the text derive both from its appropriation to musical settings and its subject—Thyrsis' catalogue of the delights of Elysium could be extended indefinitely according to the ingenuity of the poet (or poets), as the charming verses in the 1663 printed version show.[14]

Despite the poem's seeming artlessness, conforming to the seeming artlessness of the two speakers, the fair Dorinda nonetheless poses a number of queries that are both sophisticated and serious. Within the confines of her pastoral world, populated only by shepherds and nymphs, sheep and goats, wolves and foxes, how can she envision a locale so distant as Elysium or an activity that can occupy an everlasting day? The future delights which her lover catalogues are simply present delights with all contraries removed, a would-be situation which adds considerable ambiguity to Thyrsis' flat assertion that "heaven's the centre of the soul" (l. 18). In his catalogue of pastoral pleasures, the line comes to suggest that their heaven is almost, if not quite, where they are. In the context of his specific speech as well as in the total context of the poem, it suggests that heaven is the home to which they intuitively know the way. Eager to reach the enticing world he has projected, Dorinda with unerring logic demands proof of its reality, a proof that can only be demonstrated by his willingness to give up the world which has itself determined the character of that far-off one. In responding to her demand, Thyrsis' abrupt compliance is an ironic reversal: having gained a convert, he agrees to comply not because of the nature of the Elysium he has projected but because he can conceive of *no* world without her. The concluding lines of the Chorus, which must be the most novel adaptation ever of the *carpe diem* motif, thus represent conclusions that are inevitable from the vantage point of the two speakers. In Dorinda's view, if one's destination is an appealing heaven, why not accelerate the rate of progress to it? From Thyrsis' view, if their rural cell—in Dorinda's query, "Is it Elysium?" (l. 8)—will be unendurable without her, why stay behind? Softening these conclusions is the means of death proposed—poppies steeped in wine to induce intoxication, followed by a smooth "passing away" in sleep. In this brief lyric, overtones of both a classical and a Christian ethos are held in admirable equipoise (whether or not one agrees with George Lord that it should be classed among the *dubia* because of its advocacy of suicide—inconceivable to a Puritan Marvell?).[15]

More enigmatic if equally simple in form is the dialogue "Clorinda and Damon." Taking its point of departure from the pastoral invitational mode exemplified by a number of Renaissance female figures—Scylla in Lodge's epyllion, Oenone in Heywood's, and Phoebe in Drayton's—"Clorinda and Damon" presents a remarkably pared-down version. To the reluctant Damon's anti-*carpe diem* attitude that "Grass withers; and the flowers too fade" (l. 7), Clorinda offers prospective joys in an "unfrequented cave." Her words call up the Virgilian *spelunca* from the episode of the union of Dido and Aeneas, but Marvell, perhaps echoing Surrey's language in rendering the response of heaven and earth to their union (IV. 212–15), makes Damon counter with, "That den?" In any case, in Clorinda's view, the term signifies "Love's shrine"; in Damon's view, "Virtue's grave." Rather than a notion of an Elysium with an everlasting day, Clorinda proffers a spot free from the intrusion of the (busy old) sun, but Damon's punning rejoinder—"Not [from] Heaven's eye"—by means of three words makes that natural world subservient to his moral one. The explanation of his encounter with great Pan, which has altered his perspective on the "enticing" aspects of "pastures, caves, and springs" and results in his singing only of him, is curiously undercut, however, by Clorinda's concession

—"Sweet must Pan sound in Damon's note." One wonders, only then? Equally curious is Damon's concession that "Clorinda's voice might make it sweet." One wonders, since when? Or is he reversing his earlier stance? Even more curious is Clorinda's response—"Who would not in Pan's praises meet?" Has her invitation been contravened by Damon's words or is she now simply content with a conjunction in song? The concluding lines of the Chorus emphasize that the pastures, caves, and fountains, "formerly" so enticing, once again "sing," "echo," and "ring" but this time of great Pan: the world has become *his* choir. The reader is left to speculate whose perspective has changed—Clorinda's, Damon's, or, as the allotment of the final lines to the Chorus would indicate, the perspective of both.

"Daphnis and Chloe" provides marked contrast in theme and form. Its title suggests a dialogue, but what we have, in fact, is a narrator setting forth a dramatic scene and commenting on its causes and results and a Daphnis delivering a very odd lover's complaint. Presented only indirectly in the words of the two speakers, Chloe remains a non-participant. This unusual structure tacitly underscores the point that in love poetry the lady often exists only as a catalyst to elicit the reactions of her lover. Though framed by the observations of an omniscient narrator, the poem is thus in part a dramatic monologue. Daphnis reveals himself in his words as a lover struggling *in extremis* to maintain his fiction of love, while his actions exhibit one kind of logical result of maintaining that fiction. The narrator in his comments reflects on the psychology of male and female, suggesting why it is as it is.

Like the Nymph, Daphnis is presented at a crucial psychological moment, the dismal hour when he "must" from Chloe part, with the consequent loss of his former hopes, labor, and art. "Why" he must do so is the substance of the poem. The reason first stipulated (by the narrator) is that Dame Nature, a foe to her own sex, has taught Chloe to be coy, so that she knows neither how to keep nor how to relinquish her lover. But as a precautionary measure to prevent the world from separating, Nature admits a new response: Chloe drops her scruples. Well-skilled in acting the besieging lover, Daphnis, however, cannot recognize that to give up the siege is to gain the fort. Why not? He is, the narrator explains, so possessed with the grief of parting that he lacks the "sense" to do so.

Torn between joy and sorrow, he not only acts in demented fashion (like the Unfortunate Lover) but looks like a soul scarce dead, aghast at the shrieks of his friends which serve to send him on his way. This "lover's ghost" then delivers his paradoxical "complaint," which in itself is constructed on paradoxes. Why should heaven and hell be joined? Why should Chloe now grow "kind," that is, compliant (but also recalling the narrator's explanation that her behavior has been dictated by Nature's laws, sts. 2, 4)?

In his "manly stubbornness," Daphnis refuses to credit to his departure what his presence could not "win" or to increase "his losses" by a "late fruition." He then expatiates on the psychological result of what it would mean to gain that which he has been so fervently seeking all along, projecting his conception of himself and his beloved in a series of bizarre analogies: consummation would be like wearing an expensive jewel at his execution (to be bestowed on his executioner) or like being fatted up for a sacrifice (to be consumed by a cannibal) or like the ravishing of a dead but still warm body or like erring (in both senses) in the desert like the long-dead Hebrew or becoming invisible like the witch at midnight on St. John's Day. In metaphors that go far beyond the "sweet foe" of Petrarchan poetry, Chloe in his conception is thus seen as "executioner" and "cannibal." Following these extreme analogies, Daphnis succinctly voices his rationale (and it is one that strikes at the inherent fallacy of the lover's pose):

> Joy will not with sorrow weave,
> Nor will I this grief pollute.

(ll. 91–2)

His acknowledgment, like that expressed in abstract terms by the lover in a "Definition of Love", is that a perfect love (at least for a literary lover) is so only by virtue of its never being fulfilled. But unlike that lover, who concedes that in order to maintain the fiction his love must ever remain in process, Daphnis' future actions—sleeping with Phlogis and keeping a night for Dorinda—exemplify another kind of logical response. He consequently achieves, as it were, the best of two possible worlds: refusal to interweave joy with sorrow or to pollute his grief, on the one hand, keeps alive in him "all the fire / That Love in his torches had" (ll. 95–6); sexual gratification, on the other, permits (or necessitates?) a series of Phlogises and Dorindas. Even so, this parodic literary lover is compelled to shift the onus from himself to the lady, his excuse being, "Why did *Chloe* once refuse?"

In appropriating a literary stance that is then followed by an extrapolation of its causes and effects, Marvell has, in effect, evolved a new subject matter. It is one that has its equivalent in the skillful construction of a religious lyric like "The Coronet," a poem which exists only because the poet has made an artful construct out of his questioning of poetic motivation. Were it not for the "fiction," there would be no poem. "The unfortunate Lover" provides a related example.

Highly emblematic and conceited, "The unfortunate Lover" offers some indication of its date (after 1648 or '49) in that two lines from a lyric by Lovelace are echoed. Beginning with a general thematic statement that is then successively particularized, the lot of one unfortunate love comes to be seen as paradigmatic. And in giving this capsule biography from birth to death, Marvell both derides and commends poetic convention.

The first four lines convey a sense of idyllic, if mindless, youthful love, the poet obtaining his tonal effect by the utmmost economy of language. The lovers are never specified as *persons*; they are simply "sorted by pairs" (like the animals marshalled into Noah's Ark), played with by the "infant Love" (in contrast to the "tyrant Love" who persistently batters the breast of the Lover), and are a constant—"still are seen / By fountains cool, and shadows green." The very first word of the poem alerts the reader to question this idyll and to accept the next four lines in explanation of its introductory "Alas": the flames of such a love are quickly exhausted ("Like meteors of a summer's night"), nor can they ever "climb" to that region which makes an "impression upon time." However fantastic the account of the "poor lover's" birth and nurture is, it seems a veritable embodiment of the frustrated figure of literary tradition. Always wearing bitter tears, with sighs roaring through his breast, he is fed with hopes and air that (in one of the more outrageous puns) "soon digested to despair"; famished and feasted, consumèd and increased, he becomes, in brief, the "amphibíum of life and death." Subjected to fight with fortune with unbaited sword, while being plied with the "winged artillery" of the tyrant Love, his fierce reaction—"Torn with flames, and ragg'd with wounds"—is precisely the one that best pleases any other suffering lover. And his reward for undergoing these hyperbolical experiences is that Love, now acknowledged as sovereign, dubs him alone a banneret, a title conferred for deeds done on the battlefield in the presence of the sovereign. Furthermore, in dying, he "leaves a perfume here, / And music within every ear."

An inherent ambiguity characterizes the first line of the concluding couplet: "And he in story only rules." Depending on the placement of "only" as a modifier, the line can mean that, on the one hand, the lover has a place only in history-as-fiction or, on the other, that he has his place in history only because he is a paradigm of all unfortunate lovers. As with the two dialogues having a concluding chorus, the (reversed) structure of this poem again suggests the resolution: in contrast to those who are merely sorted in pairs, it is only an unfortunate lover who can attain that literary region that makes an "impression upon time."

The handling of these last two lyrics, it seems to me, indicates ways in which Marvell makes use of an earlier mode of poetry and advances beyond it. The posture of the masochistic lover had of course been ridiculed as early as the 1590's by satirists and dramatists alike, but it was left to such a long-practicing sonneteer as Michael Drayton to exploit the satiric mode *in* the service of love poetry. In his sonnet To the Reader in the 1599 version of *Idea*, he proclaims that there will be no farfetched sighs, no ah-me's in his sequence but that he will sing as "(A libertine) fantastically," a "literary" libertinism that Marvell was also to follow. In order to revitalize the by then well-worn tradition, Drayton both exploits a variety of psychological responses to erotic experience and introduces many jarring figures of speech and thought—"dung-bred scarabies," the comparison of his mistress experimenting on him to surgeons' experimenting on corpses, the assertion that a lover's fame is to be gotten only by his death, etc. Marvell follows also these practices of exploiting multiple psychological responses and relying on jarring figures of speech and thought; there is no question that he knew Drayton's poetry since he appropriates almost an entire line in his "Fair Singer." The result in Drayton was a tonic counter to the earlier Petrarchan vogue both in terms of the kind of language employed and the *idée fixe* of the lover's stance. The result in Marvell is to tease the reader since the discontinuity of the lyrics, in contrast to the organization of the *Idea* sequence, leaves him reckoning with multiple themes. A further Marvellian technique is that of establishing a kind of self-contained dramatic context so that the figures populating his poems seem in themselves to have a concrete existence—the Coy Mistress, the Chlora in "Mourning," or in the "Gallery" in all her multiple embodiments, etc. By being at one and the same time both specific and abstract, Marvell the poet, like the prose writer, remains elusive, indeed, "unhoopable."

In stressing the thematic element of four of the early lyrics, I have not intended to scant the poet's remarkable verbal dexterity or metrical skill but simply to point up different literary attitudes he exploits. Other lyrics afford other examples. Rather than lock him into such categories as Cavalier, Puritan, or satirist, one ought to consider him as the ultimate Renaissance poet, that is, as a distinctly "literary" poet; otherwise he would not have made traditions so conspicuously the subjects of his song. He is also very much the Renaissance poet in that, at least so far as the evidence indicates, he considered a poem to be a literary construct needing no further justification than that it was pleasing—if to no one but himself.

Notes

1. The material on which the early pages of this essay is based derives in large part from my forthcoming volume on Marvell in the Critical Heritage Series.

2. A "mixed" copy which belonged to Hastings's mother, the Countess of Huntingdon, and recording in manuscript her own elegy on his death, though dated 1649 has Marvell's poem in its reset position, a fact suggesting that the two issues appeared very close together.

3. Inevitably his surname, and to a lesser extent his given name (as "merry-Andrew," that is, a mountebank's assistant, or its synonym "Jackpudding," or "little Andrew") lent itself to punning allusions. Thus we find "*Pick-thank-ness* [Marvell's coinage], in which word (to keep our Rhyme) there is a peculiar *Marvelousness*"; "It is a *marvel* . . . what you will make of this *New Author*"; "that which is *admirable*, and a greater *Marvel*, is the skill and cunning of the man"; "*Marvel of Marvels*, for that is the Character given you"; "the Lord raised up a *Merveil* to fight [Parker]"; "The Author of the *Rehearsal Transpros'd* speaks marvellously." He is sometimes referred to as "The Transproser" (and by one opponent simply as "Trans") or as "The Rehearser."

4. One should exclude the last of them (in defense of John Owen), published four months before Marvell's death and the only one principally concerned with theological doctrine, since it seems to have evoked little comment then or later.

5. *The Transproser Rehearsed*, 1673, p. 55. From this point on, all seventeenth-century quotations are modernized.

6. *The Poems and Letters of Andrew Marvell*, 2 vols., 3rd ed. rev. P. Legouis (New York: Oxford University Press 1971), 2:328.

7. *The Rehearsal Transpros'd and The Rehearsal Transpros'd The Second Part*, ed. D.I.B. Smith (Oxford University Press, 1971), p. 76; henceforth abbreviated *RT*, 1 or 2 or Smith.

8. *His Majesty's Declaration Defended*, which since 1935 has been accepted as Dryden's, and Preface to *Religio Laici*, 1682. Several reasons can be invoked to account for Dryden's hostility: his shift in literary allegiance from the panegyrist of "Old Noll" to that of Charles II; in religious allegiance from Puritan to Anglican and, ultimately, to Catholic; and in personal reaction to the continued implication of the literary "Bays" behind the ecclesiastical "Bayes." Marvell of course deridingly refers to him in the verses on *Paradise Lost* as "the *Town-Bays*."

9. Inevitably, one recalls the military imagery used to describe the garden in *Appleton House* (sts. 34–46), as well as the "grove of pikes" (a phrase lifted from Edmund Waller), contrasted with the woody grove at Bilbrough.

10. Cf. the allusion to Cromwell as the sun (*The First Anniversary*) and the comment of Parker, p. oo below.

11. *Bishop Parker's History of His Own Time*, trans. Thomas Newlin, 1727, pp. 332–33.

12. In a nice conflation of political and sexual morality, Captain Thompson a few years later was to name his mistress's nephew "Andrew Marvell" in order that the name might inspire him to be virtuous.

13. A fifth edition of the poems was published in Boston in 1857 with a brief but judicious evaluation by J.R. Lowell added to the earlier biographical memoir or Henry Rogers (1844); it was to be reprinted many times both in the United States and in England. Emerson, Poe, Whittier, Lowell, and Bryant all expressed their admiration of the poet *and* patriot, with Emerson, Whittier, and Bryant including selected lyrics in their collections.

14. Line references to this poem are keyed to my edition (London: Penguin English Poets, 1972; New York: St. Martin's Press, 1974); elsewhere to Margoliouth's edition revised by Legouis.

15. George deF. Lord, ed., *Andrew Marvell: Complete Poetry* (New York: Modern Library, 1968), p. 261n.

"IT IS MARVEL HE OUTDWELLS HIS HOUR"

Some Perspectives on Marvell's Medium

THOMAS CLAYTON

I

MARVELL'S POEMS matter today, as do all works and experiences of art that we attend to often by virtue of their timeless timeliness, their classic character, their living monumentality—in a trio of poetry-appreciational truisms: their capacity aesthetically to renew themselves and us simultaneously. I feel obliged to express my own kind of persistent responsiveness to Marvell, first by displaying a petrified chestnut from Horace (to which I mean to return), then by commenting on some lines that do not seem especially to demand or reward the kind of attention I am going to claim is quite consistently Marvell's due and overdue as a poet.[1] First, Horace:

> *Exegi monumentum aere perennius*
> regalique situ pyramidum altius,
> quod non imber edax, non Aquilo impotens
> possit diruere aut innumerabilis
> annorum series et fuga temporum.
> non omnis moriar multaque pars mei
> vitabit Libitinam: usque ego postera
> *crescam laude recens. . . .*
>
> (*Odes*, 3.30. 1–8)[2]

And the first two stanzas of *Upon Appleton House*:

> Within this sober Frame expect
> Work of no Forrain *Architect*;
> That unto Caves the Quarries drew,
> And Forrests did to Pastures hew;
> Who of his great Design in pain
> Did for a Model valut his Brain,
> Whose Columnes should so high be rais'd
> To arch the Brows that on them gaz'd.
>
> Why should of all things Man unrul'd
> Such unproportion'd dwellings build?
> The Beasts are by their Denns exprest:
> And Birds contrive an equal Nest;
> The low roof'd Tortoises do dwell
> In cases fit of Tortoise-shell:
> No Creature loves an empty space;
> Their Bodies measure out their Place.

(ll. 1–16)

Marvell dazzles and dazzles again with the brilliance, freshness, piquancy, and relevance of his perceptions and their expression. It is more than a case of "True wit is nature to advantage dressed; / What oft was thought, but ne'er so well expressed," and also more than a "tough reasonableness beneath the slight lyric grace." Marvell has something of a lesser-daVincian word-painter's verbal vision that makes the reader-auditor see through his ears and enlarge his own world of experience by sharing the poet's intuitions. And the disjunctions suggested by Pope's and Eliot's formulations seem less apt characterizations of the Marvellian aesthetic experience than Coleridge's difficult but suggestive conception of the esemplastic power of the primary and secondary Imagination (*Biographia Literaria*, Ch. 13), of which Marvell has his own imaginative version in "Eyes and Tears" (ll. 1–4).

In the first three of four stanzas of *Upon Appleton House* the *données* of theme, genre, historical subject, and other orders of convention, counter-convention, and innovation are evident enough. The poem is eventually seen in full to be Marvell's Country-House

Anniversary poem, with its respective antecedents in Donne's Anniversaries and poems in the tradition of Jonson's "To Penshurst". These lines of descent and fields of vision are epitomized in two lines of the concluding apostrophe to the landscape: "... as all *Virgins* She [Maria Fairfax] preceds, / So you all *Woods, Streams, Gardens, Meads*" (ll. 751–52). The stanzas concern the transcendent modesty of the house explicitly of Nun Appleton and implicitly of Fairfax, and by contrast the generic vanity of Man, who characteristically builds in a vacuous spirit abhorrent to nature. What particularly interests me now is less what Marvell is talking about as such, than how he is writing, but his primary concerns cannot be suppressed. The first stanza contrasts Appleton House with "prodigy houses" and grounds of a kind designed by foreign architects.[3] The second demonstrates by example of bird, beast, and tortoise that "no creature loves an empty space," except man; it is "surprisingly modern" in its ecological spirit, according to which a dwelling for each creature has come to be in relation to its need and nature; Marvell's examples have a permanent sociobiological relevance. A "sober Frame" and structural, here.

The life of Marvell's design is in the stuff of his creative contrasts, in the interrelationships—the intratextualities—between the sober-framing members and the rest of Marvell's "House," and in those parts that especially gratify the mind's eye. Marvell's art properly astonishes after the beginning, because it calls so very little attention to its artfulness and resonance at first. Nevertheless, by an attentive reader and certainly by a retrospective reader, "this sober Frame" must be taken to refer not only to Appleton House but to "Appleton House," each a work of native English artistry: "sober" half personifies "Frame" even as it qualifies its varied metonymies; and "Forrain" means not only—for example—Italianate but also irrelevant and superfluous, and in this context it makes "Architect" a pejorative word. Of course, the sense and syntax don't stop at the end of line 2, despite the semi-colon, but the effect of the line is to force to the fore the implicit counter-line of sense, "[expect] Work of an English poet," in the original sense, "maker." Also implying their counter-lines, lines 3–4 characterize the "work" of the "Forrain Architect": he "drew" (in two simultaneous senses) "the Quarries," nature's store of building materials, "unto Caves" (by art misusing nature further to misuse nature by copying it in extravagantly artificial gardens); and a "*For*rain Architect" naturally would nature's "*For*rests ... hew," with a striking metonymic reduction of the architect's office to that of a woodcutter who murders to erect. Inordinately detailed as they seem, these comments barely scratch the surface of the first quatrain. It is like Marvell to mete the eye with more than meets the eye, and appropriate, I think, for a reader of poetry for poetry's sake to cooperate with the medium.

It is the second quatrain that truly and probably first astonishes any reader—and by its lightning stroke suggests revision of the original reading of the ostensibly straightforward first quatrain. What we have here is verbal architecture and the projection of the mind into several frames of space, of which the best visual counterpart, perhaps, is to be found recently in some Surrealist paintings; earlier in those dizzying inner-spatial constructs of prisons by Piranesi; and still earlier—before and in Marvell's time—in some versions of dimorphic representation, with a human head as one expression and a landscape or any combination of objects as another, as in paintings by Giuseppe Arcimboldo, Frans Floris, Athanasius Kircher, and De Momper (Dali's imitation of the type is called "Paranoiac Face, Double Image"; see figure 1 for Archimboldo's "Landscape Head"). The complex of ambiguities in this second quatrain awaits others' exploration: I wish to emphasize only the grotesque verbal-pictorial dimension of "in pain / Did for a Model vault his Brain," which has several ways to convey at once related ideas through such senses of *vault* as (1) overarch, (2) make a vault of, and (3) overleap; and through the compound antecedence and connection of "Whose Columnes," which attach both directly to the "Model" and to "his Brain," and also indirectly to his brain through the model, in such a way as to make the design in more than one sense the precise function of the designer. Here "*Architect*" finds a wry fulfillment in English and Latin connections, through "vault" (*arcus*; *arcuo*, v.) and "Brain" (*tectum* is roof, ceiling, and such). Such high-rise columns reflexively and variously "arch the Brows that on them gaz'd"— raising to take the height, expressively to disapprove, or archly to share in the vanity by reflection.

FIG. 1. *Landscape-Head.* Probably by Matthäus Merian [1593–1650]; in the tradition of Arcimboldo, to whom it was formerly attributed (when the painting was cleaned in recent years, "Merian" appeared at the lower left). 39 × 30 cm. Private collection, New York.

II

Marvell's poetic vision, like Shakespeare's and Joyce's, is deep and multifocal: it comprehends things, ideas, colors, feelings, tones, and verbal formulations in two or more languages at once. The labor of love to appreciate Marvell requires something of a love of labor as well as art to accomplish itself. But it seems worth hinting at a way, by waving in the direction of the models of Barthes' *S/Z* and Genette's *Figures*, for example,[4] although the principles and practice of the kind of attention I advocate here do not require access to contemporary French criticism for precept or example. Over fifty years ago, in his essay on Marvell (1921), T.S. Eliot wrote that "to bring the poet back to life—the great, the perennial, task of criticism—is in this case to squeeze the drops of the essence of two or three poems; even confining ourselves to these, we may find some precious liquor unknown to the present age. Not to determine rank, but to isolate this quality, is the critical labour."[5] Many aspects of the current structuralist and semiotic effort were either evident or implicit in the work of the unjustly maligned New Criticism, too. And Stephen Booth has given a fine example of several orders of detailed critical analysis of verse in *An Essay on Shakespeare's Sonnets*.[6]

To add a few details on the stanzas: Easy ingenuity can find multiple significance in "Why should of all things Man *unrul'd* / Such unproportion'd dwellings *build*?" (italics mine): "unrul'd" manifestly works partly in terms of the architectural connection, so the false rhyme prosodically expresses the sense of the aborted couplet— except that the rhyme was just as likely true in Marvell's day.[7] In such circumstances, scholarship cares about the probability that approximates truth where certainty is beyond reach; the Barthesian— and, earlier, often Empson's—"projection" couldn't care less; and the analytical reader can often have it both ways, by entertaining— and being entertained by—the apparent effect and design without sacrificing awareness that Marvell's design probably stopped short of expressive false rhyme.[8]

A fixed focus of unexamined assumptions has its virtues of convenience and concentration, but I am supposing here that there can also be value in rotating the reading stance upon its axis to some of the "intertextualities" of the primary text, the work of Marvell. In ranging as I do, I am conscious of procedural affinities with

Aristotle, Dryden, and Barthes, for example. Defining his subject early in the *Poetics* (1447a), Aristotle allows as how he will look "similarly into whatever else falls within the same inquiry." According to Dryden's thumbnail poetics of the genre in *Preface to Fables Ancient and Modern*, "the nature of a preface is rambling, never wholly out of the way, nor in it." And in *S/Z* Barthes divides his critical activity between the 561 *lexies* of "Sarrasine" and his 93 numbered digressions; *Le Plaisir du texte* as a "whole" is a series of "phylacteries."[9] Robert Scholes identifies Barthes as a "high structuralist"; Dryden, "often 'high,'" was sometimes, as Genette is, a "low structuralist."[10] I am content to be a sub-structuralist. What I intend here is a series of *petites thèses* or more accurately, perhaps, *petits fours*, *petits huits*, or the like, and I shall try to maintain decorum on the way to a concluding view of Marvell's "Mourning."

Returning to Horace, *Exegi monumentum aere perennius*, and *usque ego postera / crescam laude recens*. Poetry—mimesis, fiction, verse, fine language, whatever pleases—lives and dies in the eye and ear of the believer, has its form in the nature of the belief, and fulfills its functions in corresponding practices. Or "the category of literary texts is not distinguished by defining characteristics but by the characteristic use to which those texts are put by the community," and "the definition of literature must, like the definition of weed [or, as some might prefer, 'flower'], bring into a definition in a very central way the notion of value."[11] Marvell continues a poet because he is seen to be, and a great poet because he is said and shown to be. His *monumentum* will have remained *aere perennius*; but it must also have changed in order to be at all, as Horace percipiently wrote, merging artist, work or art, and artistry in proclaiming that "I shall grow young by praise." This standard model of perpetuity, the living monument, as in "The Nymph Complaining," gives equal emphasis to the maker and the wonderer: it is the art of human life that gives human life to verbal art.

Frank Kermode recently propounded a view of *The Classic* that has not yet been widely accepted in Anglo-American criticism and that would probably have been unthinkable two or three decades ago, when the "affective fallacy" was widely current, but its time has surely come.[12] As Kermode adapts it from Lévi-Strauss, the view in brief is that "the survival of the classic must ... depend upon its possession of a surplus of signifier; as in *King Lear* or *Wuthering Heights* this may expose them to the charge of confusion, for they must always signify more than is needed by any one interpreter or any generation of interpreters" (p. 140). Earlier, "one may speak of the text as a system of signifiers which always shows a surplus after meeting any particular restricted reading ... " (p. 135). This new critical stance involves "the by-passing of all the old arguments about 'intention.' And even if we may hesitate to accept the semiological method in its entirety we can allow, I think, for the intuitive rightness of its rules about plurality. The gap between text and meaning, in which the reader operates is always present and always different in extent" (p. 136). The attitude expressed here is very close to my own, very apt (as I think) for the reading of a poet like Marvell, and very far from E.D. Hirsch's sometime view, as expressed in *Validity in Interpretation* (1968), that recovery of the author's meaning (intention) is the proper work of criticism, as distinct from interpretation, which is concerned with the much more uncertain matter of significance.

Kermode's view of "the classic" is essentially a structuralist and semiotic one, and its value, in general, seems to me essentially that of the New Criticism: it liberates the work from the question-begging that can accompany attention to authorship, origins, and historical context, as such, and proportionally obscure the work; and a poem is no more enslaved by the limitations and predilections of the critic than it would be in any case, since these are merely redirected and differently engaged. It is perhaps an open question whose limits and predilections are better left with or without the impedimenta of orthodox literary history. But, unless literary history is primarily the end (obviously a legitimate scholarly end), there is a limit to how much of it is necessary or useful for many kinds of purposeful engagements with literary works. It has been laid to the charge of the New Criticism that to practice "it," all that was required was a poem and the *OED*: A pleasantry that omits the "intermedium of affinity," the human head through which the work comes to mean in relation to all the work's perceived intertextualities, and the reader's experience—including the *OED*—perhaps as fine a "guide to Marvell," these days, as one could recommend for a poet with such a "surplus of signifiers." Marvell may be allowed to stand a classic poet now as heretofore, and such characteristic traits as "timeless timeliness" and "genius" retain their relevance and recognizability.

The future of the informed reading and critical analysis of the lyric has much to gain from attention to recent French criticism, whether identified as hermeneutics, poetics, semiotics (earlier, semiology), or structuralism. For all the complications, which look to some outsiders like confusion worse confounded, there is a body of extraordinarily penetrating theory here, and there are provocative examples of what can be done in the reading of works—as with "Sarrasine" by Barthes, and Proust by Genette. But, interestingly, most of the theory and practical applications have been addressed to narrative. Thus "structuralists have done relatively little work on poetry, . . . and with the exception of Paul Zumthor's monumental *Essai de poetique medievale* [Paris: Seuil, 1972], which sets out to reconstruct the conventions of poetry in the medieval period, there has been no attempt to produce a systematic account of the operations of reading or the assumed conventions of the lyric."[13] The potential for mutual contributions to understanding of Marvell's poems and a structuralist theory of the lyric seems to me to point a sure direction for fruitful literary inquiry. Structuralism is not "the light that never was, on sea or land, / The consecration, and the poet's dream," but it does represent a thorough analytical inquiry into system and structure that is new in the sphere of much Anglo-American literary study. There is much to be learned from it, if doctrinal and liturgical excesses are recognized for where they are, on the fringe—which is admittedly sometimes difficult to differentiate from a frontier. Its conscious affinities with extra-literary spheres give it an invigorating social circumspectness and depth of perspective, and its evolving terminology directly if sometimes darkly reflects the complex epistemologies of our time.

III

To locate my subsequent remarks on particular poems within the larger frame of Marvellian reference, I shall briefly survey "the whole." Marvell the satirist holds a second-class citizenship on Parnassus, and to the majority of readers familiar with the poet he wrote approximately thirty-three poems, none a satire or occasional poem of the Restoration type. These thirty-three are the range of my reference here, as the received canon of Marvell's texts, and the ordonnance is approximately as follows. By these, or more often a selection of them, Marvell has his poetical majority and identity, and he is probably first, last, and always, or at least preeminently, the poet of "To His Coy Mistress." After that his majority and his familiarity rest on several classes of poem constituted according to different principles. His biggest poem is *Upon Appleton House, to My Lord Fairfax* (776 lines), a poem that has some claim to being his "greatest," not on grounds of size alone. Another major poem, and as some think Marvell's greatest and certainly one of his most complex, is *An Horatian Ode upon Cromwell's Return from Ireland*. Close to this for its capacity both to afford endless enlightened pleasure and to sustain an immense body of learned commentary is "The Garden," which has been all but manured to death, as some wag has said, after the reproach of "The Mower Against Gardens": "[luxurious man] a more luscious Earth for them did knead, / Which stupefied them while it fed" (ll. 7–8).

In the next group, such mixed company might be found as "The Nymph Complaining for the Death of Her Fawn," the suite of four Mower poems, and "Upon the Hill and Grove at Bill-Borrow." At this point—and even before—sub-sets become as difficult as arbitrary. Two separate but more or less equal ones might be such as the two "Soul and" dialogues; the three notably hieroglyphic poems, "On a Drop of Dew," "The Coronet," and "The Definition of Love"; and "Bermudas" and "The Picture of Little T.C. in a Prospect of Flowers." The other sixteen are "the rest." One or several will turn up in most anthologies, most likely "Eyes and Tears," "The Unfortunate Lover," "The Fair Singer," and "Music's Empire." The remaining twelve are definitely fugitive pieces in the anthological consciousness. One turns up, now and again, but not often. Thus the three pastoral dialogues and the pastoral narrative usually don't make it. Nor do the four slight occasional and "relational" poems, consisting in two wedding songs, an epitaph, and a translated chorus. Leaving four poems—"Young Love," "The Gallery," "Mourning," and "The Match"—at least two or three of which seem to me especially interesting, in spite or perhaps because of their persistent though not invariable neglect. Youthful works, probably, but the youth of genius has its moments.

Since so much has been written elsewhere on Marvell's poems, I restrict my comments here mostly to poems other than the anthological masterpieces. These observations should be regarded as not quite random, but nearly so, by design. The first of the *Miscellaneous Poems* of 1681 is "A Dialogue between the Resolved Soul, and Created Pleasure," (pp. 9–12), than which nothing could be much further from a burning issue in our day. What strikes one—once the inevitable note on *Ephesians* has been flushed from consciousness—is what a vivid and vigorous "Onward, Christian soldier" this is. It belongs more immediately to the vision of Homeric epic-combat than to symbolic Christian dialectics. The "whole armor of God" is there, all right, but it is armor, and what is equally there is the arming of a champion in the face of a hostile army, something of a slight and fledgling champion, at that, since the soul has need of fortitude and substance "to wield / The weight of thine immortal shield." The first verse paragraph is in the nature of a general's harangue, and the reader is invited to an initial sense of the weight of the armory and the ostensible opposition to be faced, in order to appreciate the particular appeal of pleasure. Could anything be less appropriate for resistance to the temptations of the flesh than a gladiator's or a champion's trappings? Whatever the allusive force of the whole armor of God, the real temptations are not on the field of choler but where green thoughts tend to the wrong green shades.

"A Dialogue between the Soul and Body" (pp. 21–23)—like poems of the kind by others—is deeply rooted in religious, social, literary, and pictorial antecedents and conventions, but no one who has read much Marvell could mistake it for anyone else's, because the wit is Marvell's and his alone, as *poeta ludens*, the mimetic creator at play. Marvell's letters—naturally more than his poems—assure us of his faith, but the poems don't require the biographical datum of belief or even the eternal verities themselves to give force and validity to the metaphysic struggle of the poem. "A Dialogue" creates the soul and body: we "know" we have the latter (*sentio ergo sum*), and if "mind" allows us even hypothetically to have a soul then this is how soul and body would be at odds and evens. The poem is brilliant, powerful, and witty as a whole, as well as part by part—as soon as we are past what is a *compositio loci*, in effect: "O who shall, from *this Dungeon*, raise / A Soul *in*slav'd so many wayes?" (italics mine). The question is rhetorical, of course, since the answer is obvious; but souls have something of bodies' idiom and character, as indeed they must if human nature is to be identified by its generic "intertextuality"—the *tertium aliquid*, the subtle knot that makes us man. The dance of death that life consists in has its duets, and the poem is one such.

But the master-stroke of the poem, otherwise made up of alternating decastichs, may well be the concluding pair of couplets that bring the number of the poem's lines to forty-four. Legouis writes: "Leishman notes . . . that the anonymous corrector of *T2* has drawn his pen through the last four lines of the fourth stanza and has written below: *"Desunt multa."* The poem may originally have continued through several more ten-line stanzas, of which only the last four lines of the poem in its present condition survive" (1:249). Perhaps, but it is like Marvell to give the last word to Soul through Body's mouth. The poem concludes with a sentiment that exactly characterizes the relationship between soul and body in the nature-art dialectic, and neatly characterizes each.

> What but a Soul could have the wit
> To build me up for Sin so fit?
> So Architects do square and hew,
> Green Trees that in the Forest grew.

As body, Body complains of Soul's craft and heartlessness, and in its obtuseness is made to concede the capacity—not the fact, in mid-life—of superiority to Soul: "What but a Soul *could* have the wit / To build me up [, otherwise] for Sin so fit?" The syntactical ambiguity of "for Sin so fit" is surely designed as well as functional, at the same time expressing and answering Body's own complaint. "So Architects do square and hew, / Green Trees that in the Forest grew"—an easily felt reproach, even more so now and for better reason than in Marvell's day, but also containing its own answer, since the architect, in the image of the Creator, is the type of purposeful man constructively artifacting nature, even if (as in *Upon Appleton House*) a "forrain Architect" is made guilty of idle artifice. There may be a lost poem in which there are more than the present forty-four lines, but there is a completed poem here, too, happily by dafault if not by design: Body's tongue exceeds the formal bounds implicitly set for the ten-line form of "meaningful" dialogue and thus admits its need for Soul's curbing. And as the poem stands there is no more to say.

One of the most complex, perfectly balanced, elusively circum-spect, and perspectively illusive poems ever written is *An Horatian*

Ode upon Cromwell's Return from Ireland (pp. 91–94). The title alone establishes intertextualities of time, space, and issue, and heralds a historical-literary event of extraordinary consequence—a consequence due in no small part to three hundred years' subsequent history, to which, however, the literary idiom owes nothing in origin however much by way of explication. This is arguably the most attitudinally poised poem in all literature, an astonishing accomplishment for the forces brought to equilibrium and yet kept in motion in the poem. The poem's complexities perfectly reflect those of the ethical and political judgment of the conflicts, events, and issues they are concerned with, and it is easy enough to see why critics have been able to find the poem a paean to Cromwell, an elegy on Charles I, a political satire, and withal an ode on events of lasting moment, in history and here also in art.

The Ode is a prime example of a dialectical equivocation that in different ways is also characteristic of George Herbert's (and of Shakespeare's) poetry. By any other name this is perspective and attitudinal ambiguity entailed by lexical and syntactical ambiguities. The answer to the question, "What does Marvell think of Cromwell and Charles I, respectively?" can only be answered by inference from biographical data and detailed attention to what the poem says, which is equivalent to what Marvell "thought" in the sense that what he didn't think he couldn't write. Otherwise, the poem is a poetically formal study in epistemology, by which one is forced to consider the terms of evaluation in the act of analysis, unless the poem is to be read selectively as a projection of aprioristic Royalist or anti-Royalist assumptions. By the former, Charles's tragedy (ll. 47–66) is at the heart of a vehemently ironical poem; by the latter, "the Royal Actor" plays a part—well—in an obsolete ceremonial subordinated to the true realities of biography and history, where Cromwell's will, God's, and the nation's met as he came, saw, and overcame. No doubt the latter reading is nearest what Marvell the man thought: given his life and the times, what else could he have thought? What is of interest, however, is the poetical shape of "belief," and by the epistemological imperatives of apparent ambiguities Marvell forces a series of recognitions that seem to culminate in a comprehensive conviction that Cromwell is for the best in this bettering of possible worlds. Whatever the poem's comprehensive attitude, to read it is to be confronted with conflicting ironical testimonies, and it is the kind of work well suited to sustain and reward an exhaustive analysis of the structuralist kind. This seems so especially because almost every detail in the poem looks different, depending upon how much context, before and behind in the poem, and in all directions beyond, one draws upon for the interpreting.

IV

Several poems that seem to me especially interesting for their perspective epistemology are—in their order in *Miscellaneous Poems*— "The Coronet," "Eyes and Tears," "A Dialogue between the Soul and Body," "The Nymph Complaining for the Death of Her Fawn," "To His Coy Mistress," "The Unfortunate Lover," "The Gallery," "Mourning," "Daphnis and Chloe," "The Definition of Love," "The Garden" (with *"Hortus"*), and *An Horatian Ode*. These have in common a complex verbal vision of a kind that shifts its "faces," its effects, its dimensions, its meanings, and its significances, depending upon how it is looked at—and I am talking not about the fancifully subjective propensities of the reader, but the craftily designed and finely cut facets of Marvell's own making, which irresistibly draw the eye. The epitome of these hard, smooth, and polished conspectuities is the *Horatian Ode*, as already suggested; it is in fact a perfect compound of general, conventional, attitudinal, and linguistic subtexts: it has simultaneous faces and directions and must be circumambulated like a sculpture to be comprehended either in full or in detail.

In some of these poems a prominent technique of Marvell's poetic is a verbal art of illusion approximating the graphic devices of anamorphosis: "Le système est établi comme une curiosité technique, mais il contient une poétique de l'abstraction, un mécanisme puissant de l'illusion optique, et une philosophie de la réalité factice."[14] Almost from the discovery of the art of receding perspective in the fifteenth century to the present time, systematic distortions of perspective have fascinated graphic artists not only as a matter of "technical curiosity" but as a means of reconstituting reality and revealing aspects and modalities ordinarily concealed. Two of the best-known paintings wholly or partly anamorphic were well known in Marvell's day, too. Marvell probably didn't write as he did under the influence of such paintings, but his writings and the paintings are artistic manifestations of the same complex and penetrating sensibility, and there is pronounced anamorphosis in the visual aspects of some of his poems as well as in the verbal analogues of ambiguity and equivocation. These are the fully anamorphic portrait of Edward VI by William Scrots in the manner of Holbein (1546, fig. 2, 3), and Holbein's own portrait of "The Ambassadors" (1533, fig. 4), a masterpiece of ultra-realistic portraiture with an unrecognizably anamorphosed *memento mori* afloat between and near the feet of the ambassadors (fig. 5 gives a resolution): a mirror held at the proper angle to the right of the distorted figure puts it into clear

FIG. 2. William Scrots. *Portrait of Edward VI.* 1546. 42.5 × 160 cm. National Portrait Gallery, London.

FIG. 3. William Scrots. *Portrait of
Edward VI.*

perspective, and all the rest of the painting slips into distortion and incoherence; the significance is obvious, the effect startling.[15]

E.H. Gombrich describes examples as follows. "All these skewy configurations would still present from one point of view the same aspect as the straight ones. The geometry needed for our construction is called 'the art of perspective,' and the technical term for oblique or curved images that fulfill this condition is 'anamorphosis.' The sixteenth-century portrait of Edward VI is such an 'anamorphosis.' Seen from in front [fig. 2] it presents a weird appearance, but seen from very close to the edge, the distortion is rectified, and we see the head transposed into the normal view [fig. 3]. . . . From a fixed viewpoint, any distortion in perspective can be made indistinguishable from the normal image."[16] The subtextual implications of such "oblique arts" are various: what the eye sees requires a certain perspective for resolution (an ideological proposition, at bottom); holding the mirror up to art—a means of resolving some anamorphic distortions—yields nature (the tenet of mimesis); "mortal space" is metaphysically four-dimensional (death-in-life figured by the skull in "The Ambassadors," with which compare some of the wittily lugubrious grotesqueries of "To His Coy Mistress"). Such implications poise rather obviously between the medieval Christian and the modern humanistic empirical vision.

The powers of the art of perspective, and the distorted vision of those who attempted to see from the wrong perspective, clearly did have a direct and complex impact beyond the sphere of the graphic arts, as, for example, in *Richard II* (Bushy to the Queen):

> Each substance of a grief hath twenty shadows,
> Which shows like grief itself, but is not so;
> For sorrow's eye, glazed with blinding tears,
> Divides one thing entire to many objects,
> Like perspectives, which, rightly gazed upon,
> Show nothing but confusion—eyed awry,
> Distinguish form. So your sweet majesty,
> Looking awry upon your lord's departure,
> Find shapes of grief more than himself to wail,
> Which, looked on as it is, is nought but shadows
> of what it is not. . . .

> (2.2.14–24)

Three poems especially interesting in this connection are "The Gallery," "Eyes and Tears," and "Mourning" (to which I shall give detailed attention below). "The Gallery" (pp. 31–32) is interesting not because it very directly employs the arts of "curious perspective," but because it artfully spatializes the mind's eye in articulate portraits of (and for) Clora that exhibit the sum total and accumulated complex

FIG. 4. Hans Holbein the Younger. *The Ambassadors*. 1533. 206 × 209.5 cm. Reproduced by cour of the Trustees, The National Gallery, London.

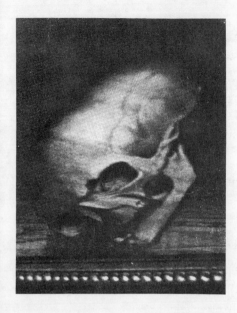

FIG. 5. Hans Holbein the Younger. *The Ambassadors.* [Detail]

of the speaker's feelings and experience in terms of distinct and simultaneous representations, or "systems," of temporality. The poem's "first" and directly representational time-scheme is that represented by the poem as utterance: its seven octaves of octosyllabic address have a beginning, a middle, and an end. The beginning invites Clora to "come view my Soul," where, "for all furniture, you'l find / Only your Picture in my Mind" (st. 1, ll. 1, 7–8; n.b. singular "Picture"). The middle (sts. 2–6) is in effect a guided tour through the gallery of the speaker's soul, where Clora's moods are variously figured as "an Inhumane Murtheress" (l. 10), "Aurora in the Dawn" (l. 18), "an Enchantress" (l. 25), and "Venus" (l. 33); the sequence is from "Here Thou art painted in the Dress" through "These Pictures and a thousand more" to "thou alone to people me, / Art grown a num'rous Colony" (ll. 9, 41, 45–46)—symbolic spots of time with allegorical representations of images left on the retina of the mind's eye, as though amorous experience were artistic perception. The end: "But of these Pictures and the rest, / That at Entrance likes me best . . ." (ll. 49–50). Wherever Clora came in, we don't arrive at "the Entrance" until the last stanza.

The second time-scheme is that of the span of experience condensed and selectively represented in the poem; this has a beginning (the first meeting with Clora) and a middle (the present, the moment of the poem's address), but no end is in sight. The third time is in effect a counter-scheme. It is a timeless present that the force of beauty's impression upon the memory effects, the perpetuity of the experience of first meeting. The power of the image of loveliness over time is an easy allegory of the poet's art, if one wants one (all of Marvell's poems are in one way metapoems), but the poem has potent charm simply as a pastorally stylized mimesis of experience: for all the vicissitudes of years of experience for worse as well as for better, the image of the beginning endures, smiling extremity out of act:

> But, of these Pictures and the rest,
> That at the Entrance likes me best:
> Where the same Posture, and the Look
> Remains, with which I first was took.
> A tender Shepherdess, whose Hair
> Hangs loosely playing in the Air,
> Transplanting Flow'rs from the green Hill,
> To crown her Head, and Bosome fill.
>
> (ll. 49–56)

"Eyes and Tears" (pp. 15–17) is emphatically a genre and convention poem that is difficult to attend to without thinking of Crashaw's "Weeper" and the many commonplaces which settle this poem into its traditional place. What interests me, however, is Marvell's art of dialectical equivocation, which is especially prominent in this poem and in "Mourning." The purport of the equivocation is perfectly clear, and the equivocation indeed conveys it. There is a shared significance in "Eyes and Tears" and what lies behind the passage from *Richard II* quoted above, since, despite Bushy's comforting insistence that eyes "glazed" with tears falsely multiply causes of grief, the Queen's tearful eyes foresee truer than either knows. On the subject of tears, Marvell is scarcely less eloquent in a letter, written in 1667 to console Sir John Trott on the death of a son:

I know that the very sight of those who have been witnesses of our better Fortune, doth but serve to reinforce a Calamity. I know the contagion of grief, and infection of Tears, and especially when it runs in a blood. And I my self could sooner imitate then blame those innocent relentings of Nature, so that they spring from tenderness only and humanity, not from an implacable sorrow. The Tears of a family may flow together like those little drops that compact the Rainbow, and if they be plac'd with the same advantage towards Heaven as those are to the Sun, they too have their splendor: and like that bow while they unbend into seasonable showers, yet they promise that there shall not be a second flood. But the dissoluteness of grief, the prodigality of sorrow is neither to be indulg'd in a mans self, nor comply'd with in others. . . .

(2:311–12)

In "Eyes and Tears," the world as a vale of tears, with grief and penitence as the proper human reflection of the fallen condition is the basis of a detailed "argument," and the essential relationship between "Eyes and Tears" is in touch with the spirit of *Venus and Adonis*:

> Here overcome, as one full of despair,
> She vailed her eyelids, who, like sluices, stopped
> The crystal tide that from her two cheeks fair
> In the sweet channel of her bosom dropped;
>   But through the floodgates breaks the silver rain
>   And with his strong course opens them again.
>
> O, how her eyes and tears did lend and borrow,
> *Her eye seen in the tears, tears in her eye,*
> Both crystals, where they viewed each other's sorrow—
> Sorrow that friendly sighs sought still to dry;
>   But like a stormy day, now wind, now rain,
>   Sighs dry her cheeks, tears make them wet again.
>
> (ll. 955–66)

Marvell's "Tears" are the ultimate reality of eyes. As the first and last stanzas differently insist, both suggesting by analogy the continuity between the primary and secondary imagination as

Coleridge characterizes them: as the esemplastic power sees, dissolves, and recreates, so eyes, "having view'd the object vain," naturally will "be ready to complain." (A resonance of "reddy" is not to be denied, I think, and complaining eyes are an all but violent metonymy.) It is crafty of Marvell to have Nature decree at once for herself and implicitly for us "with the same Eyes to weep and see," and were she not so economical we might have to have separate pairs of eyes, or at least an auspicious and a dropping eye, since both seeing and weeping are anatomically and spiritually integral functions of eyes. Indeed, the second line seems to suggest what the last stanza of the poem spells out, that in the view of heaven the sight of fallen earth is instant and simultaneous cause of grief and regret: "How wisely Nature did decree, / With—the same—Eyes to weep and see!" It is Marvell's habit of inversion that suggests this secondary reading of the syntax, which cannot be proved. In any event, the end of weeping, as it is expressed in the last stanza, is for "Eyes and Teares [to] be the same things," so that "each the other's difference"— and thus likeness—"bears." The ambiguity of the last line trenchantly expresses the dissolution into identity: "These weeping Eyes, those seeing Tears"—where "these" and "those" are at once demonstrative adjectives and relative pronouns, "these [tears] weeping eyes, those [eyes] seeing Tears." Thus subject and object are syntactically as well as naturally one, and state and action are the same, eyes-tears that characteristically see-weep actively in the process of seeing-weeping. Marvell's last line, here, seems to me to epitomize the complex simplicity of his poetic art: what he is doing is easily enough apprehended, but it defies paraphrase and it belabors comment. Which is, of course, what poetry is supposed to do.

V

"Mourning" (pp. 33–35) is a poem often omitted from anthological representations of Marvell, yet it seems to me an amazing minor accomplishment.

Mourning

1   You, that decipher out the Fate
      Of humane Off-springs from the Skies,
      What mean these Infants which of late
      Spring from the Starrs of *Chlora's* Eyes?

2   Her Eyes confus'd, and doubled ore,   5
      With Tears suspended ere they flow;
      Seem bending upwards, to restore
      To Heaven, whence it came, their Woe.

3   When, molding of the watry Sphears,
      Slow drops unty themselves away;   10
      As if she, with those precious Tears,
      Would strow the ground where *Strephon* lay.

4   Yet some affirm, pretending Art,
      Her Eyes have so her Bosome drown'd,   15
      Only to soften near her Heart
      A place to fix another Wound.

5   And, while vain Pomp does her restrain
      Within her solitary Bowr,
      She courts her self in am'rous Rain;   20
      Her self both *Danae* and the Showr.

6   Nay others, bolder, hence esteem
      Joy now so much her Master grown,
      That whatsoever does but seem
      Like Grief, is from her Windows thrown.   25

7   Nor that she payes, while she survives,
      To her dead Love this Tribute due;
      But casts abroad these Donatives,
      At the installing of a new.

8   How wide they dream! The *Indian* Slaves
       That sink for Pearl through Seas profound,   30
       Would find her Tears yet deeper Waves
       And not of one the bottom sound.

9   I yet my silent Judgment keep,
       Disputing not what they believe:
       But sure as oft as Women weep,   35
       It is to be suppos'd they grieve.

The poems will repay detailed analysis from "You" to "grieve," but I want to attend here mainly to "Perspectives in 'Mourning,'" a poem in which the medium and message are reciprocally oblique and depend upon the reader's resolution to set them straight. The poem's persistent ambiguity of perspective is wittily conveyed in another medium by Man Ray, in "Eyes with Glass Tears," a photograph of 1933, a close-up portrait of a young woman's nose and eyes (fig. 6). Her eyes, cast upward, are graced with very long, mascaraed, apparently artificial lashes; what at first appear to be tears are five transparent glass beads, four carefully placed at the corners of the eyes and one just to the left of the left nostril. The Surrealistically ironic spirit of the photograph is, in part, the spirit of "Mourning," and the differences are more a matter of medium than of period, school, or "attitude."

In its rhetorical situation, "Mourning" is an inquiry by the speaker into the causes and significance of Chlora's weeping and retirement. More generally, since Chlora is a—half-urbanized—pastoral archetype of Woman, the poem inquires into the meaning and significance of Woman's Tears. The poem either settles all the issues it raises, or it settles none; in fact, in doing both, it unsettles easy settlements, dissolves perspectives, ironically exposes others' and its own irony, and keeps reconstituting itself for further viewing: it is an anamorphic study in poetical epistemology. The effect of sustained ambiguity in the poem is the verbal, "ethical," and oral-aural equivalent of the usual pictorial methods of representing space and volume: the perceptual, as they are seen at a particular time and from a particular angle; and the conceptual, as they are "known" by measurement or "supposed" by experience and probability to be.

If Marvell's assumptions about the character of men and women

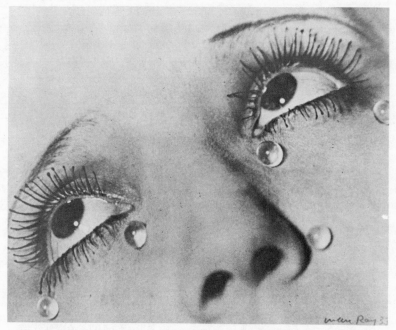

FIG. 6. Man Ray. *Eyes with Glass Tears.* 1933. Photograph. 23 × 29 cm.
Copyright Arnold H. Crane Collection, Chicago.

and the relationships between them were conventional in the seventeenth century, they are either reactionary or radical in the 1970's—depending upon how they are viewed, and how the poem is read in full. The generalizations about manners are gender-bound, but what is said about the underlying nature is that one can't be sure what that nature is. Assuming that men and women are different, Marvell demonstrates an interesting complementarity: the inscrutability of a woman's expressive gestures is complemented by the deliberate—gallant? ironical? but reciprocal—ambiguity of the male speaker, as though one perplexing turn deserved another. The most balanced intertextuality between men and women is—from the man's point of view—an ambiguous mutuality.

Some epigraphics to the purpose of a viewing of "Mourning" are these:

Be such mere women, who with shrieks and outcries
Can vow a present end to all their sorrows,
Yet live to vow new pleasures, and outlive them.
They are the silent griefs which cut the heart-strings:
Let me die smiling.

Calantha in Ford's Broken Heart, 5.3.72–76

"Not Tears of Grief; but such as those
"With which calm Pleasure overflows;
"Or pity, when we look on you
"That live without this happy Vow.
"How should we grieve that must be seen
"Each one a *Spouse*, and each a *Queen*;
"And can in *Heaven* hence behold
"Our brighter Robes and Crowns of Gold?"

One of the "Suttle Nunns" in Upon Appleton
House, ll. 113–20

And Stars shew lovely in the Night,
But as they seem the Tears of Light.

"Eyes and Tears," ll. 43–44

The tree ere while foreshortned to our view,
When fall'n shews taller yet then as it grew....

A Poem upon the Death of O.C., ll. 269–70

though he be painted one way like a Gorgon,
The other way's a Mars.

Antony and Cleopatra, 2.5.116–17

One face, one voice, one habit, and two persons—
A natural perspective that is and is not.

Twelfth Night, 5.1.208–209

The plots or projects of "Mourning" are four: in the order in which we meet them, the speaker's (he speaks), Chlora's (she weeps), Marvell's (behind the scenes, he makes the speaker speak and Chlora weep, whate'er he meant thereby), and the reader's (he—or she—comprehends all). The speaker at first apostrophizes astrologers to ask "what mean" the tears that "of late / Spring from the Starrs of *Chlora's* Eyes?" He describes events and offers possible interpretations (Chlora's tears "*seem* bending upwards," l. 7, and it is "*as if* she ... / Would strow the ground where *Strephon* lay," l. 12); epitomizes the interpretations of cynical observers, the second school "bolder" than the first (sts. 4–5 and 6–7); exclaims impatiently over the interpreters' shallowness and the depth of Chlora's tears (st. 8); and then bows out coyly and apparently without committing himself (st. 9). The poem invites close inspection of its means, since, while we hear—and through vivid accounting "see"—much of Chlora, we have not met her, and we "know" no more than what we would project from experience and what we are told at third hand, the speaker's: he reserves judgment. Does Chlora weep for Strephon's loss? Does she weep in self-pity and to "soften near her Heart / A place to fix another Wound"? (ll. 15–16). Or does she weep for joy—out with the old tears, in with the new?

The interface of the poem is between the perceptions of psychologically and morally ambiguous behavior and the "data" of the behavior, about which there is no doubt: Chlora weeps, and Chlora has withdrawn "Within her solitary Bowr" (l. 18)—either in ceremonious as well as real mourning, or (so the skeptics) in "vain Pomp," self-entertainment, and jovial and reginal bliss: "She courts her slef in am'rous Rain; / Her self both *Danae* and the Showr" is nothing if not leonine Metaphysical gossip. No wonder one so accomplished as all that, uniting heaven and earth in her own life and person, should weep such profound tears that pearl-divers—here an Eastern type of the seeker after the goodly pearls of the kingdom of heaven—would be at a loss to take their measure.

The poem is ashimmer with particular ambiguities, with meanings that come forward and recede as the poem progresses, but the pivotal ones are at the beginning and the end, though the earlier ones tend to come into relief—as courses of human action do in retrospect—after one has come to the end of, or at any rate got further into, the poem. Without an aprioristic judgment, none of the ambiguities can be certainly resolved on one side or the other, as one in stanza 8 finely suggests: in the primary reading, the grammar, syntax, and sense are "The *Indian* Slaves ... / Would find her Tears yet deeper Waves" and not sound the bottom of one of them; the secondary reading, prompted by a cogent if unchivalrous skepticism, has "The *Indian* Slaves ... find[ing] her Tears yet Deeper Waves" than are their "Seas profound" of custom, and not one of these tear-waves of sound bottom.

The last stanza is apparently a well-mannered refusal to express judgment, to enter into dispute, or to doubt without good reason: an expression, in short, of perfect courtesy. It is also reserved in other ways, and supplies its own ambiguities for the ironical resolution of the poem still available to cynics. The content of the first two lines actually concedes nothing, since the speaker could refrain from "Disputing ... what they believe," whatever the "silent Judgment" kept, and there is a judgment. It is in the last two lines that doubts arise and proliferate for the reader, but presumably not for the speaker, whose tongue cannot be seen in or out of his cheek. In the last two lines,

> But sure as oft as Women weep,
> It is to be suppos'd they grieve.

the ambiguities glister and afford resolution only according to formula and perspective. *Contra Chlora (et feminas)*: "women weep so often that they must do so disingenuously, in order to elicit sympathy by being thought to grieve." *Pro Chlora*: "however often women weep, it is reasonable to suppose they grieve." There are other ambiguities, but these are primary.

One might ask about the cautious speaker, which of these resolutions, or neither, represents his "silent Judgment" (and the still more mysterious Marvell's), but one is not to have an answer. Still, the poem supplies one or two other counters, in the name of the lady and in the title. χλωρός, ά, όν means "greenish," with varying applications and connotations; the primary figurative meaning was "fresh, tender, delicate," and of wine "sparkling." "Mo[u]rning" is an exquisite example of the radiantly ambiguous title: even when one wakes up to the two-in-one title, which compounds a set of notions that can only partly be comprehended in such a portmanteau word as "matutinalachrymation," the range and character of the significance are still not clear: what we have is "mourning" is (or may be) "morning" is (in a manner of speaking, or a way of looking at things) "mourning" is. ... The dawning of a new day. What then?

Marvell's verse invites both the eye and the ear, if it is to be fully appreciated. Addressed to the ear, its ambiguities—like "Mo[u]rning"—are most alive and tentative until either resolved or revealed as far as they are to be revealed; seen by the eye they can be better understood, but they must almost always be heard, too. "Mourning" is very accessible to modern readers, and one of its prime virtues is that it continues delightful and rewarding upon rereading even when it is quite fully understood; it does so, I think, because as a complex perspective poem it continues to look different as its elements rearrange themselves in our perception, even as those in a painting do when we look at it now one way, now another, and now both ways at another time retrospectively. Moreover, the poem is about something, it is not merely an agreeable formal tour de force: it is about persons and attitudes, and it is wittily and genially about all of the persons that it is essentially about, but especially Chlora, who has her grace and charm whatever the meaning and motives of her tears. Her tears have significance and value, both within the fiction of the poem and in the making of the poem: she is not only witty in herself (if she is witty as charged, as her tears are deep), but causes wit in her observers, "some" (l. 13), "others" (l. 21), the speaker, Marvell, the reader. If the poem may be said to have a moral, the moral is, all things being equal in an aesthetic state of equilibrate ambiguity, let's see it both ways and let the doubt be generous. The poem is playful, sociable, "open," perhaps as a circle is open, since its ending invites return to the beginning, but open, nevertheless; it enjoys what it says and what it sees, and it invites the reader to do the same. Turning on their axes, art and nature hold the mirror each to each.

Marvell's tutelary deity was surely Janus, the spirit of the doorway, seeing before and behind, vigilant in war and peace, visionary in space and time. Although Milton didn't know it (no more do we), his elegist in "Lycidas" was Marvell, awaiting his time to move on from the pastoral world of civility and wit to which he had given so much. When he heard the strain of higher mood, sometime in the second decade of the Interregnum, "he rose and twitches his mantle blue: / Tomorrow to fresh woods, and pastures new." And tomorrow he was a man of an age, of public life and verse. And yesterday and today a poet for all time. It is Marvell. He outdwells his hour.

Notes

1. *Salerio:* His hour is almost past. *Gratiano:* And it is marvel he outdwells his hour" (*Merchant of Venice*, 2.6.2–3). David Farkas, of Texas Technical University, Lubbock, and Arthur Walzer, of the Department of Rhetoric, University of Minnesota, St. Paul, kindly read this essay in draft. I am indebted to them for what they took away and for making valuable suggestions; what is left I owe to their generosity, but I am bound to take responsibility for it.

2. "I have finished a monument more lasting than bronze and loftier than the pyramid's royal pile, one that no wasting rain, no furious north wind can destroy, or the countless chain of years and the ages' flight. I shall not altogether die, but a mighty part of me shall escape the death-goddess. On and on shall I grow, ever fresh with the glory of after time" (C.E. Bennett's Loeb Classical Library translation; *Odes and Epodes*, rev. ed., 1927; reprint ed., Cambridge, Mass.: Harvard University Press, William Heinemann, Ltd., 1968). Libitina is actually goddess of burials, and *crescam laude recens* needs the emphasis on life, motion, and activity of "I shall grow young by praise" (Cicero has *in laude vivere* in his letters to friends, 15.6.1).

3. "The most stiking [domiciliar] phenomenon of the period [1570–1620] is the gigantic country seat, the so-called 'prodigy house.' The work of the Court aristocracy of the late Elizabethan and Jacobean age, many of these fantastic edifices still lie heavily about the English countryside like the fossilized bones of the giant reptiles of the Carboniferous Age. Their sole justification was to demonstrate status, their sole function to entertain the sovereign on one of the summer progresses"; Lawrence Stone, *The Crisis of the Aristocracy* (Oxford: At the Clarendon Press, 1965), p. 551; see pp. 551–555, condensed as pp. 252–254 of abridged ed. (1967).

4. Roland Barthes, *S/Z* (Paris: Editions du Seuil, 1970), a 200-page study of "Sarrasine," a thirty-page story by Balzac. Gerard Genette, *Figures I–III*, 3 vols. (Paris: Éditions du Seuil, 1966–72), a study of Proust. There is a useful brief commentary on these works in the chapter on "The Structural Analysis of Literary Texts" in Robert Scholes, *Structuralism in Literature: An Introduction* (New Haven: Yale University Press, 1974), pp. 148–67.

5. *Selected Essays: New Edition* (New York: Harcourt Brace & Co., 1960), p. 251. Elsewhere Eliot stigmatizes "lemon-squeezing," but, since the "precious liquor" here seems nearer Emily Dickinson's "liquor never brewed" than to lemonade, the yield must depend equally on the squeezing and the fruit, and one cannot get blood from a turnip.

6. New Haven: Yale University Press, 1969.

7. There is evidence that [y:], as in German *grün*, was sometimes the vowel sound in both "rule" and "build"; see E.J. Dobson, *English Pronunciation*, 1500–1700, 2nd ed. (Oxford: At the Clarendon Press, 1968), 1:266 ("rule"), and 2:654 ("build").

8. I don't intend "analytical reader" to characterize a privileged status of any kind; I mean one who reads critically for pleasure with a respect for truth.

9. *Le Plaisir du texte* (Paris: Éditions du Seuil, 1970); in English as *The Pleasure of the Text*, trans. Richard Miller (New York: Hill, 1975).

10. Scholes identifies "high structuralism" with the work of Barthes, Lévi-

Strauss, Michel Foucault, Jacques Lacan, and Jacques Derrida: "whatever contributions of these men are absorbed by the general culture, their texts will not suffer the same absorption but will remain—like philosophical texts, which they are, and literary texts, which some of them aspire to be—as unique objects to which later thinkers must return. . . . This is what we may call 'high structuralism'—high in its aspirations and in its current prestige" (*Structuralism in Literature*, p. 157). "The low structuralist"—e.g., Saussure, Propp, Genette—"writes to be immediately useful, to be ultimately superseded. He makes a considerable distinction between creative and critical activity. . . . In a sense, . . . the achievement of the formalists, like that of Aristotle, will be permanent because it will have to be incorporated in any later poetics of fiction. Poetics is, in fact, the discipline par excellence of low structuralism" (p. 158).

11. John M. Ellis, *The Theory of Literary Criticism: A Logical Analysis* (Berkeley and Los Angeles: University of California Press, 1974), pp. 50, 51.

12. *The Classic: Literary Images of Permanence and Change* (New York: Viking, 1975).

13. Jonathan Culler, *Structuralist Poetics: Structuralism, Linguistics, and the Study of Literature* (Ithaca, N.Y.: Cornell University Press, 1975), p. 188; an excellent introduction to the subject.

14. Jurgis Baltrušaitis, *Anamorphoses ou perspectives curieuses* (Paris: Olivier Perrin, 1955), p. 5: "The method has the status of a technical curiosity, but it contains a poetic of abstraction, a powerful mechanism for optical illusion, and a philosophy of artificial reality."

15. The portrait of Edward VI is pl. 3.b in *Anamorphoses*; it is also reproduced in E.H. Gombrich, *Art and Illusion: A Study in the Psychology of Pictorial Representation*, 4th ed. (London: Phaidon, 1972), p. 216. For "The Ambassadors" see pl. 13 and chap. 6, "'Les Ambassadeurs,' de Holbein," in *Anamorphoses*: "Un singulier objet, pareil à un os de seiche, flotte au-dessus du sol: c'est l'anamorphose d'un crane qui se redresse lorsqu'on se place tou près au-dessous, en regardant vers la droite" (p. 58): "A strange object resembling a cuttlebone floats above the floor: it is the anamorphosis of a skull, which rectifies itself when one places oneself nearly underneath, while looking at it toward the right". Since this essay was written, Michael Schuyt and Joost Elffers have assembled an exhibition of anamorphic paintings that opened at Boston's Museum of Fine Arts the week before it was reported on in an article in *Time* magazine (4 October 1976, pp. 92–93) that includes color reproductions of these two paintings, together with resolutions. The *Time* heading, "Fun-Fair Illusions," bears out the accuracy of Baltrušaitis's comment on the usual interpretation of anamorphosis as a technical curiosity. The catalogue, *Anamorphoses: Games of Perception and Illusion in Art* (New York: Harry N. Abrams, Inc., 1976), contains a valuable introduction and essay on pictorial anamorphosis as well as many reproductions in color and black and white.

16. *Art and Illusion*, pp. 213–14.

Marvell's "Soul" Poetry

Joseph Pequigney

Placed, respectively, first, second, and ninth in Marvell's *Miscellaneous Poems*, the volume published posthumously in 1681, "A Dialogue between The Resolved Soul, and Created Pleasure," "On a Drop of Dew," and "A Dialogue between the Soul and Body" share more than a common topic in the human soul. J.B. Leishman can find in these poems "nothing incompatible with Christianity" or "with a kind of Platonic Deism."[1] Although Marvell does occupy both positions, he neither holds them in suspension nor takes an attitude of impartiality toward them. In the design of each work the philosophical yields to a theological perspective; or, in more classic Christian terms, as those, say, of Dante, Reason comes to be completed, and even corrected, by Revelation. Virgil conducts Dante the character in the *Divine Comedy* by the light of Aristotelian reason —Marvell's thought has a more Platonic cast—as far as it can go on the journey to God, and Beatrice can conduct him the rest of the way because she additionally possesses the truths of faith. Marvell expressly introduces the Christian viewpoint with "Humility" in one and "Sin" in the other "Dialogue" and with the conceit of "Manna" in "On a Drop of Dew." Commentators have failed to recognize the determinant effect that those notions and that conceit exert structurally as well as thematically.

I

Prior to the "Dialogue" proper the "Resolved Soul," preparing to contend with "Created Pleasure," defines the point at issue:

> Now, if thou bee'st that thing Divine,
> In this day's Combat let it shine:
>
> (ll. 7–8)

The second-person address does not indicate a man's communicating with his psyche as an "other," for the powers of thought and feeling inhere in the psyche and the personality is inseparable from it, but rather indicates the Soul at soliloquy engaged in self-exhortation. The couplet quoted is one of five, all iambic and octosyllabic, in the prelude, and we soon come to recognize that meter/rhyme combination as the hallmark of the protagonist's utterance. The imagery in ll. 1–10, from the opening word "Courage," through the girding of armor, to the sighting of the "Army, strong as fair / With silken banners" to be opposed, is martial, the opponent being identified as "Nature" with whatever seductive "Art" lies at its command. An "immortal Shield," a "Helmet bright," and a "Sword" are donned in ll. 2–4, and from this detail commentators, among them Legouis[2] and Kermode,[3] have supposed an allusion to a passage in Ephesians 6, verses 16 and 17 of which read:

> above all, taking the shield of faith, wherewith ye shall be able to quench all the fiery darts of the wicked. And take the helmet of salvation, and sword of the Spirit, which is the word of God.

Though Marvell's knight is equipped in like manner, any impression that an allegorical gloss is furnished here will be dissipated upon further investigation. The armor, for one thing, would be incomplete, lacking from Ephesians 6:14–15 "loins girt about with truth," and a "breastplate of righteousness," and "feet shod with preparation of the gospel of peace." St. Paul enjoins his warriors (6:11–12) to "Put on the whole armour of God"—not merely part of it—

that ye may be able to stand against the wiles of the devil. For we wrestle not against flesh and blood, but against principalities, against powers, against the rulers of the darkness of this world, against spiritual wickedness in high places.

The adversary warned against is supernatural and demonic, while the adversary that Marvell depicts and names "Nature" and "Pleasure" is strictly mundane and does not belong to the diabolic hierarchy. The distinction is consequential. The design of the poem would be perceived amiss by a reader led into believing that an alleged Pauline allusion establishes Soul's Christian commitment at the outset. Soul will prove himself a Christian, but ultimately rather than immediately, in due time and by other means.

Pleasure is personified as the tempter throughout, and the measure first heard in his greeting below, trochaic and heptasyllabic, is exclusively his:

> Welcome the Creations Guest,
> Lord of Earth, and Heavens Heir.

> (ll. 11–12)

Though begun on an unexpected note, with hospitable rather than hostile words, the "Combat" is actually underway. The epithets, whose aims are to elicit pride by means of flattery and to lay the groundwork for temptations ahead, can be understood in a right way as well as in the wrong way intended by the speaker. Soul is rightly a guest in the sense of a temporary visitor on earth, and wrongly a guest in the sense that creation is there for his entertainment. Soul may be a "Lord" who has dominion over inferior creatures but is not one in the intimated sense of a "God below" (l. 28), a false divinity. In context the phrase "Heavens Heir" less refers to final felicity than imputes superhuman attributes. Pleasure entreats, "Lay aside that warlike Crest," but this is an attempt literally and figuratively to disarm his opponent upon presenting the first temptation. It is gustatory, an invitation to "Nature's banquet . . . Where the Souls [essences] of fruits and flow'rs / Stand prepar'd to heighten [elate] yours," i.e. Soul's soul.

With six lines devoted to the first and a quatrain to each of the next eight, the temptations appear prolix alongside the retorts, which, with one exception (ll. 41–44), have the relative conciseness of a single couplet. The earliest of these retorts typifies all nine of them metrically and the first five, those in response to the tests of the senses, tactically.

> I sup above, and cannot stay
> To bait so long upon the way.
>
> (ll. 17–18)

In a terse, witty, epigrammatic style, the protagonist declines the invitation by pleading a prior engagement. He chooses to be a guest "above," at the heavenly and spiritual banquet rather than at "Nature's," which would be vegetive and appetizing. He makes corrective reference to the epithet in l. 11, for he will not be "*Creations* Guest," and to the word "heighten" (l. 16), for he will "sup" not to become "high" but on high. More than declining, he converts the terms of the invitation from literal to metaphorical, thereby defining an unworldly outlook and loftier goal. The verb "bait," which means "to stop for rest and refreshment when traveling" (*OED* 7), introduces the figure of a journey; it is that of life and is made by one who must push on so as not to miss his figurative and supernal dinner appointment. Milton's "true wayfaring Christian" from a section of the *Areopagitica* in which aspects of Marvell's theme can find remarkable elucidation comes to mind here:

> He that can apprehend and consider vice in all her baits and seeming pleasures, and yet abstain, and yet distinguish, and yet prefer that which is truly better, he is the true wayfaring Christian. I cannot praise a fugitive and cloister'd virtue, unexercis'd and unbreath'd, that never sallies out and sees her adversary. . . .

The imagistic and conceptual congruities between this and the "Dialogue" are obvious. The noted editorial crux of Milton's having written his Christian "wayfaring" or "warfaring" hardly matters, for both participles apply to Soul, "wayfaring" in the case of the first retort (ll. 17–18), "warfaring" in that of the prelude (ll. 1–10).[4] But Soul is never called a Christian, and whether or not he is to be considered one as yet remains an unresolved question.

In part 1 (ll. 1–50) Pleasure tries the three lower senses of taste, of touch (with ease), and of smell, and then the two higher senses of sight (with vanity) and hearing. Soul rejects "downy Pillows" and a bed of roses in favor of the metaphorical and moral "gentler Rest" of a tranquil conscience, and rejects the olfactory sensation of "fragrant Clouds" of incense in favor of the "perfume" of eschewing presumption. The two remaining sensory trials take a mildly idiosyncratic turn. A mistress would ordinarily serve to elicit the lust of the eye; she being reserved for a later occasion (ll. 51–54), however, a "Crystal" mirror serves the purpose (l. 34). The fact that Soul is to gaze upon his own "face" in the glass underscores his being incarnate. The narcissistic slant of the test suggests that Marvell assumes a high degree of vanity to beset human nature. In his response the hero presupposes his corporeality and tenders a remedy for narcissism. He discriminates what whould be "priz'd" in the human form, the "Creator's skill," from what should be contemned, "Earth disguis'd," repudiating the diversions of sight for the insight that can penetrate to the origin of flesh in dust (Gen. 2:7). By assigning to hearing rather than to more customary vision the dignity of final place in the series, Marvell may be injecting, as he may also with the weight put on vanity, a subjective, confessional note into the otherwise impersonal morality drama. At any rate Soul shows himself, momentarily and as nowhere else, flustered. He acknowledges his predilection for music, spreads the reply over four verses instead of his accustomed two, and his aphoristic and metaphorical skills can here bring forth nothing more witty than the pun on "chordage" (l. 44) as both musical chord and binding cord.

The fifth temptation over, an unanticipated, third voice sounds (ll. 45–50), that of a Chorus. Not otherwise identified, its members, because expressing the viewpoint and "delight" of "Heaven," would seem to be celestial spirits. They reveal their partiality toward Soul not only in sentiment, applauding his abstentions and counseling him to "persevere," but also through the imagery, martial like his in the prelude, and through the meter, like his iambic, of their song. They hold out a recompense: *"if thou overcom'st thou shalt be crown'd."* The crowning of a victor—and with a garland, as indicated here (cf. "The Garden," ll. 1–4)—alludes to the custom of classical antiquity. In New Testament epistles the triumphal garland does on occasion provide a metaphor for the reward of the saints—as "a crown of glory that fadeth not away" at 1 Pet. 5:4, or the "incorruptible" crown at 1 Cor. 9:5—but Marvell refrains from designating the compensation "everlasting." That adjective, though forthcoming, is reserved for the ultimate verse, also to be assigned to the Chorus. By then Christianity will have had an epiphany, which in turn will certify the choral membership as angelic. Now at most a glimmer of the Christian stance is afforded, a foreshadowing of the later development. This italicized song concludes part 1.

The verse is most artfully orchestrated, each of the three voices having a distinctive prosody. That of Soul alone consists, and invariably, of iambic tetrameters rhyming in couplets. This verse form in the prelude is strong evidence of his being its speaker. The prosody of the chorus, though similar, for also iambic and usually tetrameter, differs from Soul's in two respects: the tetrameters are arranged in quatrains (rhyming ABBA at ll. 45–48, ABAB at ll. 75–78), while pentameters compose the one choral couplet, at ll. 49–50, just where attention is shifted to part 2 and the only place in the text where the norm of four stresses is exceeded. All trochees belong to Pleasure; though of seven syllables rather than eight, his trochaic lines meet this norm, but the iambic lines that he intersperses with them in the later temptations fall short of it. In his five speeches of part 1 he favors couplets, with the exception of his initial four lines (11–13), which rhyme ABAB, as do his four quatrains in part II (ll. 51–78), where the B lines are the iambic trimeters. The dominant pattern in which iambic meter comes to have "heroic" and trochaic "iniquitous" associations is subtly varied when the tempter adopts the former meter. His prosody exhibits the most fecundity, to suggest shiftiness, and that of Soul the most uniformity, to suggest steadfastness. Pleasure's iambs, however intermittant and aborted, seem to have been expropriated from the Chorus as well as from Soul, as if to win him more congenial accents and to befit the grander temptations of the second series. Instead of the previous approach to each several sense, the new approach calls for offering the entire world as a lure.

The proposal of a mistress (ll. 51–54) may seem to undermine that distinction, since like the earlier temptations and unlike the later, the focus remains on sensual indulgence. This "Beauty" will gratify not one but all of the senses, being "fair" (to the eyes), "soft" (to touch and hearing),[5] "sweet" (to smell and taste). This enticement might appear quantitatively but not qualitatively different from the earlier sense enticements and so properly to belong with them as a synthesizing culmination. True enough, but this sixth temptation is transitional, also inaugurating the second type, as the contrasting words "scatteringly" and "meet" will attest. The sensuous phenomena that "scatteringly doth shine" through the length and breath of creation will "meet" in the female "Beauty." She is a microcosm in whom all the kinds of sensation derivable from the macrocosm are epitomized. To have her would be to possess the world though the mode of the senses.

Pleasure can produce a Helen-like Beauty as tantamount to one aspect of the world, and in his next three attempts proffers control of it. He would win Soul by supplying him with gold for purchasing it, or with glory—that of vanquishing it in war or that of ruling it in peacetime—or with scientific knowledge. By synecdoche the sum total of natural philosophy is evoked: geology would "Try what depth the Center [= that of the earth] draws" and astronomy would "then to Heaven climb;" the knowledge is both theoretical (to "know each hidden Cause") and practical ("to see the future Time"). The antagonist proposes prideful and pleasurable —Faustian—exercise of types of power: that of vast wealth, military and political power, and scientific power over nature.

Soul must alter his strategy of reply once he no longer receives sensual proposals that he can transmute through metaphor into ethical propositions. He now turns more to refutations, often phrased as rhetorical questions, but he persists in enunciating spiritual values. He can acknowledge woman's beauty as visibly heavenly and regard it, in the Platonic vein of l. 56, as but a pale reflection of the true beauty of invisible, immaterial heavens. The retorts of the second series become highly compressed essays, as does the one on "Gold" (ll. 61–62). It is valued not for itself but for its commercial function of determining "price," only, since the salability of goods betokens their materiality and consequent worthlessness, gold will purchase mere trash; and by implication that is invaluable which has no economic value, for example goods of the spirit such as virtue. As to friendship and slavery (ll. 67–68), both originate within. On friendship Soul, reminiscent of Polonius, maintains that he must be true to himself, that is, constant in adhering to right principles, in order not to be false to others. One is untrue to oneself who submits to the sensual desires or worldly ambitions urged by Pleasure, the tempter upholding a contrary scheme for self-realization. The two lines of the reply are not quite parallel: "What Friends [can I have] if . . . "; "What [have I to do with] Slaves, unless. . . . " The latter verse admits of mutually reinforcing readings: Soul might "captive" and so enthrall Pleasure, or might himself become a slave, if enthralled by Pleasure.

In the last and noblest temptation, that of knowledge, with the clause "And then to Heaven climb," Pleasure adverts to astronomy. The rejoinder revises the notion of heaven from the celestial spheres to the abode of God: "None thither mounts by the degree / Of Knowledge, but [by the degree of] Humility." The different end requires different means. Science enables one to gain knowledge of the skies, virtue to attain salvation. The "degree" is the "step" or "rung" (*OED* 1) and the "manner" or "way" (*OED* 2) by which in either case one proceeds upward. Since the sense of "lowliness" persists in English from the Latin root *humilitas*, a paradox is conveyed, to "mount" by lowliness, and this paradox derives from that reiterated in the Gospels of Matthew (23:12, 18:14) and of Luke (14:11, 18:14): "He that shall humble himself shall be exalted." It is by electing and exemplifying humility that Soul proves his Christianity.

St. Augustine writes that Christians are "named . . . from Christ, whose Gospel no one studies carefully without finding in Him the Teacher of humility," and writes, further, that "*the whole Christian way of life wages war above all against pride*, the mother of envy, *for it inculcates humility*, by which it acquires and preserves charity . . . " (italics mine).[6] Not only is the "war against pride" pertinent to the poem, but so is the compass that virtue has for Augustine and for other authorities to be cited. "Humility," though named only at the end, is the central and pervasive idea, and Soul from the first has been expounding its scope.

In his initial reply he had designated heaven as his destination ("I sup above"), and in the last reply posits humility as the sole means of ascent. In the third reply he refuses godlike ministrations with incense:

> A Soul that knowes not to presume
> Is Heaven's and its own perfume.

> (ll. 29–30)

The "perfume" of negating presumption is, in more positive terms, the odor of humility, the virtue opposed to that vice. The next reply, the fourth, makes a recondite allusion to the stem of *humilitas*. The Latin word *humus*, which means "ground, earth," lies at the stem, as moralists are fond of pointing out, in such reflections as the following:

> La signification étymologique du terme *humilité* nous ramène à la pensée de notre origine terrestre. *Humilitas dicitur ab humo*, disaient les anciens. L'homme, issu de la terre ... est destiné a retourner en son sein.[7]

This quotation helps us to realize that the protagonist, coaxed to view his own face in a looking glass, has humility in mind in the rejoinder:

> When the Creator's skill is priz'd,
> The rest is all but Earth disguis'd.

(ll. 35–36)

The word "degree," though singular, yet as "rung" recalls the famous Ladder of Humility, with twelve rungs, in the seventh chapter of the Rule of St. Benedict. The following instructions are included by the *humilitatics doctor*[8] under the first degree or *gradus*: "constantly [to] turn over in [one's] heart the eternal life which is prepared for those who fear [God]" and to "check the desires of the flesh."[9] Thus can we learn from St. Benedict, as we might also from St. Bernard of Clairvaux, whose *De Gradibus Humilitatis et Superbiae*, especially the first part, is based on the Benedictine Rule,[10] that Soul's resistance to "The Batteries of alluring Sense" in part I can be comprehended under humility. With regard to the temptations of part II, St. Thomas Aquinas has a doctrine that they neatly fit, for according to him it belongs to the virtue of humility "to temper and restrain the mind, lest it tend to high things immoderately" and to "restrain the appetite from aiming at great things against right reason."[11] These high and great things are imagined by Marvell as the financier's, conqueror's, dictator's, and scientist's modes of wielding supreme terrestrial power.

But Soul does more than spurn power and sensual indulgence.

A new light is cast over all previous retorts by the last, so that retro-spectively we can recognize that he has been constructing his own ladder of humility. He does so by means of those retorts, each of which in turn contributes a rung, for a total of nine rungs disposed as follows: (1) to seek heavenly rather than earthly feasts; (2) to do one's duty; (3) to avoid presumption; (4) to regard material goods, including the body, as God's handiwork but otherwise negligible; (5) to keep the mind free from sensual entanglements; and to prefer (6) invisible to visible paradises, (7) moral values to economic or material values, (8) self-mastery to the fame of mastering the world, and (9) to pure and practicable understanding of the universe, salvific virtue.

When humility is proclaimed his sovereign principle, then is Soul distinguished from a deistic Platonist, who would not espouse that ideal and would have chosen the "degree" of knowledge, and then does he shine forth "that thing Divine" in a Christian sense, for during all of "this day's Combat" (ll. 7–8) he has followed the admonitions and example of the God-Man who said, "learn of me, for I am meek and lowly in heart" (*humilis corde* in the Vulgate—Maat. 11:29).

The shield, helmet, and sword initially taken up can now be interpreted as the armor of "Humility." The mention of that virtue at l. 74 silences the antagonist, ends the dialogue, and serves as cue to the Chorus—composed, it has now become clear, of angels—whose song concludes the second as it had the first part of the poem, with the difference that the closing quatrain (ll. 75–78) is purely celebratory:

> *Triumph, triumph, victorious Soul;*
> *The World has not one Pleasure more:*
> *The rest does lie beyond the Pole,*
> *And is thine everlasting Store.*

"Rest" carries the dual senses of "tranquility" and of "remainder" or "other." In the iambic measure of Soul, with its "heroic" asso-ciations, the choral stanza also has something in common with Pleasure's versification, not the "iniquitous" trochees but the alter-nate rhymes: ABAB. This fusion of prosodic facets of both dialogists lends support to the words, which express partisanship with Soul along with the pledge of a pleasurable "Store," though of eternal rather than temporal delights, and the reward hereafter for present abnegations.

II

In octosyllabic couplets throughout and thus simpler in prosody than the poem just examined, "A Dialogue between the Soul and Body" offers Soul once again, or another character so designated, in confrontation with a different opponent and issue and, in the changed circumstances, unable to succeed as before.

The discussion unfolds in a quite orderly manner. Each speaker considers himself victimized by the other and this attitude remains a constant throughout. Though for the most part neither addresses the other, each listens attentively to the other's charges, and rather than offering refutations reciprocates with charges of his own. Each describes his own punishing plight in his first speech (ll. 1–20) and in his second (ll. 21–44) specifies the ills peculiar and intrinsic to the opponent.

Soul's plight is physical because he is "inslav'd" in a fleshly "Dungeon"—a variation on the ancient conception of the body as a prison house—and miserable because of the "many wayes" of his being racked. The bodily organs become, with wordplay, shackles (bone bolts; feet, fetters; hand[L. *manus*], manacles) or instruments of torture: paradoxically the eye blinds (sensory sight impedes intellectual vision) and the ear deafens (hearing obtrudes external noises); "Nerves [sinews], and Arteries, and Veins" enchain and suspend him; and finally he must undergo torment in a "vain Head and double Heart." The "Head" and "Heart" are bodily parts, and the adjectives have the senses they take when qualifying physical objects: "vain" means worthless, or empty, void; "double" means "having some essential part double" (*OED*, 1, c). The moralistic senses of "conceited" and "deceitful," though connoted by the speaker for the rhetorical effect of diminishment, must be excluded from denotation, for immorality is not attributable to the body but to the soul alone, a point to be stressed later in the poem.

Body's opening remarks are modeled on those he has just heard, in form (a rhetorical question beginning, "O who shall . . .") and substance (a plea for deliverance), and in the variation on a commonplace figure for the opponent (the soul not as ruler but tyrant). He complains of standing as if a spiritual stake, "stretcht upright, impales me" and of an acrophobic reaction to walking, "That mine own Precipice I go." This challenges Soul's complaint that he is the one "hung up" in "Chains." The torments Body suffers, besides those of posture and carriage, are consequent upon the life contributed in "spight" by the vivifying soul, namely biological warmth and death. The invective escalates when the death-dealing tyrant is recast as an evil spirit whose diabolical possession keeps the organism incessantly restless.

Soul picks up this motif of diabolic arts to portray himself the party hurt by them, by the black "Magic" that has doomed him "Within anothers Grief [sickness, disease] to pine." The woes innate to and inflicted by the body are its maladies. It also inflicts health, the "Care" of which Soul resents for immersing him in material things to his spiritual detriment (ll. 25–26); and the "Cure" is "worse" than the "Diseases" for being the disaster in which he is "Shipwrackt into Health again" and kept from the "Port" of death.

The ills intrinsic and proper to the soul are passion and, worst of all, sin. Body's second speech has a singular features that signalize its importance, among which are direct address to the opponent ("Thou" at l. 32 being the sole second person pronoun in the text), length (14 lines rather than 10), and, especially, finality of position. The motif of "Maladies" is now picked up, with the term converted from a literal to a metaphorical sense. "Cramp," "Palsie," "Pestilence," and "Ulcer" stand respectively for "Hope," "Fear," "Love," and "Hate." In the case of "Joy" and "Sorrow" the figurative vehicle changes from somatic to mental illness, that of (manic and depressive?) "Madness." The repugnance attaches not to the malfunctioning of the emotions but to the agitations of their normal operation. Body is compelled to partake of Soul's "Knowledge" and to "know," or be aware of, the emotions within. Cognition intensifies and "Memory" prolongs the organic concomitants of passion—a psychosomatic insight of some astuteness.

Body cunningly reserves his most cogent thrust for the end:

> What but a Soul could have the wit
> To build me up for Sin so fit?
> So Architects do square and hew,
> Green Trees that in the Forest grew.

(ll. 41–44)

In this analogy "a Soul" is to the body ("me") as the "Architects" are to the "Trees." Soul and the "Architects" alike possess intelligence or "wit" and alike are efficient causes as builders. Their buildings— the formal causes—differ in material causality, Soul's being made out of bone, tissue, blood (ll. 1–10, esp. 3, 8), and those of the architects out of timber. Final causality is expressly ascribed to Soul, whose intention is "To build me up for Sin so fit" at l. 42, and when l. 43 begins, "So Architects . . . ," the implication is, plausibly, that the edifices for which they ravish forests will likewise serve sinful purposes. The first stanzas of *Upon Appleton House* lend support to this supposition. The squared and hewed timbers and architect's plan intimate the kind of mansion—that of a "Forrain *Architect*" who "Forrests did to Pastures hew" (ll. 2, 4)—which is there disapproved as ecologically exploitive and expressive of human pretension and pride. But whether or not such aims are imputed to the art of the "Architects," what matters is that the aim of sin is imputed to Soul's architectural art.

Body's logic and rhetoric are calculated not only to put the opponent in a bad light but also to put himself in a good light, which he does by analogically juxtaposing himself with the "Green Trees." Green, for Marvell the most agreeable of colors to judge from frequency of elicitation, has a range of significance in his verse, and here appears connotative of the trees' pristine natural condition. We may infer that Body is as harmless as trees growing in a forest, as subject to mind-directed violation as they when squared and hewn, and as guiltless in the sinful use Soul may put him to as they are guiltless of any bad human ends for which their wood may be utilized.

During the course of the controversy some of the chief of soul's functions—intellectual, sensitive, and vegetative—though not the entire complex of them, are surveyed. The powers of memory (l. 40), reason (ll. 39, 41), and volition (l. 42) reside, as do the emotions (ll. 32–38), in the soul, which informs the organism as a vital principle and endows it with self-moving capability (ll. 13–14), physical development ("build me up"), and life (ll. 15, 18). All differences between a living man and a corpse are due to this spiritual constituent. Sensory response emanates from it, as the "Soul/Pleasure" rather than this Dialogue makes plain. Neither poem takes up the vital function of sexual reproduction. The erotic potential of the soul is not disregarded, but neither is it exhibited with the emphasis, approval, and ardor, of the last section of the "Coy Mistress," wherein her "willing Soul transpires / At every pore with instant Fires." Pleasure's sixth temptation, baited with the "Beauty," is obviously directed to the erotic imagination. The passions listed by Body, hope and fear and joy and sorrow as well as hatred and love, while not necessarily so restricted in focus, might all be conceived of as concomitants and products of eros. The mower knows most of these emotions—though not joy, which tends to elude Marvell's pastoral lovers—when enamored of Juliana. The soul in "The Garden" can achieve a contemplative ecstasy and momentarily divest itself of the body (ll. 49–56), but that type of exaltation does not happen in either of these dialogues. One, that with Pleasure, lays stress on the heavenly aspirations of the immortal spirit; the other, that with Body, fleetingly refers, at l. 29, to death as "the Port," where the spirit gains release from fleshly confines and where it gains entrance to a happier state. The yearnings of Body are more enigmatic. The closing verse may hint that he, like Herbert's persona in "Affliction" (I), though with a rather different import, can "wish I were a tree." He seems to entertain the reverie of a placid arborial existence, one spared the pains of ambulation, emotions, memory, and consciousness, as well as sin, to wish for a more elementary vegetable soul as a welcome alternative to the human. It is obvious which of the two dialogists enjoys the greater range of possibility and superiority of faculties. That, however, is not the question in controversy.

The word "Dialogue" has a different signification in each title, even though in both works Soul and a personified abstraction engage in conversational conflict. "Soul / Pleasure" resembles a play, not only in the dialogic mode in which the action is presented and the chorus, but the kind of characters and theme of salvation give it affinities with morality plays. A plot composed of temptations can recall Milton, particularly *Samson Agonistes*, where the form also is dramatic but the adversaries multiple, or *Paradise Regained*, where though the form is epic and the personages supernatural, the hero confronts but one tempter. Like Satan, Pleasure has the role of endeavoring to induce the protagonist to submit to him, and Soul, like the Son, must not only resist blandishments—many of the same ones—but also persuasively enunciate the grounds of his resistance. Body and

Soul relate to each other in quite another way. Neither has any delusions about swaying the other's decisions or conduct. The interchange between them has marked affinities with the formal debate. The "Dialogue" in "Soul / Pleasure" is dramatic, in "Soul / Body" disputatious.

The situation rendered in the latter "Dialogue" exhibits, along with aspects of the debate, those of a personal altercation. Each participant looks upon himself as the injured party, detailing the miseries of his own experience and acrimoniously inculpating the other. A quarrelsome pair, they come across somewhat as a mismated man and wife and indeed are even more indissolubly joined "until death do them part." Like Adam and Eve in *Paradise Lost* when fallen and bickering, "they in mutual accusation" spend their time, "but neither self-condemning." The narrator adds, "of their vain contest appeared no end." This verse, that ends Book 9, will do as a motto for some critical misapprehensions of Marvell's poem. Harold Toliver considers it "a dramatic contest between antagonists who need each other," and either might have the "final word, which by the nature of their fusion cannot be final."[12] J.B. Leishman, going still farther, holds that the work is "almost certainly incomplete," and must originally have "continued through several more ten-line stanzas."[13] If a mere altercation it might indeed have proceeded on or stopped inconclusively, but the contention has another facet, that of the debate, which is the delimiting factor and key to the arrangement.

As an undergraduate at Cambridge, Marvell would have assisted at and participated in the academic disputations embedded in the curriculum, and the imprint they left on his mind is apparent in this composition. He by no means reproduces a disputation in its elaborate totality,[14] but he includes sufficient particulars to suggest a performance of the type, particulars such as: the set speeches; their equal length, as if time limits had been fixed, except that the last runs slightly longer; their being addressed, except again for the last, not to the opponent, though exerting a determinant effect on his subsequent discourse, but to some third party, either directly to the reader or else to some other judge or a moderator supposed present at the occasion; the orderly presentation of the arguments; and the impressive command of formal devices of logic and rhetoric in the argumentation. I have space for no more than a sampling of these devices, some of which have already been noted. The four causes belong to the "topic" of "cause and effect,"[15] and these figures of speech in the poem can be related to various other "topics of invention"[16]: metaphor, paradox, puns, meiosis, which "belittles,"[17] at ll. 15–16 and elsewhere, and martyria, which "confirms a statement by one's own experience."[18] Besides those figures of "logos" there are these of "pathos": the interrogatio that commences each of the first three speeches, or, more specifically, epiplexis, where "one asks questions, not in order to know, but to chide or reprehend"; categoria, when "one lays open the secret wickedness of another before his face";[19] and ara, "by which the Orator detesteth, and curseth some person or thing, for the evils which they bring with them, or for the wickedness which is in term".[20] An enthememe can be discerned at ll. 41–42, where the implied premise, so well known to the auditors that they can be depended on to add it themselves,[21] is that the greatest evil man can perpetrate or suffer is sin. Furthermore, all four speeches are germane to an implicit thesis, which admits of some such formulation as the following: "In the human compound of body and soul, the body inflicts greater evil than the soul." This question might be phrased the other way around, but I chose this way because it makes Soul, who speaks first, the defendent, who in the scholastic debates at Cambridge gave his speech prior to an opponent's, whose part would become Body's here. However these roles are assigned, the interest very much lies in the skill of argumentation on both sides of the question.[22]

The debaters of the thesis are personifications of two of the terms. They postulate kinds and degrees of offenses. Body offends with physical, Soul with psychological and moral evil. The latter kind is, in the values of the poem, the gravest, far more grievous than any bodily affliction, and the word "Sin" has religious implications, presently to be examined, that extend beyond moral evil. Soul affirms these values by having no comeback when charged with sin, he tacitly acknowledges defeat. Body's second speech, its significance hinted at by the special features earlier remarked, proves, by virtue of this charge, conclusive, and for him a disputatious triumph. Critics approach the poem with so fixed an expectation of a triumph by Soul that they are unable to respond to the reversal of that expectation.[23] The reversal can have been calculated by Marvell as the crowning touch of wit in a performance witty throughout. At any rate, the parts cannot be rearranged, and the "Dialogue" is autonomous and complete.

The conception of the soul through l. 40 as a spiritual form, able to exist independently, and an immortal being, is philosophical, accessible to reason without faith, and the pagans of antiquity could and did share the conception. Then the reference to "Sin," in the decisive analogy of the last four verses, introduces a new perspective, one including the ethical and extending to the religious and even into the realm of Christian faith. Just how far this perspective extends depends on the way "Sin" is to be defined. The applicable definition in the *OED* is recorded under *sb.* 2: "Violation of a divine law; action or conduct characterized by this; a state of transgression against God or his commands." This, the ordinary sense of the term when and as employed by Marvell, comprehends the ideas of a personal God and his will. For Milton sin is a "transgression of the law" because so "defined by the apostle" at 1 John 3:4.[24] St. Augustine's definition is classic: "sin is a word or deed or desire contrary to the eternal law," and the law is "eternal" as deriving from God.[25] The notion of sin in the text carries such religious implications and may carry additional theological implications as well. When Body speaks of the "wit / To build me up for Sin so fit," he seems to allude to transgressions that involve him, him as instrument or as victim. Now the body is a "fit" instrument and potential victim if the sin alluded to entails, as is probable, an excess of sensual indulgence requiring the body's agency and often causing its deterioration. But the body would be victim in another way, for at the Last Judgment it too would be condemned to suffer forever the pains of hell. The doctrine of the resurrection of the body would be implied by "Sin" at l. 42 if the term brings into play the range of Christian meanings, including infernal damnation, the lack or loss of grace, and the violation not only of the Deity but of the person of Christ. Marvell expresses the latter belief in "The Coronet," the poet imagining the (erotic) sins he repents of as piercing thorns that "My Saviours head have crown'd." The poems on religious themes, most of them grouped together with "Soul / Body" at the beginning of *Miscellaneous Poems*, lend support to our apprehending "Sin" with the word's full theological significance.

The naming of "Humility" spells the failure of Pleasure the tempter and casts a Christian light upon that "Dialogue." The naming of "Sin" spells the defeat of Soul the disputant by injecting a new note, ethical and religious and arguably Christian, into this "Dialogue."

III

"On a Drop of Dew" presents the soul, not as a speaking character in dialogic encounter with an antagonist, but as the immaterial object of speculation placed in analogic relationship with a material object observed. A single persona discourses throughout—monologue in contrast to the "Dialogues"—but eschewing first person pronouns, he calls minimal attention to himself. Nor does he employ second person pronouns, and only once does he use a form of direct address, the imperative verb "See," but it is the opening word. The implied listener is less likely the reader than a fictive person assumed at the scene who can "See" what is pointed out. But the dramatic relationship between poet and auditor is obscure, low-keyed, overshadowed by the comparison and contrast that contribute both structure and subject.

The poem divides into three sections: the first eighteen lines describe the drop of dew along with its movements and setting; the next eighteen lines draw a parallel between the human soul and the dewdrop; then four final lines bring in the conceit based on manna. As Frank Kermode remarks, "The poem has been criticized on the grounds that the comparison with manna enters too late, and forms a sort of appendix."[26] The chief task of criticism is certainly to give a satisfactory account of how this late-added comparison is incorporated into the overall design.

The poet begins by directing the eyes of another where his are fixed, on the "Orient ['out of the dawning east' and 'lustrous'] Dew"—and the noun, to judge by the title, should refer to a single dewdrop—that lies on the purple petal of one of the "blowing Roses." The season is spring or summer, and the time extends from the cool just after sunrise on a sunny day till warmth later sets in. The semi-personified spherical drop is disdainful, on the one hand, of its terrestrial habitat, shrinking from its floral base, feeling "Restless," and fearing contamination, and is nostalgic, on the other, for its "native Element"—that is, its birthplace in the sky or air—

straining to reflect what light it can of that "clear Region," and with sad looks appealing to the sun for compassion and rescue.

The first eighteen lines by themselves establish, despite the meticulous visual examination they contain, that the poet's concern is less imagistic than emblematic, the dew holding his interest not in and of itself but for its fitness to represent the human soul. The impression can be strengthened by the position of the lyric, which in the first and most subsequent editions comes just after "Pleasure / Soul," and Soul there shows the same attitudes as the dewdrop here, *contemptus mundi* and aspirations toward heaven. But that congruity aside, the emblem is made so transparent as to risk rendering redundant the carefully paralleled treatment of the soul that follows. Redundancy is avoided, however, principally by contrasts disclosed along with the similarities in the next phase of the extended simile.

The soul and dew have both originated above and have descended to earth, find it uncongenial, and yearn to reascend. Like dew the soul has properties of light ("that Ray"), liquidity ("that Drop"), and sphericality (ll. 27–28, 35–36), but has them metaphorically. If perhaps a bit curious as a salient attribute of the soul, sphericality is introduced to make it conform to the dewdrop and also to signify its perfection. That idea traditionally attaches to spheres and circles. Thus "in pure and circling thoughts" the soul expresses "The greater Heaven in a Heaven less." The greater is the abode of God, the thoughts of which are "circling" to comprehend not only perfection but eternity as well. The "Heaven less" is a paradise of contemplation within. The wateriness implied by "Drop" is also curious as an attribute of the soul, and also adduced for conformity with dew. In this instance Marvell invents the modus operandi of making the figurative water coalesce with light through their common referent, soul, and their common source in "the clear Fountain of Eternal Day." The dewdrop, "shed from the bosom of the Morn," stays within temporal and material confines. The soul's "Ray" is an emanation of everlasting and divine rather than a reflection of diurnal, solar light. "Receiving in the Day" means that the spirit is open to the supernatural, and "bright above" that it meditates heavenly truths. The dew alights on a "purple flow'r," an actual rose, while the soul resides "within the humane flow'r" of "sweet leaves and blossoms green," tropically the body. It is associated with verdant vegetation in the "Dialogue" too, there with the "Green

Trees." Color and plants go together to symbolize the body's status as a creature of the natural world, and the green, particularly as against purple, may carry overtones of relative purity—but more on this later.

Although the dewdrop is endowed with human feelings, I called it semipersonified above because it retains something of "thingness" in its passivity, its characteristic of undergoing rather than initiating action. The soul, on the contrary, is truly a person, self-moving, a center of energy, exercising volition.[27] The "Orient Dew," subject of the subordinate clause introduced by "how" at l. 1, still has no verb when a semicolon appears at the end of l. 4. In the correlative lines, 19–23, the soul, subject of an independent clause, takes a verb of decisiveness, "shuns." The distinction I am now concerned with is conveyed largely by verbs and verbals. The drop is "Shed from," "Frames as it can" (the sky), "does slight" (disregard), "lyes," "Shines" (with refracted beams), "roules" (with the external motion of the flower), and is pictured as "Scarce touching," "gazing back," "Trembling," and waiting to be "exhaled" (drawn up) by the sun. More active and deliberate, the soul "shuns," "Does . . . express," "turns away," "does upward bend," and exercises its powers of memory ("remembering," "recollecting," which also means "again gathering together"), of intellect (in the "pure and circling thoughts"), and of will ("excluding," "disdaining," "in Love"). The dew, moreover, appears frightened ("Trembling," "insecure") and sad ("Shines with a mournful Light;/Like its own Tear"), while the soul is wholly free of those pathetic emotions.

The dew has a means of returning to the sky, for the "warm Sun" will "exhale it back again" (l. 18). The soul is "girt and ready to ascend," but the readiness is all, for when the lengthy analogy ends at l. 36, no ascent has occurred and no means of it is in evidence. The analogy of the soul to dew is left incomplete, or can be said to break down at a critical juncture.

Marvell skillfully modulates the prosody from one section to the next. The poem gives the intital impression, even by its shape on the page, of some disarray. This is not free verse because of the metrical regularity, though eight trochaic lines are admitted among the thirty-six that are iambic, but the verse is free from fixed or recurrent formalities in regard to the arrangement of rhymes, the diversity of line lengths, and the mode of indentation. However, a pattern, apposite and evolutionary, does gradually emerge. Each section has nine pairs of rhyming words. In the first (ll. 1–18) the rhymes may be separated by two lines; in the second (ll. 19–36) they are separated by no more than one, and the rhyme scheme now exhibits uniform units, each consisting of a couplet followed by a quatrain of alternate rhymes. In the first section four verse measures appear (one dimeter, five trimeters, eight tetrameters, and four pentameters); in the second only two (fourteen tetrameters and four pentameters). In the first section the identation follows no set plan, and one line, 13, is both the shortest and most deeply indented of the text; in the second only the pentameters are flush left, and the first ten tetrameters, in separated groups of one, three, and six lines, are aligned and in double indentation, and the last four are also aligned and in single indentation. The trochees do not constitute a leitmotif as in "Pleasure / Soul." Here the earliest line in that meter tells of the "Trembling" and fastidious dewdrop, the next such lines of a more self-confident and vigorous soul, thus accenting the contrast of characterization. The single trochaic verse (16) in the first section strikes one as anomalous; the seven in the second—one (l. 19) at the outset and six in succession (ll. 27–32)—come to seem integral to the metrical artifice. The increasing orderliness of versification and format observable from the first section to the second belongs to a process that reaches its culmination in the third. That brief stanza (ll. 37–40) has no indentations, with all the lines flush left, and is unvarying in meter (iambic), rhyme scheme (couplets), and measure (pentameter).

At l. 36, where the developing prosodic pattern is about to enter its last stage, another pattern, that of symmetry between tenor and vehicle, breaks down. The soul "does upward bend"—in the geometrical sense of a sphere curving from its "point below" and in the psychological sense of intentness on Heaven—but fails to move upward. At this moment these lines intervene:

> Such did the Manna's sacred Dew destil;
> White, and intire, though congeal'd and chill.
> Congeal'd on Earth: but does, dissolving, run
> Into the Glories of th' Almighty Sun.

(ll. 37–40)

Marvell surprises not only by interjecting the new conceit but also by recapitulating with manna the entire cycle of descent ("did . . . distill"), abiding "on Earth," and reascent ("Into the . . . Sun"). The language is figurative, with the soul continuing on from the second section as the subject, of which manna now becomes the surrogate. "Such" refers to the prior treatment of the soul. The stanza, moreover, does finally supply the correlative factor missing from the analogy, ll. 37–40, with their "Almighty Sun," corresponding to ll. 18–19, with their "warm Sun." The soul "thither mounts," but only after a figurative transmutation into "Manna's sacred Dew."

This, in contrast with the "Orient Dew" of nature, is "sacred" because sent directly from God, and perhaps also because taken from sacred scripture. Exodus 16, the source of the trope, provides much of the descriptive detail. In that account manna is associated with dew, the two falling together each morning in the wilderness, and lay on the ground in round white grains, like hoarfrost, and melted as the sun grew hot.

The thermal images are among those suggested by the source. "Congeal'd and chill," below, the manna seeks out the implicit warmth of the "Sun," above. The color spectrum is enlarged from purple in the first section (l. 9) to green in the second (l. 23) to white in the third (l. 38). The colors pertain in diverse ways to creatures in an ascending scale and also suggest degrees of purity. The purple is a literal quality of a "flow'r"; green is a quality of "leaves and blossoms" of the metaphorical "humane flow'r," the animal and soul-animated body; the white is descriptive of the manna that symbolizes the redeemed soul. White stands for purity. Purple, as the darkest of the three hues, in this context carries opposite overtones. Some corroboration is furnished by the dewdrop's fear of growing "impure" (l. 16) from contact with the purple petal, from which it is "dark below" (in a phrase transposed from l. 31). Green falls between white and purple in terms of chromatic brightness and purity value. The green "humane flow'r," by virtue of the soul "within" (l. 21), unites with spiritual being as the material rose cannot, and thus enjoys a higher degree of purity; and yet the wholly immaterial and so purer soul—purer by nature, sin is not in question—"Shuns" the gross, corporal "leaves and blossoms" (l. 23).

Light changes in kind and significance from one section to the next. In the first it is either direct, as in "Morn," "clear Region," "the Skies," and "the warm Sun," or reflected, as in "Shines with a mournful Light," and in both cases is solar, that perceived by the sense of sight. In the second section light is invisible and of two kinds. One, that of "the greater Heaven" that God illuminates with his own Light, is referred to in the words "the clear Fountain of Eternal Day" and "Light" at l. 24, "Day" at l. 30. The soul, the "Heaven less," is illumined by the second kind, the light of reason, and so is referred to as "bright above" and as "that Ray." This term postulates the source of intellectual light in divine light, and the two are connatural. The soul is in the "World" but not of it, and "excluding" and "disdaining" it, "turns away"; it rather deploys its faculties to preserve and deepen otherworldly awareness, a project that entails "remembering," "recollecting" (memory), "pure and circling thoughts" expressive of "Heaven," "receiving in the Day" (intellectual), being "there in Love," and the primed and eager postures recounted in ll. 32–35 (the will). The third section, in its own and the poem's climactic line (40), discovers "the Glories of th' Almighty [an attribute of the Godhead] Sun" / Son—that is, Christ in glory. This was a common pun in seventeenth-century religious verse. Herbert made it the topic of a sonnet, "The Sonne," which concludes:

> For what Christ once in humblenesse began,
> We him in glorie call, *The Sonne of Man.*

The sun as a traditional symbol of Christ is traceable to the *Sol justitiae* in the prophecy of Malachi 4:2. Shining in Heaven, *lumen gloriae* is apprehended not in this life by meditation but in the afterlife by the beatific vision of the saints. They, in the imagination of Dante at the end of the *Paradiso*, seated in the Celestial Rose and contemplating the three circles of *luce etterna*, behold in the second *nostra effige*—the incarnate form of the glorified Word (33: 124, 131). This supernatural goal lies beyond the capacities of unredeemed man, and so in order to attain it the saints have to undergo a process of rebirth or of—Dante's word—"transhumanizing" (*Paradiso* 1:70).

In addition to the manna itself, its documental source and its displacement of dew are meaningful in the terminal conceit.

The Biblical source, with a kind of synecdochic effect, brings Revelation to bear. The poet begins with sense data, inspecting the dew on the rose (ll. 1–18); the sense perception generates a purely intellectual activity, reflection on the concept of the soul, on its origin (ll. 19–20), its way of being in the world (ll. 21–32), and its immortal longings (ll. 33–36). Through l. 36 he reads the "universal and public Manuscript" of Nature "that lies expans'd unto the eye of all"—including, for Sir Thomas Browne, "Heathens." "Heathen" philosophers might peruse the book of creatures much as the poet does, the faculties of sense and intellect being equal to the task, and they can comprehend the "Hieroglyphick" of the dew, can grasp the correspondence between it and the soul. But just when heavenly salvation emerges as the imminent issue, the poet abruptly turns to another book, "that written one of God,"[28] the scriptural repository of Judeo-Christian history and belief. With the soul set to ascend, an impasse occurs, out of which he finds a way by recourse to passages in the old Testament,[29] passages he interprets as a Christian, his figure of the "Almighty Sun" serving to demonstrate that interpretation.

The spiritual transformation essential to Christian experience, miraculous rebirth or regeneration, receives most inventive treatment in the closing stanza. For Milton—to stray no farther from Marvell—regeneration, "operated by the Word and Spirit," is "that change . . . whereby the old man being destroyed, the inward man is regenerated by God after his own image, in all the faculties of his mind, insomuch as he becomes as it were a new creature. . . ." A plethora of supporting quotations follows this definition, as is Milton's wont in *The Christian Doctrine*, among these the first two that follow:[30] "Lie not to one another, seeing that ye have put off the old man . . . and put on the new man (Col. 3:9–10); "if any man be in Christ, he is a new creature: old things have passed away" (2 Cor. 5:17); "be ye transformed by the renewing of your mind" (Rom. 12:2).[31] Regeneration is presented in the poem by a kind of figurative reenactment. To get to heaven the soul-as-dew must be transformed into the soul-as-manna. The "old" metaphorical vehicle differs significantly from the "new": the one is an ordinary and universal phenomenon, occurring in nature, dropping from the sky, commonly perceived by sight and touch; the other is a miraculous substance, occurred in a particular region and period and for the special purpose of feeding the Israelites, came directly from Yahweh, and is known from Biblical accounts. God-given, "sacred" (l. 37), and miraculous, manna introduces religious connotations. The old image of dew is discarded and the soul is regenerated in the image of manna to become a new creature. Marvell has the soul put off the old dew and put on the new manna to gain salvation.

Traditionally an Eucharistic symbol, manna for Milton, as for St. Paul (1 Cor. 10:3–4), typifies the Lord's Supper. Jesus, expressly comparing himself with manna in John 6:31–51, established it as a type of himself as "the true bread from heaven" and "the living bread." He said, "For the bread of God is he which cometh down from heaven, and giveth life unto the world." Exegetes, however, have always understood the "bread" of this discourse in either of two ways: as that of the truth that he divinely reveals, or as that of the sacrament. These have been labelled the "sapiential" and eucharistic interpretations.[32] Milton allows for both, leans toward the "sapiential," and expounds the Lord's Supper in the light of it, holding that the bread of the sacrament, "which Christ calls his flesh," is "but the food of faith alone" and "can be nothing but the doctrine" of the incarnational redemption, belief in which ensures eternal life."[33] The manna in the final section of "On a Drop of Dew," literally the "bread from heaven" in the Old Testament, figures the "living bread" of the New. Transfiguration into manna means that the soul "puts on Christ" (Rom. 13:14), becomes an *alter Christus*, either by faith in him, or, in addition, by the bread of communion (with whatever position on the Eucharist the Puritan author may have held (probably Milton's or one similar).

The manna first "did . . . distill" (fall in drops), and last "does, dissolving, run" sunward. The verbs shift from the past tense of historical reference to the present of the generalization about the action of souls upon entering eternity. The Biblical event is at once literally itself in time and an allegory of the redeemed in time and eternity. The arrival upon "Earth" of the manna at l. 37 parallels that of the dewdrop at ll. 1–2 and that of the soul adumbrated in ll. 19–22. The soul, then, undergoes a second birth, a regeneration in the guise of manna. It also undergoes the death implied by "dissolving." Unlike the soul in the second section, the dewdrop has a return in the first, one in which the sun acts on it to "exhale it back again." The manna-as-soul "does run," returning with contrasting kinetic imagery, with the rush of desire, and runs, upon mortal dissolution, toward the exalted Savior, "Into the Glories of th' Almighty Sun."[34]

And "so the Soul" resembles the dewdrop. Insofar as this analogy suffices, the poet's thought proceeds in accordance with philosophical Platonism. Platonic thought, without the aid of Revelation, is cognizant of the immortal soul, its "recollection" of origins elsewhere, its yearning to return to the eternal world of the supernal forms, and, moreover, posits its innate power to regain that world after release from the body. If the analogue of the dewdrop had availed for the final felicity of the soul, descent and ascent would have been as natural for it as is falling and evaporating for dew. A Christian critique of Platonism can be discerned in the last four verses as they shift the poem from a philosophical to a theological framework, from reason to faith. The goal is not contemplation of the eternal Ideas but union with Christ, both the goal and the "way" (John 14:6–7). The soul as dew is in the order of nature, that of Virgil in Dante's conception alluded to in my opening paragraph, and as manna is in the order of grace, that of Beatrice, who can guide Dante on the Christian and only way to God. Section by section Marvell's poem moves from sphere to higher sphere, from the phenomenal realm to the purely human realm to the Christian realm of Revelation and redemption, and section by section the versification assumes increasing regularity in answerable style.

IV

All three of the poems consider the condition of the soul, either as virtuously "resolved" against the corruptive currents of the world ("Soul / Pleasure"), as more victimizer than victim of the body through a capacity for vice ("Soul / Body"), or as a spiritual creature seeking the way to Heaven from an alien material environment ("Drop of Dew"). The three have, also, an organizational kinship. Marvell's viewpoint is a humanistic-rationalistic one until the moment, which comes near the close, when he adduces, respectively, the Christian virtue of "Humility," "Sin" in, most probably, the fullness of its Christian sense, and the "Manna" Christianized in a many-sided figurative and symbolic manner. It is not the mere presence of these notions, but the critical and suffusive effect they have on theme and structure, that entitles these poems to be categorized—"Soul/Body" less obviously but I think legitimately so—as religious rather than philosophical verse.

Notes

1. J.B. Leishman, *The Art of Marvell's Poetry* (London: Hutchinson University Library, 1966), p. 193.

2. Pierre Legouis, ed., *The Poems and Letters of Andrew Marvell*, ed. H.M. Margoliouth, 1:242 (Commentary). Margoliouth did not bring in Ephesians to annotate the lines in the first two editions.

3. Frank Kermode, ed., *Selected Poetry* by Marvell (New York: New American Library, 1967), p. 49. Other texts of St. Paul will illumine others of Marvell, and will be considered later.

4. *Works*, ed. Frank Allen Patterson et al. (New York: Columbia University Press, 1931–37), 4:311, 367, n. 8.

5. "Her voice was ever soft/Gentle and low, an excellent thing in woman." *Lear*, 5.3.272–73.

6. St. Augustine, "Holy Virginity," trans. John McQuade, S.M., *Treatises on Marriages and other Subjects*, *The Fathers of the Church* (New York: Fathers of the Church, Inc. 1955), 27:179, 182.

7. "Humilité," *Dictionnaire de Théologie Catholique* (Paris: Librairie Letouzey et ané 1903–50), 7:322.

"The etymology of the word *humility* brings us back to our earthly origins. *Humilitas* comes from *humus* (= earth), the ancients used to say. Man, sprung from the earth, living and depending on it, is destined to return to its bosom."

8. Hubert van Zeller, *The Holy Rule* (New York: Shead and Ward, 1958), p. 98.

9. *The Rule of St. Benedict* (chap. 7), trans. Abbot Justin McCann (London: Burns Oates, 1952), p. 39.

10. *The Twelve Degrees of Humility and Pride*, trans. Barton R.V. Mills London: Society for Promoting Christian Knowledge, 1929). Louis L. Martz sees the soul as "basing its stand firmly on the view of St. Bernard" in the "final couplet," (*The Poetry of Meditation* [New Haven: Yale University Press, 1962], p. 131). From this cryptic statement I am unable to say how much or precisely what Martz perceives. He does not remark the dependence of the Bernardine treatise on the Benedictine Rule, does not note the monastic focus of both documents, and so leaves the possible impression that the Puritan poet would embrace without qualification the instructions meant for monks in a religious community.

He fails to observe that the issues of the second part of the "Dialogue" do not come into the purview of St. Bernard. Harold E. Toliver cites St. Bernard too, quite specifically and in connection with his own view that in "Soul / Pleasure" the "Christian framework prevails over the Neoplationist elements" with the evocation of humility (*Marvell's Ironic Vision* [New Haven: Yale University Press, 1965], p. 71).

11. The *Summa Theologica* (2-2, Q. 161, Art. 1), trans. Fathers of the English Dominican Province (London: Buns, Oates, and Washbourne, Ltd., 1932), 13:216–17. In the sixth article of this question St. Thomas examines and approves the "twelve degrees of humility" in the Rule of St. Benedict (pp. 227–31).

12. Toliver, p. 82.

13. Leishman, p. 216. His evidence, extremely tenuous in any case, is nullified by the demonstrable autonomy of the poem.

14. See William T. Costello, *The Scholastic Curriculum at Early Seventeenth-Century Cambridge* (Cambridge, Mass: Harvard University Press, 1947), pp. 14–31.

15. Sister Miriam Joseph, C.S.C., *Shakespeare's Use of the Arts of Language* (New York: Columbia University Press, 1947), pp. 333–36.

16. Ibid., Chapters 3 and 7, both entitled "Logos: The Topics of Invention," passim.

17. Ibid., p. 151; Rosamund Tuve, *Elizabethan and Metaphysical Imagery* (Chicago: University of Chicago Press, 1947), p. 207. I find her discussion of "Soul / Body" along rhetorical lines at pp. 162–63 and 207–208 to be desultory and misdirected.

18. Sister Miriam Joseph, p. 310.

19. Ibid., pp. 256, 257.

20. Henry Peachem, *The Garden of Eloquence* (London, 1593), quoted by Sister Miriam Joseph, p. 393. It is noteworthy that aspects of the quarrelsome interaction turn up as rhetorical techniques.

21. Aristotle, *Rhetoric*, 1:2, 1357ᵃ 16.

22. Sister Miriam Joseph, pp. 203–204.

23. Joseph Summers is aware that Body with the final four lines "wins and ironically resolves the argument" ("Marvell's 'Nature,'" *ELH* 20 [1953], 128). Yes, but why ironically?

24. *The Christian Doctrine, Works*, 15:179.

25. "Péché," *Dictionaire de Théologie Catholique*, 11:158.

26. Kermode, p. 53. He adds, "but there is an old association between manna, dew and grace, and Marvell remembers it, probably, throughout his development of the analogue between the soul and dew." This clue could hardly be more misleading.

27. Toliver, pp. 73–74, discusses this contrast.

28. *Religio Medici*, 1:16.

29. Manna is referred to at Num. 11:7–9, Deut. 8:3,16, Neh. 9:20, Ps. 78:24, Ps. 105:40 as well as at Ex. 16.

30. *Works*, 15:366–75.

31. The citations, which could go on and on, need not be restricted to Paul. See, e.g., John 1:13, 1 Pet. 1:23.

32. Raymond E. Brown, S.S., ed., trans., *The Gospel according to John (i–xii)*, The Anchor Bible (Garden City, N.Y., Doubleday, 1966), pp. 272–73.

33. *Works*, 16:192–97. Milton writes that John 6 "does not relate exclusively to the Lord's Supper, but to the participation in general, through faith, of any of the benefits of Christ's incarnation" (p. 193).

34. J.E. Saveson, "Marvell's 'On a Drop of Dew,'" *N&Q* 203 (1958), 289–90, introduces, in a brief reading of the passage on manna that diverges from my own, points along lines similar to some of mine. Patrick Cullen, *Spenser, Marvell, and Renaissance Pastoral* (Mass.: Harvard University Press, 1970), offers, on p. 178, a few inchoate glimmerings of the function of the passage. Ruth Wallerstein, *Studies in Seventeenth-Century Poetic* (Madison: University of Wisconsin Press, 1950), p. 164, also touches upon some connections between the manna and Christ.

Marvell's Songs and Pictorial Exhibits

Harold Toliver

> Words move, music moves
> Only in Time; but that which is only living
> Can only die. Words, after speech, reach
> Into silence. Only by the form, the pattern,
> Can words or music reach
> The stillness.
>
> (T.S. Eliot, "Burnt Norton")

ALTHOUGH THE METAPHYSICALS clearly prefer definition to silence, Eliot has some precedent in them for thinking that the poet should somehow reach beyond words and music into stillness. They are pulled two ways in this regard—toward discipline and intellectual precision, and toward the transcendence of these and, in certain moments, perhaps even toward the abandonment of form and pattern. This is most obviously true of Vaughan and Traherne, who pursue a fugitive spirit that they never find fully manifest in the world's body. It is more problematically true of Marvell, who is frequently alert to the difficulties that nature and art present as formal revelations of an origin that lies beyond them—nature as a set of analogies to that origin and art as an expression of nature's underlying principles of order, symmetry, harmony, and logic.[1] Like Milton in "Ad Patrem" and "At a Solemn Music," Marvell realizes that "disproportion'd sin" has "with harsh din / Broke the fair music" of creation and thereby clouded our perception of what lies beyond. Ordinary music shares in that fall, as do the other arts. When Marvell regards the arts comparatively or measures them against the soul's unmediated intuition of its origins, he is likely to notice the impact they have on what they present: the medium crowds between the mind and its proper object in all created forms. As "On a Drop of Dew" suggests, he sometimes manages to have it both ways, first, the expressive precision of highly articulate images, then the soul's dissolution and escape from natural forms "Into the Glories of th' Almighty Sun." For him it often boils down to just such an affair of forms, held in "pure and circling thought" and then dispersed. The distortions, the yoking of incongruities, and the sheer wreckage of his poems are a surprising violence committed against forms established on a seemingly calm and graceful surface.

Marvell also realizes that images, metaphors, architecture, music, and painting, when they stay within the guidelines of decorum, are capable of expressive accuracy. When the neoclassicist in him prevails, one thing is seen as a well suited substitute for another, as "Beasts are by their Denns exprest." Where "These *holy Mathematicks* can / In ev'ry Figure equal Man," he remarks about the house of Fairfax; one has the satisfying sense of a fully located exponent. Thus even where the fit is tight and the embodiment slightly comic, greater things may be "in less contained." One sees even heaven in the spherical dew drop, in so "coy a Figure wound." Indeed, the mind may be displaced and homeless if it cannot find expressive terrain: to be known, paradise must be rendered by nature's surface, as Pan is in "Clorinda and Damon" by the songs of fountains, pastures, and caves.

Hence fitness of expression is partly a matter of keeping concealment and revelation in balance and finding a compromise between the desire for mathematical precision and the soul's desire for the removal of obstructive mediation. When he is not shattering forms, Marvell searches out a compromise between matching and mismatching, as the dew drop is and is not the soul, is and is not heaven. Objects are compromised not only by the threat of dissolution but by classification and recasting. While a given object strives to hold its assigned form, like the fish in *Upon Appleton House* that lie fixed in water "As *Flies* in *Chrystal* overt'ane," it is subject to the analysis of metaphor and must yield its uniqueness to join the world of uniform geometrical and mathematical shapes. Molding and casting, fitting one thing to another, yet also scaling down, squeezing, changing sizes and shapes, looking through the microscope or telescope, straining for optical clarity (as Rosalie Colie has described[2]) are frequent form-making and form-shattering stages on Marvell's way toward a balancing of definition and dissolution.

Although Marvell's unease over matching and mismatching cannot be limited altogether to his concern with the radical of presentation in the different arts, we can see its impact there with special clarity. Three basic modes locate in many of the difficulties he finds with form: argument or the thematic and rhetorical mode that governs the debate poems; the iconic mode that governs pageantry and picture gallery poems; and the melodic mode. The latter two, which are my main concern, Marvell sometimes isolates for separate attention, as in "Musicks Empire" and "The Gallery," and sometimes combines, as in "The Fair Singer." More broadly, he exploits their organizing and expressive principles in poems threaded by rhetoric and logic. In the long run he abandons the ambitious uses he finds for them in panegyric and lyric poems and reduces them to the service of satiric portraiture. There they shrink to illustrative devices and drop the metaphysical complexities that make the earlier lyrics so richly enigmatic.

Music Reaching into Stillness

Marvell's distrust of music is evident in a number of places, but he also makes concessions to music's access to the order of creation. "A Dialogue Between The Resolved Soul, and Created Pleasure" (pp. 9–12) is especially ambivalent. Music provides both the highest sensory pleasure set before the soul and the formal framework of the poem itself. It marks a climax and a turning point in pleasure's temptations:

Pleasure

Heark how Musick then prepares
For thy Stay these charming Aires;
Which the posting Winds recall,
And suspend the Rivers Fall.

Soul

Had I but any time to lose,
On this I would it all dispose.
Cease Tempter. None can chain a mind
Whom this sweet Chordage cannot bind.

(ll. 37–44)

Against the soul's otherworldly inclinations, created music amounts
to a counter proposal. Rising out of the primitive monotony of the
sounds of wind and water, it organizes them into airs and presents
them as pure harmony. If music can suspend a river's fall and recall
the posting winds, might it not also reach into the quiescence of
eternity? The poem itself celebrates the soul's victories in choral
music and obviously could not function were it not for the melodic
devices of meter, interval, rhyme, and other sound effects. Even
as the soul makes its point against music, music sustains the rhetoric
and undermines it, dividing it into tuneful phrases and marking its
divisions into stanzas. The nature of argument, too, demands the
movement of the mind through dialectical stages to the moment of
hymnal triumph. Hence though the soul may not need stages of
any kind, the poet and the reader require the serial form of verse
and rhetoric, even if it must deny its own special benefits.

Less ambiguously in fefense of music, Marvell in "Bermudas"
sees no conflict between the holy, cheerful note of the pilgrims and
the spiritual heights they seek. The winds listen, and the rocks sound
God's name, as do the heavens themselves. Again in "Clorinda and
Damon," the chorus suggests the expressive value of music. Like
the Resolved Soul, Damon is moralistic and aloof, but he has strong
attachments to the tradition of pastoral song. As a chorus of natural
objects joins him in singing of Pan, the universal god is duly "noted,"
in a harmony reminiscent of Orphic and Pythagorean traditions.
The singers in effect extract from nature's mute suggestions of
divinity a foreground exponent of the sacred. The pilgrims and
shepherds mark time as the soul in "The Garden" does, preparing
for longer flight by the practice of an art in which nature and the
supernatural join on easy terms.

More singular than these poems in exploring the special powers
of music is "Musicks Empire," (pp. 50–51), which adds another

dimension to the serial existence that music leads. Marvell constructs the poem along incremental lines, beginning with a simple monotone instrument (the cymbal), adding various technical advances in sound-making (the organ, lute, viol, and coronet), and coming to a cosmic music in full consort. He holds rhetoric and argument to a minimum in what is essentially a song in praise of song and its historical process. The poem is not without implications for the soul's retreat from nature, but these reverse the implications of "A Dialogue": the evolution of music forestalls the soul's quest for another world, or at least conducts it through the evidence of this world with some sense of achievement. Whereas the Resolved Soul resists all sensory contamination, the world here is delivered through sensory perception. The various instruments extrapolate its inherent harmony, refining nature's crude sound and drawing out an ideal latent in it. The pace, coordination, and opposition of musical composition not only control the raw materials of nature but extract life and human feeling from them—as though in the discovery of order, one stumbled upon a kind of social and spiritual power imprisoned in the silence of the source. The instruments are virtual deliveries of the Logos, finishing the creation, building out hints, exploiting time as though in extension of the six original days. Whether or not, as Jonathan Goldberg has suggested,[3] the poem goes beyond that tribute to music, prepares for a typological reading of Jubal, and makes Christ into the "gentler Conqueror" of the last stanza, the progressive view of history obviously favors civilization over an untamed and unfinished nature. Music's pleasure is both created and binding; its "chordage" wraps up a universe for delivery to the ear's perception.

By reversing the notion of the fall of man and other versions of history as a decline, music thus makes possible a progressive view of the human arts. By division and arrangement, a sullen monotony spreads into a whole colony as though in imitation of the spread of European nations to the primitive world:

> Then Musick, the Mosaique of the Air,
> Did of all these a solemn noise prepare:
> With which She gain'd the Empire of the Ear,
> Including all between the Earth and Sphear.

(ll. 17–20)

The introduction of "Heavens quire" suggests one further thing about music's empire: progress is not only numerical and spatial but hierarchical. The poem endorses everything the Resolved Soul and its heavenly choir find unnecessary, degrees as well as created pleasure. As music advances upward into its kinds and voices, so concepts rise toward abstraction and godlike vision. The final stanza indicates that though the ultimate music may lie beyond the lute and the viol, it is nonetheless analogous to theirs:

> Victorious sounds! yet here your Homage do
> Unto a gentler Conqueror then you;
> Who though He flies the Musick of his praise,
> Would with you Heavens Hallelujahs raise.

(ll. 21–24)

If the earlier pun on "Mosaique" suggests a holy testament written in the air parallel to the writing of Moses, the power of music seems no less than redemptive here.

But it is also true that redemptive conquest cannot be as meaningful where no paradise has been lost to begin with; if Christ is the "gentler Conqueror," as Jonathan Goldberg surmises, what he has to overcome in a world without discord is not altogether clear. In subordinating argument to the imitation and praise of music, Marvell narrows the poem's range and silences the counter voices that test the expressive forms of other poems. "Musicks Empire" gains its victories by discarding the ambivalence toward art that animates other comments on music. Where "A Dialogue" and "Musicks Empire" are mutually exclusive in this respect, "Bermudas," "Clorinda and Damon," and "A Dialogue between Thyrsis and Dorinda" consider a middle ground. In the last of these, Thyrsis seems to argue for a dissolution of form as radical as that of "On a Drop of Dew." Taking the view that "No Oat-pipe's needfull" in Elysium, where "thine Ears / May feast with Musick of the Spheres," he urges instant transport there by suicide. But until one actually arrives, the "slender Oate" and a chorus of fountains and pastures are presumably better than many things one could imagine; they at least supply estimations of what an ultimate music might be.

Taken altogether, these poems on music entertain variances and sustain pluralities in exploring music's access to certain realities.

Marvell is consistent in supposing those realities to be partly beyond expressive form, but no less consistent in being tempted by the delight music offers before it dissolves into stillness. The poet's difficulty is to catch what lies beyond from the flowing away itself. The lyric Marvell, as opposed to the witty Marvell of pictorial exhibitions and eventually of satiric counterpunches, might be said to proceed under Milton's view of the descent of heavenly demarcations into the marriage of airs and immortal verse, which paradoxically both entangles and frees the soul—as "the meeting soul" pierces verse in notes,

> with many a winding bout
> Of linked sweetness long drawn out,
> With wanton heed, and giddy cunning,
> The melting voice through mazes running;
> Untwisting all the chains that tie
> The hidden soul of harmony.

("L'Allegro")

If the final music is an unexpressive nuptial song, to Marvell in his less rigorously Platonist moments it can nonetheless be approached through the conducted labyrinths of sound.

Frozen Images on Display

Perhaps the more crucial question is not whether nature and the expressive forms of music give the Resolved Soul pleasure or merely contaminate it but what implications music carries in contrast to other forms, what kind of world it is capable of setting up and maintaining. Marvell unobtrusively introduces into the lyrics that concern music a recurrent struggle between the serial, blending, harmonious, sensory method of musical perception and the dividing, classifying, analytic intellignece of debate and exhibition, compounding the tension between dissolving and expressive form by a competition among forms themselves. In its capacity to sweep the listener along and direct each stage of his feelings as part of an ascending or descending sequence, music demands uncritical empathy and linear plotting: one surrenders to its intricacy. A rhapsody both makes and disbands acoustic forms; it is a progressive dissolution that predicts its final silence. Marvell also knows all the Cavalier devices of recurrent sound, stanzaic form, and rearranged syntax that give musical support to precise definition and constantly reconfirm the solidity of previous acoustical moments. More forceful counters to the dissolving runs of music are Marvell's theoretical, argumentative, and metaphysical tendencies. His brand of juxtaposition is often contrastive and dialectical. Where music would blend the soul with nature, erase distinctions, and make a train of perceptions into a fluid course, iconic and rhetorical modes pose pictures and theses side by side. Even if we did not know Marvell's frequent recourse to them, we might guess that a poet so fond of rival systems and devices of wit would find gallery portraits, monuments, and debates as attractive as music's power of entrancement—and equally dangerous from the Resolved Soul's viewpoint. He understands the guided museum tour as well as the concert, and he realizes the differences between them.

What the visual artist at his best displays before us is basically symbolic moments or epitomes in frozen form that allows us to scrutinize things that are otherwise fleeting and evasive. The guide's function is to arrange an intellectual or visual itinerary, dissecting and analyzing as he goes. Even a relatively simple picture poem such as "The Gallery" follows several principles of assembly, including an unstoried sequence of prospects, implicit persuasion, and glancing effects of metaphor.[4] A similar guide arranges *Upon Appleton House* almost like a sequence of painted scenes, playing in the meadow portion, for instance, with the notion of nature as a pure white tablet on which the creation paints its multitude of objects—as though the filling of a blank mind through the optic nerve were equivalent to the making of a cosmos. Certainly the painter figure in Marvell is expected to assemble a world whose plenty is at least to be acknowledged if not inventoried and carefully arranged. Hence it is not surprising to find Marvell drawing upon the traditional reinforcement of painting and poetry, as when the instructor concludes to the painter, "*Painter* adieu, how will our Arts agree; / Poetick Picture, Painted Poetry." As though fulfilling that program, certain poems proceed almost like emblems connected by argument or narrative— or like photos flashed at a pace timed to suggest stillness within movement and thus to "make our Sun / Stand still." "On a Drop of Dew" begins with an indicator or guide pointing to sharply visual symbols carefully delineated in close focus and organizes its movement as a two-phase iconic realization of the soul's incarnation. The argument of "To his Coy Mistress" is also strongly pictorial and especially skillful in alternating a sense of speeded up and stopped time. Although "A Dialogue Between The Resolved Soul, and Created Pleasure" contains elements of the debate poem and is punctuated by musical outbreaks, it, too, begins with a speaker pointing out a visual pageant. Created Pleasure then proceeds to make a programmed demonstration of the advantages of embodiment, each of which falls into place as part of both a tightening logic and an exhibit. Marvell treats even the execution of Charles in *An Horation Ode* (pp. 91–94), as a spectacle—not quite a pictorial display, to be sure, but a kind of ritualized exhibition climaxed by Charles's assumption of a classic, almost painterly pose for a gallery of watchers:

> *He* nothing common did or mean
> Upon that memorable Scene:
>   But with his keener Eye
>   The Axes edge did try:
> Nor call'd the *Gods* with vulgar spight
> To vindicate his helpless Right,
>   But bow'd his comely Head,
>   Down as upon a Bed.
>
> (ll. 57–64)

In effect, the episode is set off as an interval; a gap falls between it and the moment in which the contemporary audience stands. It is therefore of no use for that audience to try to recross the gap, which would be as difficult as entering the frame of a picture or the staging of a masque: what's done is done. Meanwhile, Cromwell himself lives on, still sitting for a not-yet-finished portrait.

In these and other instances, Marvell realizes the detachment of pictorial art, as though by framing and museum installment a portrait is disengaged not only from its subject but from the logic and the pressure of serial time. He also appreciates the fact that pictorial detachment can suppress dramatic, rhetorical, and musical elements. Subordinating forensic technique to visual display, he emphasizes the escape of the picture from the controls of logic and persuasion. No direct exchange accompanies the exhibit in "The Gallery," for instance. The speaker does not give Clora a chance to reply; he merely lectures her on the portraits arranged in his own mind. Moreover, as an instrument of the arts, the eye is potentially as dangerous as the singing voice. The subtle nuns of *Upon Appleton House*, like the fair singer, mix rhetorical skills with a display of visual adornment in tempting the virgin Thwaites with a richly rewarding innocence, as Satan himself is entwined in the flowers of "The Coronet." The nuns in elaborate needlework, inscribed saints' lives, and fancy linen seek to ensnare their victim with the intricacies of design. They conclude their temptation with a portrait of the virgin as herself already a saint, seated in a holy, sensuous picture of flattering radiance:

> 'I see the *Angels* in a Crown
> 'On you the Lillies show'ring down:
> 'And round about you Glory breaks,
> 'That something more then humane speaks.

(ll. 141–44)

Other instances reinforce the impression that Marvell distrusts the lure of art. Though Damon the Mower is not a reliable guide in such matters, his rhyming of "paint" with "taint" carries a similar fear of the trap that visual ornament weaves for the eye. Even the little pictures of "On a Drop of Dew" are a bit like stage props or artifices that we are eventually urged to transcend if we are to grasp the soul's true state—not by the eye but by pure "recollection" beyond all discursive or iconic exponents. From a viewpoint that Marvell returned to several times, any sort of embodiment or expression is captivity, just as to the dew-drop soul nature itself, though a beautiful flower, is contaminating.

The fixity of visual art, like its detachment and its concretion, is both a strength and a weakness. By stopping an action for contemplation, it frees the mind from time, but it also emphasizes even more the corporeality of surfaces and creates a problem of gaps that neither rhetoric nor music has. In music, of course, as an interval and a necessary part of rhythm, a hiatus presents no special problem: silence is a heard part of the sound. But in pictorial display, the eye is left with teasing breaks in logic between parts of an exhibit. Marvell's poems are filled with the implicit violence of those severed connections. The hiatus between the stanzas of poems like "The Garden" or between poems in a possible group like the Mower poems leaves the structure of the whole for us to fill in as we can.

In *Upon Appleton House* the hiatuses between scenes are especially puzzling, and even within each scene and between the components of a given metaphor we discover problems of transition. While yielding hints of some underlying purpose, for instance, the forest keeps its distance from the systematic intellect; it is on display, but the guide cannot provide all the necessary keys. He realizes that the exhibits of a sanctuary are of a different sort from those of other galleries; they possess talisman powers and work in a hushed atmosphere. At the same time, this is not quite a true gallery poem, since the Fairfax possessions and activities cannot be reduced to monuments, and the emblems of the forest and meadow remain living and moving. They bring with them awareness of certain universals and a deepening time, as mystery, not as certain knowledge. History itself is a combination of picture and hiatus:

> Out of these scatter'd *Sibyls* Leaves
> Strange *Prophecies* my Phancy weaves:
> And in one History consumes,
> Like *Mexique Paintings*, all the *Plumes*.
> What *Rome*, *Greece*, *Palestine*, ere said
> I in this light *Mosaick* read.
> Thrice happy he who, not mistook.
> Hath read in *Natures mystick Book*.
>
> (73: 577–84)

The emphasis here plainly falls on the book and its signs, and on the conversion of history into visual mosaic and painting. But that does not indicate a triumph of explicit definition. That the leaves are scattered means that the observer must assemble his own pattern from them, as feather pictures are composed not of flowing brush strokes but of particles. History is to be put together out of discrete incidents composed by the sign reader; it is not a flowing allegory by a divine compositor, not a form of music, not a continuous conceit or argument. Similarly, the aphorisms that drop into place here and there in the poem are not the products of analysis or thematic illustration. They tend to be harvested perceptions that have come to the observer like spontaneous compositions isolated in a larger prospect—or like views through the microscope of momentarily fixed phenomena. In any case, unlike linear compositions, Marvell's mosaic so affixes images that they stand in both past and future:

history and prophecy become one and the same, reduced to the smallest epitomizing form at the still point of the forest's center.

When he moves on from there, the cryptic exhibition guide wishes to be drawn into the scene himself (l. 624), as the actor becomes scene and the spectator the thing observed. When Maria Fairfax appears, her shadow is seized by the stream, which "gellies" and becomes fixed as though willing to cease flowing for the privilege of becoming an *object d'art* (ll. 673ff.). Indeed, under the influence of Maria, the topography becomes akin to a landscape painting. She works upon it as its perfecter, changing the pace of its movement, the consistency of its bodies, and the arrangement of its light, until the whole emerges as a map of paradise—perhaps the highest substitution to which a visual scene can aspire. Her commerce with heaven suggests that any portion of earth visited by such an emissary may become a symbolic index of that higher place (stanza 96), both detached from the progressive story of its earthly locality and suspended beneath another logic that collects it.

Marvell manages perhaps his best fusion of expressive modes and balance between temporal occupations and the postponed dissolution of mind and soul in "The Garden," which sorts out the difficulties of embodiment into layers and phases. The garden itself provides a splendid bodily anchoring of speculations that carry beyond the limits of form. It permits the mind to play with transcendence and imaginative creations of "Far other Worlds, and other Seas" and to annihilate all created forms, yet brings it back to the tangible matters of description and observation. It has abundant rewards for those who have left civil, literary, and amorous affairs; it satisfies the body's delight in ripening processes and the soul's delight in music. Unlike the Mower's garden, it does not corrupt the maker or the observer. Except for one explicit mention of song, the arts blend into nature and into the oblique presence of echoes and allusions. Song itself is not a snare but a gathering of nature's lights and shapes and a preparation for the soul's exodus. Half bird and half angel, the soul sits on its bough like a moving icon.

The garden allows not only the soul's pastime but a kind of measure or calculation as well, at least for the industrious bee that computes its "tyme" and those who reckon wholesome hours. The implication throughout is that the mind is busy with comparison, sorting, and other occupations of wit. However, that zodiacs and clocks are very arbitrary in their measurements reminds us that the order of the poem, too, is both rigid and loose: though Marvell's exhibition of images and delights is shaped into metrical and stanzaic units of great formal exactness, the miscellaneous collection is lifted out of the regular world and made into assorted *objets d'art*. The dial of herbs is a curious example. It converts both the movement of time and the body of botanical life into a monument of some regularity. But though time is complete on its face, it can be computed and read there only in phases; calculation is never more than a guess at the total, which is ultimately not measured but infinite, as the garden is only a surmise of the paradise the soul awaits. All the natural forms and arts do not add up to a depiction of heaven; they are materials for filling time and raising surmise. Ultimately the soul must undergo its dissolution even as the mind its annihilation of created forms.

The balance of natural and man-made forms in "The Garden," and of objects and the gaps between them that tease thought out of compass, is Marvell's most impressive. It is both enigmatic and precise, teasing and satisfying. That balance is not equaled elsewhere in Marvell, though "Bermudas" and parts of *Upon Appleton House* approach it. Marvell customarily stresses the fetters that pleasure, fair singers, or painters bring with them—the subtlety and snaring delay that art imposes on what should be the soul's unimpeded progress. He is also aware of another tension that proves to be central to the later poetry, that between the finish that art has, or seeks to have, and the indefiniteness of temporal life. The nymph in "The Nymph complaining" (pp. 23–26), foreshadows that tension when she imagines passing from the condition of narrative events into permanent art:

> First my unhappy Statue shall
> Be cut in Marble; and withal,
> Let it be weeping too: but there
> Th'Engraver sure his Art may spare;
> For I so truly thee bemoane,
> That I shall weep though I be Stone:
> Until my Tears, still dropping, wear
> My breast, themselves engraving there.
>
> (ll. 111–18)

Two impulses obviously struggle here: one is to be memorialized in absolute purity, the other, to continue to feel. The nymph cannot imagine herself as an exhibit without transporting the pathos of the "story" with her. The gesture toward pure art, or through art toward the still point, stalls against the recalcitrance of the historical process, which the imagination cannot transcend.

Similar battle lines are drawn in a crucial sequence of poems that I think of as transitional on Marvell's way to becoming the satiric painter who puts on display a multitude of contemporary sins. In these poems dominated by chronicle and by rhetoric, Marvell turns to the combination of millennarian thought and politics that informs the Puritan hope for a new kingdom and makes Cromwell momentarily the key artisan and the hope for a reconciliation of movement and eschatological completion. Working broadly and ambitiously in *The First Anniversary*, (pp. 108–19) for instance, Marvell has Cromwell combine the musician, statesman, and architect as a master of rhetoric, music, and fixed art. Since one of the purposes of the poem is to hold up for praise the accomplishments of the year, Marvell is conscious of the calendar of events and Cromwell's compression of achievements, which are equivalent to Amphion's erection of an entire city:

> While indefatigable *Cromwell* hyes,
> And cuts his way still nearer to the Skyes,
> Learning a Musique in the Region clear,
> To tune this lower to that higher Sphere.
>   So when *Amphion* did the Lute command,
> Which the God gave him, with his gentle hand,
> The rougher Stones, unto his Measures hew'd,
> Dans'd up in order from the Quarreys rude.

> (ll. 45–52)

Unfortunately, Cromwell's finished structure is a commonwealth, not a paradise. It must run by parliamentary procedures. Despite the millennarian cast of the poem, it must leave the kingdom under the sway of time and suggests not a finished map of paradise but a yearly survey. Though argument is one way to convert into lucid reason the principles required of the state, it, too, is unable to compose a clear model of the Logos and apply it to human institutions.

Rather than providing a set of stages toward the realization of truths beyond definition, the busy intellect in the later Marvell dissects, satirizes, endorses; it argues, responds to, and urges courses of action. The completion of its work lies outside the scope of its forms of expression and the arts it takes up. Perhaps even more than argument, then, certainly more than the expressive marvels of painting and music, it is chronicle that dominates the later Cromwell poems and the portraits commanded of the painter. Though we may never do better than guess why the Restoration Marvell changed his poetic allegiances from lyric to satire, the rogues' gallery of the painter poems is filled with the miscellaneous details of horse and carriage, furniture, clothing, and political dealing. The poems present exhibitions still, but of Jermyns, duchesses, and affairs of state, as the collaborations of forensic art, portraiture, and melodic art are subordinated to the daily record. The painter's scenes cast discredit on all the expressive forms that society takes, none of which approaches the paradigmatic models of *Upon Appleton House*, "Bermudas," or "Musicks Empire." Whatever marriage with temporal forms the soul might be coaxed into accepting in the garden is cut short by the new gallery of "Drunkards, Pimps, and Fools."

Notes

1. See Gretchen Ludke Finney, *Musical Backgrounds for English Literature: 1580–1650* (New Brunswick, N.J.: Rutgers University Press, n.d.). For comments on musical structure, poetry and music, and *musica speculativa*, see Leo Spitzer, "Classical and Christian Ideas of World Harmony," *Traditio* 2 and 3 (1944–45): 409–64, 307–64; John Hollander, *The Untuning of the Sky: Ideas of Music in English Poetry 1500–1700* (Princeton: Princeton University Press, 1961); Kathi Meyer-Baer, *Music of the Spheres and the Dance of Death* (Princeton: Princeton University Press, 1970); Leonard B. Meyer, *Music, the Arts and Ideas* (Chicago: University of Chicago Press, 1967); Bruce Pattison, *Music and Poetry of the English Renaissance* (Folcroft, Pa.: Folcroft Press, 1948); Paula Johnson, *Form and Transformation in Music and Poetry of the English Renaissance* (New Haven: Yale University Press, 1972); Jerome Mazzaro, *Transformations in the Renaissance English Lyric* (Ithaca: Cornell University Press, 1970); Joan Stambaugh, "Music as a Temporal Form," *Journal of Philosophy* 61 (1964): 265–80; Patricia Carpenter, "Musical Form Regained," *Journal of Philosophy* 62 (1965): 36–48; Victor Zukerkandl, *Sound and Symbol: Music and the*

External World, trans. Willard Trask (Princeton: Princeton University Press, 1956); E.H. Gombrich, "Moment and Music in Art," *Journal of the Warburg and Courtauld Institute*, 27 (1964): 293–306; John Stevens, *Music and Poetry in the Early Tudor Court* (Lincoln, Nebraska: University of Nebraska Press, 1961); Gerardus Van Der Leeuw, *Sacred and Profane Beauty* (New York: Holt, Rinehart and Winston, 1963), "The Pictorial Arts," pp. 153–92, and "Music and Religion," pp. 211–62.

2. *"My Ecchoing Song": Andrew Marvell's Poetry of Criticism* (Princeton: Princeton University Press, 1970), pp. 205ff.

3. Jonathan Goldberg, "The Typology of 'Musicks Empire,'" *Texas Studies in Language and Literature* 13 (1971): 421–30; see also Hollander, pp. 309–15.

4. Rosalie Colie comments on both the hiatus problem in "The Garden" and the picture gallery principle in Marvell, pp. 196, 175–77; on pictorial traditions, "The Gallery," and *Upon Appleton House*," pp. 106–17, 192–218. From a quite different quarter, I have also found interesting and useful Philip Fisher's "The Future's Past," *New Literary History* 6 (1975): 587–606.

MARVELL'S "TOUGH REASONABLENESS" AND THE COY MISTRESS

FRENCH FOGLE

IN THE THREE HUNDRED YEARS since Andrew Marvell's death he has been many different things to different generations of critics.[1] From primary renown during the late seventeenth and eighteenth centuries as uncorrupted Parliamentarian and patriot, satirist and wit, he emerged only slowly to his present standing as preeminently a poet. In this essay I shall not try to cover the whole range of responses to Marvell's poetry. My purpose is by focusing attention on recent critical estimates of "To his Coy Mistress," that touchstone of Marvell's poetry, to suggest something not only about the Marvellian qualities and profundities that have become increasingly evident to critics but also about the extent to which learned and sophisticated critical approaches have helped (or hindered) an understanding of the subtle mind and variable sensibilities that inform Marvell's poetry.

Twentieth-century critics have attended to what might be called "interior" qualities of the poetry—the interaction of metaphor and image, the intellectual tone, the exploitation of traditional modes and ideas for Marvell's unique poetic purposes. It should not be surprising that this shift in critical attention from the nineteenth-century emphasis on lyric grace, love of nature, and the witty play of language seems to have come about largely through the combined efforts of Sir Herbert Grierson and T.S. Eliot, who changed our critical attitudes toward more than one area of seventeenth-century poetry. In his influential *Metaphysical Lyrics and Poems of the Seven-*

teenth Century (1921), Grierson cites Marvell as the strongest personality among the disciples of Donne and the Metaphysicals:

> " ... his [Marvell's] few love poems and his few devotional pieces
> are perfect exponents of all the 'metaphysical' qualities—passionate,
> paradoxical argument, touched with humour and learned imagery
> [quotes "As lines, so loves ... can never meet" from the "Defini-
> tion"] and above all the sudden soar of passion in bold and felicitous
> image, in clangorous lines [quotes "But at my back ... there
> embrace" from the "Coy Mistress"]. These lines seem to me the
> very roof and crown of the metaphysical love lyric, at once fantastic
> and passionate. Donne is weightier, more complex, more suggestive
> of subtle and profound reaches of feeling, but he has not one single
> passage of the same length that combines all the distinctive qualities
> of the kind, in thought, in phrasing, in feeling, in music."
>
> (Introduction, p. xxxviii)

Though this criticism may not attain the specificity of recent comment on the poetry, it is primarily concerned with the inner qualities which have become recognized as the hallmarks of Marvell's sensibility and technical mastery of his poetic art. Grierson suggests levels of meaning and resonances which had escaped earlier critics.

The seminal essay by T.S. Eliot in 1921 must be familiar to all critics of Marvell, but it might be well to remind ourselves of some of Eliot's major points which have been such powerful stimulants to later criticism. It will be remembered that in trying to define the quality that distinguishes Marvell at his best Eliot speaks of "a literary rather than a personal quality; or, more truly, that it is a quality of a civilization, of a traditional habit of life," and he further suggests that "Marvell's best verse is the product of European, that is to say, Latin, culture." He sees this elusive quality as one of the chief distinctions between the intense individuality of Donne, for instance, and the intellectual poise and detachment, the teasing elusiveness and ambivalence notable in Marvell's greatest poems. The very comprehensiveness of Eliot's formulation did not satisfy the critical thirst for greater precision, but its essential justness has encouraged attempts to recover the essentials of that European culture which shaped and tempered the mind of Marvell—not always with illuminating results, to be sure, but on the whole promoting our understanding of the complexities of Marvell's intellectual and cultural heritage.

Eliot singles out wit and magniloquence as the two dominant qualities of the high style developed from Marlowe through Jonson and passed on to the poets of the later seventeenth century. His definitions of the terms are familiar: wit as "a tough reasonableness beneath the slight lyric grace"; and magniloquence as "the deliberate exploitation of the possibilities of magnificence in language." In employing these devices of art and thought, Marvell is seen as "more a man of the century than a Puritan," as a poet speaking "with the voice of his literary age" more clearly than does Milton. In the remainder of his essay, Eliot does not develop the idea of magniloquence as it applies to Marvell (one might suggest that Marvell's use of language is magnificent rather than magniloquent), but in his attempt to delineate more precisely than ever before the wit that informs Marvell's art, he resorts to pointing out what is *not* characteristic of that wit: "... we can say that wit is not erudition; it is sometimes stifled by erudition, as in much of Milton. It is not cynicism, though it has a kind of toughness which may be confused with cynicism by the tender-minded. It is confused with erudition because it belongs to an educated mind, rich in generations of experience; and it is confused with cynicism because it implies a constant inspection and criticism of experience. It involves, probably, a recognition, implicit in the expression of every experience, of other kinds of experience which are possible, which we find as clearly in the greatest as in poets like Marvell." But even with this set of critical distinctions, Eliot is aware, with an honesty not always displayed by subsequent critics, that Marvell may well have eluded him. He confesses, "The quality with Marvell had, this modest and certainly impersonal virtue—whether we call it wit or reason, or even urbanity—we have patently failed to define. By whatever name we call it, and however we define that name, it is something precious and needed and apparently extinct; it is what should preserve the reputation of Marvell." Perhaps, like later critics, Eliot was trying to define the indefinable, but despite his confessed failure he at least staked out the grounds on which later critical effort would be expended.

In applying his critical analyses to the "Coy Mistress" Eliot makes a number of telling points which may be briefly summarized here. He finds the "voice" of the poem to be that of the literary age out of which it came, reflecting a broad literary culture rather than a set of personal responses to experience. He defines the theme as "one of the great traditional commonplaces of European literature," the theme of *carpe diem*, common to such lyrics as "o mistress mine," "Gather ye rosebuds," and "Go, lovely rose," but he characterizes Marvell's treatment of the theme as marked by the "savage austerity of Lucretius and the intense levity of Catullus." The real distinction in Marvell's handling of the theme lies in the wit whereby he invents and orders the images, the high speed and concentration of the images magnifying the pleasing fancy with which the poem opens and leading to the astonishment of "Vaster than Empires, and more slow." With the opening of the second verse paragraph ("But at my back ... vast Eternity," ll. 21–24), Eliot finds "that surprise which has been one of the most important means of poetic effect since Homer." A whole civilization, he says, resides in the lines, and he quotes from Horace and Catullus in support. The Donnean touch of"... then Worms shall try ... do there embrace" (ll. 27–32), he thinks might have been the ending point for a modern poet, but the "syllogistic relation" which exists among the three strophes calls for the conclusion, "Let us roll all ... Iron gates of Life" (ll. 41–44). The wit which dominates the poem; which "is not only combined with, but fused into, the imagination"; which controls "this alliance of levity and seriousness"; which provides "structural decoration of a serious idea," is the same wit that can be found in Catullus, Ovid, and Propertius, in Gautier, Baudelaire, and Laforgue, "a quality of a sophisticated literature."

But for all of Eliot's acute and sensitive insights into the ways by which Marvell develops his theme and the way wit manipulates imagery in the poem, later critics have not been content to accept "pleasing," "surprise," and "astonishment" as descriptive of what the poem has done to them—or what it did, apparently, to Eliot. They have exerted more particular pressures on the poem—on its structure, its images, its language, its literary background—in order to clarify the question of why the poem acts as it does on readers. Using the points raised by Eliot as centers of inquiry, it might be of some interest to examine random samples of recent criticism to explore what expanded "meaning" the poem has acquired, and the merits of today's varied critical approaches to the "Coy Mistress." In view of the amazing variety, contradictoriness, and partiality of recent interpretations of the poem, one has some sympathy for the impression of the late Pierre Legouis that the greater the recent efforts to explicate the "Coy Mistress," especially the last six lines, the less he understood them,[2] but one should not allow despair to cloud one's vision of critical effort.

On the matter of the theme of the poem there has been general, even monotonous, agreement. Apparently working on the assumption that every *carpe diem* poem must finally propose seduction as a defiant gesture against, or a witty evasion of, the threat of time and death, the great majority of critics have accepted the "Coy Mistress" as conforming to the expected pattern. Eliot himself seems to have viewed the conclusion of the poem as a reflection of the Catullian model, although he never faced squarely the implications of the violent imagery in the third verse paragraph. No critic before Eliot that I have discovered even faintly suggested that the outcome of Marvell's poem was anything other than the traditional invitation to sexual indulgence as a form of insurance against the uncertainties of life. Nineteenth-century critics may have been embarrassed by the stark realism of the scene in the marble vault and the naked appetites suggested in the third paragraph, but none, so far as I know, doubted that the poet's purpose was anything other than momentary pleasure in despite of the sterile deserts of eternity that lay ahead. Critics of the twentieth century seem to have been, by and large, dominated by the idea that (a) the resolution of a *carpe diem* poem is always seduction; (b) the "Coy Mistress" is a *carpe diem* poem; ergo, (c) the resolution of the "Coy Mistress" is necessarily seduction. In a sense the convention has been allowed to determine the "theme" of the poem. It may not be necessary to document in detail the prevailing interpretations of the poem, but some examples of recent summaries of what the poet is saying in the "Coy Mistress" may be helpful in considering the extent to which Marvell was the servant of convention, and the extent to which critics have allowed the convention to sway their judgments of the poem.

In an essay in *The New Statesman*, 2 April 1921, Desmond MacCarthy, commenting on the tercentenary celebrations of Marvell's birth, noted with some surprise that Mr. Gosse, in the Sunday *Times*, and Mr. Squire, in the *Observer*, had not even mentioned "Marvell's best and most surprising poem"—the "Coy Mistress." Attempting to make up for the neglect, he makes a claim for the poem as "one of the best passion poems in the language." After the "playful and enormous hyperboles" of the first verse paragraph, he detects the threat of passion in the second, and that passion combined with "a kind of anger" in the third, the whole accumulation of feeling culminating in the "crash" of the final couplet, like the crash of a black "mounting wave." MacCarthy is imprecise in stating what the passion and anger are directed toward or against—the coyness of the lady? or the threat of time? or the immanence of death?—but one can only assume that he accepts *carpe diem* as the admonition of the poem. At any rate he detects an intensity of passion which is outside the range of the usual seduction poem.

In the volume of *Tercentenary Tributes* of 1922, containing the famous Eliot essay, H.J. Massingham notes as a particular poetic mark of Marvell his "mannerliness, now tender, now playful, now ironical, now gallant, now reflective," all combined in a special way in the "Coy Mistress." It is more than "witty delicacy," more than elegance or grace or comeliness; it has "an imaginative gravity, which brings news and sound of the eternal concords." But Marvell, he says, is "a poet of little passion," even though he has a "sudden wildness in him," as demonstrated in the final lines of the "Coy Mistress." Again, one is uncertain as to what the "imaginative gravity," and the "sudden wildness" have to do with the statement of the poem, but one supposes that they apply in some fashion to the traditional "invitation" the poem presents. The "sudden wildness" that Massingham notes at the close of the poem contrasts strangely with the gradually mounting passion and anger marked by Mac-Carthy in the development of the argument.

Victoria Sackville-West brings the sensibilities of a poet to her commentary on Marvell.[3] She regards the "Coy Mistress" as "the peak of Marvell's achievement" (p. 17), as a complete success, so successful in fact that it has made us "covetously demand from Marvell more than he was ever temperamentally fitted to give" (p. 63). She feels that "Marvell seldom strikes the more resonant chord" (p. 60) of truly great poetry, but the central section of the "Coy Mistress" represents one of the times he does. Into the forty-six short lines of the whole poem "are crowded, but without any jostling or confusion, the maximum number of ideas and images. . . . The whole poem is as tight and hard as a knot; yet as spilling and voluptuous as a horn of plenty" (p. 52). But she provides little light on just what the ideas are and what the images convey when she comes to summarize the poem's statement:

The urgency of passion is its theme, expounded in language which moves from an apparently extravagant frivolity to an intense and menacing seriousness; then swings back to the human plea again, still decoratively presented, but sobered now and dignified by the reflections on mortality which have intervened. It is, in fact, as nicely constructed as a geometrical problem in two propositions and a solution. "Had we the whole of time before us, we might dally ingeniously and with grace; but life is short, and the grave will divide us eternally; therefore let us make the most of the moment while we can."

This is the familiar theme, the familiar solution which nearly all critics have found in all poems of the genre. If the third paragraph of the poem represents "the human plea," "decoratively presented," sobered and dignified by thoughts of mortality, it is difficult to explain the imagery of those tortured lines. One is inclined to ask just *which* passion is urgent in the poem—sexual merely? or intellectual? or the passionate questioning of passion itself as satisfying resolution? Her statement opens up more problems than it solves.

In their searching, if occasionally opaque, study of Marvell, M.C. Bradbrook and M.G. Lloyd Thomas acknowledge the presence of the *carpe diem* theme in the "Coy Mistress," but they elevate it to a quasi-philosophical or metaphysical level.[4] From the playful first section of the poem, in which "the whole macrocosm is seen in Metamorphosis" and "time's changes are jested with," they see the poet moving in the second paragraph to the concept of eternity, in which "Metamorphosis is accepted in its keenest implications", as in lines 27–29, "then Worms ... to dust." The knowledge and assurance that come from acceptance, they suggest, is able to turn the present moment into an eternity. Just how this happens, or how *this* eternity differs from the terrifying "Desarts" of line 24, is not made clear. In the final paragraph, the "Ball" into which the lovers roll all their strength and sweetness is seen as "the commonest symbol of Eternity," which should make us aware that "this is no simple doctrine of *carpe diem*" (as indeed it isn't), but a metaphysical statement of the way in which the "am'rous birds of prey" don't just make the most of time but conquer it (not each other). It is suggested that both past and future have been concentrated in the present moment, and the paradox of the final two lines "suggests that though the lovers cannot control Time, yet *a fortiori* it is their energy alone that supplies the

motive power of existence whereby Time is created." The lovers
are not mere Joshuas, but gods. And the whole poem demonstrates
the power of love "concentrated into a moment, the instant of
creative strife in which Time is devoured. . . ." This is an ingenious
analysis, one that at least tries to account for Marvell's disturbing
variations from purely conventional *carpe diem*, but it still isn't clear
just how the power and energy of love can at once both create and
devour time; nor is it easy to accept all that violent action in the
third paragraph as "creative strife." Again, it would seem that what
must be the outcome of the *carpe diem* poem has been allowed to
determine the resolution of the "Coy Mistress."

The past twenty-five years of Marvell criticism have not basically changed interpretations of the "Coy Mistress." Dennis Davison[5]
finds that in the poem "despite its urbane wit there is hidden . . . an
essentially healthy plea, against the background of 'vast Eternity,'
for the fulfillment of love as opposed to the 'crime' of fashionable
coyness. Love is not a matter of Court debauchery, or amorous
escapism, or 'Platonic' masquerade, but the uniting of Sweetness and
Strength in a defiant gesture against Time." In other words, Marvell
accepts the conventional solution to the love-time problem. Geoffrey
Walton[6] seems a bit uneasy about his interpretation of the poem.
He is aware that the images and rhythms of the "Coy Mistress"
"give a new urgency and seriousness to the traditional theme," and
he senses the sardonic, ironic elements in the second stanza. In the
final stanza, which "synthesizes all the varied shades of seriousness
and gaiety in the poem," he sees a contrast between the delicate
beauty of the lady and the fierce struggle that follows. "In the third
and fourth couplets 'carpe diem' has become a fight to the death
between wild bird and beast." It is only by "muscular effort" that
the lovers "fight themselves free of any hindrances, abstract or
concrete, to the full enjoyment of their passion. . . . Life is conquered, but the victory over time is more apparent than real. . . ."
And he points out the "blatant false logic" in the final couplet. This
would seem to be having it both ways. If *carpe diem* has become "a
fight to the death," how can there be "full enjoyment of their
passion"? Walton's uneasiness is evident in his judgment that "the
victory over time is more apparent than real," although in some
mysterious way "Life is conquered." He tries (unsuccessfully, it
seems to me) to accommodate the traditional resolution of the love-

time conflict with the difficulties Marvell throws in the way of accepting such a resolution.

F.W. Bradbrook[7] sees the main idea of the "Coy Mistress" as classical, almost a commonplace of love poetry, but in its details original, both witty and imaginative, the major effect gained by a combination of rhythm and ambiguity. In the middle section of the poem Marvell uses the ideas of desolation and death "as a means of frightening his mistress" into acceptance of the invitation to love in the final section. As Love tears its way, as it must, through the iron gates of "a humdrum passive life," "Time and death ... are conquered by love as they were conquered by nature in Marvell's other great lyric, *The Garden*." This is the conventional solution to the *un*conventional questions that Marvell poses through image and argument in the poem. J.B. Leishman,[8] concerned primarily with comparisons between Donne's and Marvell's poetry, also sees the "Coy Mistress" as a variation on an ancient theme, the theme of *carpe florem*, "an essentially rhetorical theme," in which the invitation is to "gather the Rose of love whilest yet is time." He paraphrases the poem this way: "If we had infinite time, I should be happy to court you at leisure; But our life lasts only for a moment: Therefore, in order to live, we must seize the moment as it flies." This admittedly is an oversimplification of Leishman's analysis of the poem, but it is his own. It would appear that the weight of tradition was allowed to suppress certain implications of Marvell's play of image and use of irony in the poem.

Harold E. Toliver[9] is aware of tradition, of course, but he is also aware of the ways in which Marvell adapted tradition to poetic statement in his own time. There is obvious conflict between the Catullian urgency toward the joys of the moment and Marvell's Christian Platonist impulsion to see things in the light of eternity. Eternity may not be as intimidating to a convinced Platonist as it is to a lover trapped in time, but in this poem, as Toliver sees it, Marvell deliberately denies himself the "aid of the Platonist's cosmic order" and stresses instead the force of time as an element in that "residual stubbornness of nature that Marvell insisted upon making an essential part of poetry" (p. 8). And so it is that in the "Coy Mistress" the "passive victim of time" is forced to "tear pleasure with rough strife and make the sun 'run'" (p. 10). The speaker of the poem, caught between the pressures of time and the vast deserts of eternity, "has no place to retreat *to*" except the dubious consolation that he and his mistress "can make the sun run faster, though only thus to burn up more quickly" (p. 10). But with this resort to the traditional resolution of the Love-Time dilemma—the satisfaction of passion—the result is "*self-annihilation*, a kind of symbolic suicide reversing the annihilation that's made in the process of *self-discovery*" (p. 152). In effect, the "Coy Mistress" reverses the strategies of other poems in the Marvell canon and proposes "a negation of Plantonist assumptions: the lovers are to enter the stream of time, deny providential control of the cosmos, and turn the sun and the emotions loose" (p. 154), thus exposing the limits of the *carpe diem* resolution. The radical conflict that Toliver sees between the speaker's proposition and the poet's values should alert us to the fact that "the poem's commitment to love is not unqualified," that "the speaker's come-live-with-me scherzo is interpenetrated with a dirge-like theme mixing a painful sense of loss with exuberance, disappointment with wit" (p. 156).

This attempt to place the "Coy Mistress" in the context of larger philosophical concerns intimated in the total corpus of Marvell's lyric poetry has been resisted by those critics who choose to see individual lyrics as reflections of different aspects of Marvell's poetic experience rather than as variations on a basic theme. Toliver himself appears to employ considerable ingenuity in making the "Coy Mistress" relate significantly to a supposed larger body of Marvellian "philosophy." It might perhaps have been better to leave the poem to speak for itself on the *carpe diem* theme, and to admit, as Toliver does, that "the lines would appear to deny any kind of symbolic triumph. With as much pain as joy—and with a suggestion of frenzy—the lovers can only defeat time by hurrying toward death," and that passion is only a "dissolution and tearing" (p. 157). Toliver also admits that the poem itself suggests that "the fierce common meeting place of willed passion" is a "limited accomplishment," all "that one can count on here and now. There are no timeless places to withdraw to, no rebirth, no green thought [as in other poems], but the spirit, mistress willing, can create its own way of dying" (p. 161). But the question remains as to whether the "suggestion" of the "Coy Mistress" might better be seen as an answer to traditional *carpe diem* resolution, as a criticism of conventional flimsy defenses against the tyranny of time, than as a facet of Marvell's Christian Platonism. The powerful impact the poem has made on all sorts of critics would seem in large measure to depend on how Marvell, with the grace and poise of a skilled surgeon (and a touch of anesthetic), strips man of one of his most cherished poetic delusions—the power of passion to resolve the problems of time.

To Pierre Legouis[10] the central theme of the "Coy Mistress" is that "tritest of all" themes, *carpe diem*, familiar enough in love poetry going back to ancient times. What distinguishes Marvell's handling of the theme is not the end toward which he moves, for that is seen as common to previous poets who had exploited the theme, but the manner he displays in achieving that goal. Legouis points to Marvell's impetuosity, his headlong speed, his full-bloodedness and pride: "possessed with a sensual frenzy heightened by his mistress's coyness, he means to triumph over this female reluctance through the male vigour of his intellect" (p. 34). After the "somewhat *précieux*" language of the first section of the poem, Marvell dares in the second to face the grimmest features of death and the grave in lines which "suffice to settle contemporary doubts cast on the poet's virility, and to prove that he was at least once in love—body and soul—with a real live mistress" (p. 34). The third section is seen as "defiant, headlong, and so to speak ravenous," but it results in "vehement affirmation" of the traditional insistence that "therefore we must grasp the fleeting instant for love" (p. 64). Legouis openly confesses that in 1928, when his original study of Marvell appeared, he "could not unravel the metaphors entangled in the last six lines of 'To his Coy Mistress'; they were to me as unanalysable as any cluster of images in Shakespeare, and no less powerful" (p. 70, n. 1). Modern attempts at explication had only made matters worse for him. Commentary on lines 38–44 of the "Coy Mistress" in the third edition of Margoliouth's *Poems and Letters*, revised by Legouis,[11] does not indicate any great clarification of the matter: "While the conclusion of the poem clearly aims at sexual consummation I see no evidence that the images are themselves sexual." One can only wonder how the statement of this poem can be understood without more unraveling of those closing metaphors than Legouis, perhaps overmodestly, claims to have done. And in accepting unquestioningly the aim of the poem as sexual consummation, without qualification, he would seem to have allowed the familiar voice of the tradition to speak for the poem itself.

John Press's explication[12] of the "Coy Mistress" follows the traditional line. To him it is a poem "which celebrates with passionate conviction the power and ardour of physical desire." The lover's final demand is for sexual consummation, "yet despite the uncompromising sexuality of the lines quoted above ["But at my back ... there embrace"] and of the imagery in the poem's concluding lines, Marvell has invested the old classical commonplace of *carpe diem* with an intensity and a nobility that seem to affirm the triumph of love over time, in the teeth of the evidence." The intensity is certainly there, and the lines themselves are noble; the nature of the triumph is more questionable.

In recent years four book-length studies of Marvell[13] have come up with interestingly divergent assessments of what the "Coy Mistress" says and does. In a study remarkable for its knowledge of the traditions in which Marvell worked and its sensitivity to the intricacies of Marvell's manner and method, the late Professor Colie throws much light on the workings of Marvell's mind and the manipulation of his art. His detached and quizzical attitudes toward his subjects, his adoption of widely varying personae in different poems, and his new uses of old forms and themes are seen as elements in his criticism, implied rather than stated, of the very genres and language he inherited. And she makes some telling points. But in the case of the "Coy Mistress," "Marvell's most remarkable poem of *carpe diem*" (p. 54), she appears to accept the ending of all poems in the tradition as necessarily the conclusion of Marvell's poem. In her view, the first section "prolongs fulfillment, stretches out the courtship to make more intense its short, powerful consummation" (pp. 54–55). The tomb scene in the second section is designed "to frighten the living lady into taking comfort in her lover's arms," and the whole poem "shows how to accomplish a seduction, to pluck love's day, made bright against the dark night of death" (p. 55). In this final section, which "bursts into life in a far franker sexual joy than is normally encountered in poems like these," the poet "knows" that "Strength joined to sweetness can intensify life and for a little bring time's passage under lovers' personal control. This lover is utterly confident that he can make the love-experience mean much to his mistress" (p. 60). In view of the predatory and violent imagery of that final section one can only wonder whether the experience meant the same thing to the mistress as it appears to have meant to the critic, who never faces the possibility that in this poem as in others Marvell may be offering criticism of the very genre he is employing rather than merely effecting a seduction.

Ann E. Berthoff sets herself the twin problem of defining "the thematic unity of Marvell's poetry" and of defining "the limits by which interpretations of the metaphors should be guided" (p. x). She finds the unity in the "master theme of the soul's response to temporality" (p. x), in the idea "that the absolute disparity of heaven and earth is mediated by the soul, that the separation of the realms of grace and nature, the discontinuity of time and eternity creates an opposition which the soul can resolutely seize upon, mitigating the terrible force of time through love, heroic action, and contemplation" (pp. 5–6). And so it is that she hears not many voices but only the voice of the Resolved Soul speaking out of Marvell's poems. In the "Coy Mistress," "The lover who declares that they must 'tear' their 'Pleasures . . . Through the Iron gates of life' is as clear-sighted as the 'Resolved Soul' in rejecting the feathery ease offered by 'Created Pleasure.' He labors under no delusions whatsoever and he offers no blandishments. The 'rough strife' promised is a necessary concomitant of earthly love, but by it are to be won those sweet pleasures which are the lovers' triumph" (p. 112). But if this *is* the Resolved Soul speaking in the guise of lover, it is somewhat surprising to find him accepting carnal pleasure (love isn't even mentioned in the last two sections of the poem) as any sort of meaningful answer to "the terrible force of time," even within a *carpe diem* poem. Would it not be more reasonable for him to reject this created pleasure as he had others on other occasions? And if he were all that "clear-sighted," would he be able to view the violent activities (sporting, devouring, rolling, tearing) of this concluding section as "sweet," or as any sort of real "triumph" over menacing time? Marvell invites such questions.

The unity Donald M. Friedman finds in Marvell's poetry is that of "pastoral vision, considered as one of the major ways of literary thinking that the European mind has found and followed" (p. 4). He does not limit "pastoral" to the received definitions of style, diction, subject, etc., but regards it "as a mode, literally as a way of interpreting experience, a measure of ordering that experience and giving it conspicuous artistic form" (p. 7). Marvell's range of subject matter goes beyond that usually allowed in pastoral, his lyrics being "scrupulous contemplations of the relationships between man and nature, between soul and body, between mind and matter, between the knower and the known" (p. 13), in a world of men enfeebled by the fall of Adam. Friedman finds that for the most part "the poems examine without judging, weigh without deciding; above all, they *present* the consequences of the Fall through tropes and subjects that embody those consequences in the most expressive and compelling way—through pastoral" (p. 14). But the "pastoral vision" does not seem to have been much help in cutting through the ambiguities of the final section of the "Coy Mistress." Friedman suggests that the last lines refer to more than an act of sex, and that "*Perhaps* the point is that when passion reaches its perfect state and renders Time powerless, the way that normally leads to death opens up unimaginable prospects of life—life lived so intensely in the moment that it seems to subsume eternity itself within a point of time" (p. 187; my italics). Although passion cannot conquer time or eternity, "it can create a world of its own where passion is the only sovereign force." The decline of the lovers seems to be arrested "by the timeless perfection of their union." And "the poem has sought a way to find more world and time than either the World or Time will provide for the consummation of love, and the answer has been found in consummation itself," but on the other hand the poet has attempted "to transcend the limits of life in the flesh by seeking the perfection of passion in abstract concepts" (p. 187). Friedman admits that this kind of answer is unusual in Marvell's poetry, but he sticks to it, in part, one suspects, because the tradition calls for consummation as an end to the strategy of the persuasion poem.

Lawrence W. Hyman has the temerity to depart from conventional interpretations of the "Coy Mistress." He cites as a pervasive theme in Marvell's poetry the distrust of passion, the fear of sexuality as a destroyer of the innocence which is essential to love. He sees the "Coy Mistress" as Marvell's exploration of the question of whether "a pure love can be attained by the body as well as by the 'extended Soul' [of "The Definition"]" (p. 59). But such a possibility, presented wittily in the first section of the poem, is shattered in the second by grim reminders of what time does to "the physical aspects of love" (p. 61). With the ideal desires of the first section denied by the brutal realities of the world of time in the second, a new question arises for Hyman: why is the poet "so insistent, in the final section, on a physical union?" (p. 61), when that would only seem to hasten the lovers toward their own destruction. By identifying the "Ball," into which the lovers have rolled their strength and sweetness, with their "Sun," Hyman is confronted with a new question: "why should 'our Sun . . . run'?" (p. 62). The answer: because it brings about a union of the lovers. But what a dusty answer, for "The intensity of the physical union . . . leads to death—in both senses of the word," and "The syntax of the lines indicate [*sic*] that the 'Strength' and 'sweetness' of the lovers is not intensified by the physical union but destroyed. And the imagery . . . also suggests that the ecstasy which leads the lovers out of this world . . . leads them into death" (p. 62). The concluding section is therefore not a solution to the alternatives presented in the first two, but in some mysterious way it is "a genuine resolution because it neither ignores the conditions of existence nor does it succumb to them . . ." (p. 63). One may experience some difficulty in following Hyman's logic, but at least he has taken into full account the possibility that the "Coy Mistress" confronts us with death rather than life as the outcome of passion's attempt to thwart time.

The deluge of critical articles dealing with the "Coy Mistress" cannot be dealt with adequately here, but some trends and varying viewpoints can be indicated.[14] The chief impression one gets is that increasing pressure is being brought to bear on specific elements in the poem as keys to an understanding of what the poem is all about. Discussion of the meaning of "vegetable Love," begun years ago by Bradbrook and Thomas, continues without consensus. From the relatively modest original suggestion that the term has to do with the lowest of the three levels of the soul, the vegetable, which is the principle of generation and corruption, of augmentation and decay, one critic has risen to the point of suggesting that proper understanding of the term indicates that the poem "may be read as a testament of faith in which Marvell at once rejects the materialism and determinism of Hobbes, spiritualizes the Deism of Lord Herbert of Cherbury, and cements the union of faith and reason which the Cambridge Platonists thought they had found implied in Descartes" (Hogan, p. 1). If this seems indeed to make vegetable love "grow Vaster then Empires," it is only because the Plotinian construct behind the poem calls for the soul (the "Mistress") to extricate itself from the life of the senses and eventually "run" to union with the supreme One. Hogan has no explanation as to why Marvell should have veiled such a blinding vision in a *carpe diem* poem; he just *did*. Other uses of the idea of the vegetable soul have produced suggestions that the three sections of the poem present a gradual ascent from the vegetable to the sensitive to the rational levels of the soul (Putney); or that the pattern is from the vegetable level of existence in section one, to the mineral state in section two, to the animal level of section three (Low and Pival), this latter level presumably being more appealing to the lady than the former two.

The "sun" of the final couplet has been identified with the "bridegroom coming out of his chamber" of Psalm 19 (Sedlow); with the phoenix, the ashes and worm of the second section thus becoming "life symbols just as from the ashes of the phoenix comes a worm which ultimately becomes the renewed bird" (Carroll); with the Greek sun god Helios (Gwynn) and with the rising-setting, self-renewing action of the natural sun which is a symbol of the lovers' action (Sasek). Farnham sees the final couplet as summarizing "the central conflict and compromise" of the poem: "time, like the sun, cannot be halted in its inevitable course; but by willing to squeeze the present moment to its utmost yield, man can outrun time for a short space before the final overtaking." Thus "our Sun" is identified with the "one Ball," which symbolizes "the infinitesimal point of the present moment in the vastness of eternity." The necessary compromise the lover proposes means that "time, although not in any way cheated, is put out of mind for as long as possible."

Bruce King goes considerable beyond Toliver's suggestion of "self-annihilation" and Hyman's of "death" as the ultimate threats contained in the "Coy Mistress." To him the poem is nothing more than a satire on the *carpe diem* poetry of the seventeenth century. The speaker is not merely a persona, but "a satiric mask," much like that adopted by Swift in *A Modest Proposal*, concealing "a seventeenth-century libertine pretending to hold pure materialistic assumptions." By the use of exaggeration Marvell mocks the pure skeptics assumptions that the afterlife is nothing, and in the final section of the poem he ironically exposes the supposed "pleasures" of sexual indulgence as mere bestiality, not the conquering of time. Through this caricature of the genre, King suggests, Marvell leads us to consider other values, mainly those of Christian Platonism. The "youthful hew" of the mistress is a covert allusion to the state of the innocent soul born into a fallen world. King finds Platonic indicators all through the poem, until finally he can state that "the coy mistress is clearly the soul, newly descended from heaven, innocent and tempted by the suasion of the body." The poem thus becomes Marvell's case for Christian Platonism by subtly exposing the fallacies in the libertine argument for bodily pleasure. One wonders whether the trenchant criticism of the *carpe diem* theme inherent in the poem is not sufficient to explain its power without recourse to all that Platonic scaffolding to shore it up. And what has happened to the "real, live mistress" that Legouis recognized in the poem?

Recent commentary on the "Coy Mistress" reveals increasing doubt as to the ultimate implications of the poem. Is it a *carpe diem* poem in any true sense of the term, graced though it may be with Marvell's irony, wit, and detachment? Does the poet really submit that the momentary enjoyment of passion is an answer to time or a genuine affirmation of love in a desert of eternity? Some of the reservations about accepting the conventional conclusion of the *carpe diem* poem as also the conclusion of Marvell's ostensible exploitation of the theme are intimated in questions that Louis L. Martz poses as he views the conclusion of the "Coy Mistress": "But what kind of pleasure is this? Marvell has consumed all the natural beauty out of the experience of human love. Is he suggesting that perhaps the rosebud-philosophy is self-destructive, corrosive, and ultimately empty? Is this a love poem at all? Is it not rather a poem about man's fear of Time?"[15] Such questions have aroused the varying critical responses that we have seen: it *is* a true *carpe diem* but spiced by typical Marvellian irony and wit; it is only *apparently* a *carpe diem* poem as a disguise for deep philosophical statement; it is not a *carpe diem* poem at all, but a sarcastic parody of the theme. Stanley Stewart, one of the more perceptive recent critics of the poem,[16] is convinced of the radical differences between the tone and imagery of the typical *carpe diem* poem and those of the "Coy Mistress," and hence of a difference of statement in the latter. The gravity and intensity of Marvell's depiction of the ravages of time evokes terror and horror not only in the reader but in the mistress as well, "For the speaker's argument concerns one thing and one thing only: the speed with which the lovers are to die" (p. 139). The *ars moriendi* elements in the second section of the poem, convincingly pointed out by Stewart, are designed "to remind the Coy Mistress of the certainty of death" (p. 141). Ultimately the poem presents man with only two choices: "to go slowly, gently, but abjectly into that eternal, lonely good-night, or to hurry with his lover in a state of excitement to an end that is only the beginning of loneliness. The one alternative is passive and excruciating; the other is active, and it asserts the dignity of the human will, yet it is finally more self-destructive" (p. 149). The lover's proposal to his mistress is neither Catullian nor Christian, but it is "an expression of both contexts, an argument turned in such a way as to become an ironic parody of both" (p. 150).

Criticism of the "Coy Mistress" is almost unbelievably open-ended. The poem is, and it isn't, almost anything a particular critic is capable of seeing—or chooses to see. One is inclined at times to agree with Legouis, who saw each successive critic only negating the efforts of previous commentators. But in spite of the conflicts and contradictions among various critics one comes out of such a survey as this with the heartening feeling that Marvell criticism, having followed nearly every possible approach to the poet, is about to enter a new phase, a phase in which the rigidities of the critic will be tempered by the flexibilities of the poet. Critical sight will be clear enough to perceived the nuances of the poem, but not so sharp as to limit the provocative play of image and tone that will continue to mark Marvell as one of the most exciting minds to have observed life in seventeenth-century England.

Notes

1. For useful surveys of Marvell's reputation over the past 300 years, see Pierre Legouis, *Andrew Marvell: Poet, Puritan, Patriot* (Oxford: Clarendon Press, 1965), Chapter 8, an abridged and revised version of his *André Marvell: Poète, Puritain, Patriote* (Oxford: Oxford University Press, 1928); and the Introduction to *Marvell: Modern Judgements*, ed. Michael Wilding (London: Macmillan, 1969).

2. See his *Andrew Marvell*, p. 70, n. 1.

3. *Andrew Marvell* (London: Faber & Faber, 1929).

4. *Andrew Marvell* (Cambridge: At the University Press, 1940), pp. 43–44.

5. Introduction to *Andrew Marvell: Selected Poetry and Prose*, ed. Dennis Davison (London: Harrap, 1952), p. 42.

6. *Metaphysical to Augustan: Studies in Tone and Sensibility in the Seventeenth*

Century (London: Bowes & Bowes, 1955), pp. 130–32.

7. "The Poetry of Andrew Marvell," in *From Donne to Marvell*, The Pelican Guide to English Literature 3, ed. Boris Ford (Baltimore: Penguin Books, 1956), pp. 193–204.

8. *The Art of Marvell's Poetry* (New York: Funk & Wagnalls, 1968), pp. 70, 77.

9. *Marvell's Ironic Vision* (New Haven: Yale University Press, 1965).

10. *Andrew Marvell* (1965).

11. *The Poems and Letters of Andrew Marvell*, ed. H.M. Margoliouth, 3rd ed., revised by Pierre Legouis with the collaboration of E.E. Duncan-Jones, 2 vols. (Oxford: Clarendon Press, 1971).

12. *Andrew Marvell*, Writers and Their Work, No. 98, rev. ed. (London: Longmans, Green, 1966), pp. 29–30.

13. Ann E. Berthoff, *The Resolved Soul: A Study of Marvell's Major Poems* (Princeton: Princeton University Press, 1970); Rosalie L. Colie, *"My Ecchoing Song": Andrew Marvell's Poetry of Criticism* (Princeton: Princeton University Press, 1970); Donald M. Friedman, *Marvell's Pastoral Art* (Berkeley and Los Angeles: University of California Press, 1970); and Lawrence W. Hyman, *Andrew Marvell*, TEAS (New York: Twayne Publishers, 1964).

14. Among the articles briefly referred to here are: Patrick G. Hogan, Jr., "Marvell's 'Vegetable Love,'" *SP* 60, I (January 1963): 1–11; Rufus Putney, "'Our Vegetable Love': Marvell and Burton," in *Studies in Honor of T.W. Baldwin*, ed. Don Cameron Allen (Urbana: University of Illinois Press, 1958), pp. 220–28; Anthony Low and Paul J. Pival, "Rhetorical Pattern in Marvell's 'To his Coy Mistress,'" *JEGP* 68 (1969): 414–21; Walter A. Sedelow, Jr., "Marvell's To His Coy Mistress," *MLN* 71 (1956): 6–8; John J. Carroll, "The Sun and the Lovers in 'To His Coy Mistress,'" *MLN* 74 (1959): 4–7; Frederick L. Gwynn, "Marvell's To His coy Mistress, 33–46," *The Explicator* 9, 7 (May 1953), item 49; Lawrence A. Sasek, "Marvell's To His Coy Mistress, 45–46," *The Explicator* 14, 7 (April 1956), item 47; Anthony E. Farnham, "Saint Teresa and the Coy Mistress," Boston University Studies in English, 2, 4 (Winter 1956): 226–39; Bruce King, "Irony in Marvell's 'To His Coy Mistress,'" *Southern Review*, ns 5 (1969): 689–703; and Bruce King, "In Search of Andrew Marvell," *Review of English Literature* 8, 4 (October 1967): 31–41. Further recent commentary on Marvell is to be found in Gillian Szanto, "Recent Studies in Marvell," *ELR* 5 (Spring 1975): 273–86.

15. Louis L. Martz, "Andrew Marvell: The Mind's Happiness," in *The Wit of Love: Donne, Crashaw, Carew, Marvell* (Notre Dame, Ind.: University of Notre Dame Press, 1969), p. 169.

16. See his "Marvell and the *Ars Moriendi*," in *Seventeenth-Century Imagery*, ed. Earl Miner (Berkeley and Los Angeles: University of California Press, 1971), pp. 133–50.

Logic and Rhetoric in Marvell's "Coy Mistress"

John Hackett

TWENTIETH-CENTURY REALIZATIONS about the logical mechanics of "Coy Mistress" seriously affect the meaning and force of the speaker's argument. Coextensive though hardly identical with the poem itself, the logic of that famous argument has been reconstituted by modern criticism, twice reconstituted, and this paper will ask how the poem now reads in the light of these new understandings. It reads, of course, like a different poem. The logic of the argument bears enormously on its rhetoric, though some have declared this relation irrelevant, and the modern recovery of the poem's logical form challenges standard critical opinion on such basic matters as character, action, feeling and tone. In turn, and through it gild the lily, new critical interpretation will also require due reevaluation of Marvell's achievement.

A review of modern criticism finds three or four schools of thought about the poem's logical form. The first or zero grade ignores the shape of argument: "Coy Mistress" is treated as a traditional love poem, not unreasonably classified as such in countless textbooks and tables of contents. Its speaker pleads with his mistress to love him, or rather to demonstrate her love, and more than once he professes his own love quite explicitly (though never absolutely: each declaration is thrown into the conditional and the subjunctive). Grierson and Bush and most of the earlier critics see the speaker's ardor shining clearly through the ironies, while lately to Pierre Legouis it's Marvell who's "in love—body and soul—with a real live mistress."[1] If the genus is love poem, the species is *carpe diem*, Miltonically endangered by its own perfection, while the poem's individual distinction, and fame, stems partly from the frankness of its proposition. Many a course in freshman rhetoric has wakened from abstractions to its flesh and blood insistence, while as recently as 1966 the wire services reported that community pressure led the University of North Carolina to suspend an English teacher just for assigning the poem to his class. The zero grade judgment about logical form is still commonplace. This criticism assumes, rarely states, that love and logic are inimical: "who shall give a lover any law?" It typically ignores the possibility that impassioned pleas may be reasonable, that propositions may be worded in propositional language.

Three grades of criticism address logical form proper. The first acknowledges that the poem sets out to make a case, and commends the general quality of the argument. This position is held at various levels of critical sophistication. Thus a recent introductory handbook that studies the poem from diverse theoretical standpoints pronounces "Coy Mistress" a "tightly reasoned argument," careful in its construction and characterized by "sweet reasonableness."[2] How tightly reasoned Anne Berthoff may attest. Her *Study of Marvell's Major Poetry* sees the issue resolved as foregone conclusion: "the dialectic offers no opportunity for response, much less debate."[3] In these examples the appraisal of form reflects on character, so the speaker is honest, reasonable, and sincere. Thus Berthoff follows her judgment about the conclusiveness of the dialectic with praise for the speaker's "directness of address," while the handbook expatiates less cautiously:

> The succession of thoughts is kept basically simple and straight-forward as the speaker concentrates on the simplicity and directness of his argument, an argument addressed to a foolish woman who has ignored logic and reality in her passion for coyness.[4]

The second phase of critical attention to logical form began with Eliot's statement some fifty years ago that "the three strophes of Marvell's poem have something like a syllogistic relation to each other."[5] Soon the relation was seen to be more rigorous than "something like," and critics such as J.V. Cunningham, Elizabeth Donno, and J.B. Leishman came to recognize that Marvell's argument takes the form of a syllogism proper.[6] This syllogism is hypothetical or conditional, marked not only by the strophes but also by their initial logical signposts: if p, then q; but not p; therefore not q.[7] The formal argument concludes that "we should not delay." This conclusion is tacit, the basis for the subsequent exhortations: (it follows that we should not delay), "therefore let us sport, devour, roll and tear." The pronouncement of the syllogism constitutes the first important revision in our modern understanding of the poem. It changes not only the quality of the argument but also its kind. "Coy Mistress" now professes to assert demonstrable knowledge. Its argument is no longer a question of likelihood but certitude. Evaluation becomes a matter of deductive rigor. To judge from the form he adopts, the speaker attempts not only to plead but also to prove. The form asks to be assessed not as strong or weak—or right or wrong or true or false—but according to validity.

Phase three represents a more recent development of the critique on logic, a still more drastic revision. The critics who saw the syllogism neglected to remark its type, and perhaps for this reason they failed to appraise its validity. Although Allen Tate and others had adumbrated the point,[8] it was not until 1962 that Bruce E. Miller declared the conclusion unwarranted, formally invalid, and Barbara Herrnstein Smith has since independently concurred.[9] While J.C. Maxwell claimed to vindicate the "elliptical" formulation of the major premise,[10] this finding against the poem's argument on strict logical grounds has not been disconfirmed. Schopenhauer wrote that "it would be a very good thing if every trick could receive some short and obviously appropriate name, so that when a man used this or that particular trick, he could at once be reproved for it."[11] Let it please his ghost that the short and appropriate name for this particular trick is "denying the antecedent." If p, then q; but not p; therefore not q? Non sequitur.

The fallacy is classic, but sometimes hard to detect, as the earlier stages of criticism attest. Few short poems have been as widely read or closely studied as "Coy Mistress," but the speaker's trick seems to have worked for some three hundred years. His argument would hold, of course, not if he and his mistress had but world enough and time, but if and only if—if that one condition were the sole operative consideration. Uncritical acceptance of the major, ignoring such potentially relevant variables as personal, social, or moral consequence, would indeed commit the mistress. Once both premises pass unchallenged, the conclusion is q.e.d.

The fallacy of denying the antecedent can be a very effective fraud of logic. Not long ago I saw it worked successfully on a serious issue before a readership of millions, and perhaps the analogue will instruct the analysis. Writing in his regular *New York Times* editorial page column, William Safire discussed the Nixon tapes. Dateline was 16 July 1974, as the Supreme Court decision neared. Safire anticipates a ruling against Nixon and constructs a scenario in which the President is ordered to yield the tapes. Putting the reader in Nixon's shoes, Safire writes that at this point "all eyes turn to you."

> If you defy, you would deserve to be impeached, most people would say, not realizing the obverse of their judgment: *That if you do not defy, you would deserve not to be impeached.* (emphasis in the original)

Compliance and the syllogism: "that would be my plan," Safire concludes. Marvell cloaks his argument in conceits, but for all its nakedness Safire's claim went unchallenged. The *Times* made no comment, nor did it later print any protest. In poem and polemic alike, of course, the minor denies the antecedent and the conclusion denies the consequent. Non sequitur.

But if literary criticism and the readership of the *Times* have been slow to spot this kind of thinking, there's consolation from history and hope in the classroom. Students who read "Coy Mistress" for the first time, men included, often confess malaise; many do not know why, but sooner or later most come to feel that for all the "sweet reasonableness" and the "simple and straightforward" development, there's something wrong. Dialogue and common sense can usually bring out the factors excluded, and classroom experience with the poem often proceeds from initial concurrence with a plausible argument, to vague misgivings, thence to the discovery of those other considerations in the major, and finally to mechanics, to the formal business of unpacking the syllogism and exposing the fallacy. (It helps, of course, to sensitize a class to dialectics beforehand with a session on something like *Passionate Shepherd* and *The Nymph's Reply*.)

*   *   *

Sooner or later, then, criticism brings the fallacious syllogism to the modern reader's attention. Now that he can describe logic, how shall he explain it? I suppose it's possible that Marvell just made a mistake. Safire is welcome to the benefit of the doubt, but I take it that Marvell knew exactly what he was doing. He constructed the fallacy as deliberately as he constructed the syllogism, to make a better poem. If so, criticism must ask what purpose the fallacy serves. It must ask how the logic affects the rhetoric, which in this case is to ask how form affects meaning. As the mere presence of presumably valid form once embarrassed the love poem, until Eliot and Cunningham took the occasion to disabuse criticism of that general prejudice,[12] so the fallacy now threatens embarrassment, unless it can be made consistent with a poem that remains an undisputed masterpiece.

Call the poet's mistake a zero grade hypothesis and three grades of good explanation can be distinguished. The first begins unpromisingly by saying all this talk of logic makes too much of fine distinctions. So the poet knows it but his speaker doesn't, so what? This is a love poem, the fallacy doesn't matter. "Coy Mistress" is a brilliant *jeu d'esprit*, and let us not make earnest out of game. Marvell is saved, the speaker remains trivially imperceptive. Thus when Herrnstein Smith acknowledges the fallacy, she claims that "logical validity has become irrelevant to the reader's experience —or not relevant in the same way that it would be to his experience of nonliterary logical discourse."[13] Can this be so? Let teaching the poem be the practical test. Assume validity to make no difference and neither the syllogism nor the fallacy need henceforth be called to students' attention. Should they raise the issue themselves, it could be safely dismissed. Since the logic is not relevant to their experience, whether in literature or life, the criticism that addresses it could also be dismissed. So the irrelevance reading is readily tested: the logic doesn't matter, until it's noticed. Put less empirically, the logic drives the poem into the realm of moral discourse. Introduce questions of the argument's quality, and problematic matters like intent and obligation naturally follow.

But Smith's final view of the fallacy is not dismissive; rather, she turns debit irrelevance to credit. Because of the speaker's "playful tenderness in his feeling for the lady,"[14] his mistake remains irrelevant but the irrelevance becomes appropriate. The illogical conclusion becomes, in fact, "entirely appropriate to the context of the poem, indeed *more* appropriate in this sense than a logically respectable conclusion." Add to the speaker's tender feelings his "acute and unfeigned consciousness of mutability," this view has it, and the conclusion emerges as wishful thinking. Smith moves the focus of the poem from argument to affect, using the fallacy to suggest motive and character. Her ultimate criterion in judging the argument is not its logic or even its efficacy but its "expressiveness." I like this interpretation, for its suggests a speaker tense with metaphysical passion, anxiously mortal, and yet a rather attractive romantic speaker, charmingly muddled, whose emotions rule his reason or at least temporarily neutralize his logical faculties. But I can't agree with it because the poem offers better reason to think that the speaker must be as conscious of the fallacy as Marvell himself. The poem turns decisively on the speaker's knowledge of his logical performance, turns and turns again, as I now hope to show.

★   ★   ★

A better explanation makes the fallacy relevant and the speaker aware. I take it that his mistake is deliberate. He knows that the argument won't hold, that it does not obligate the mistress. Rather, and for that reason, it mocks her. Herein lies its relevance, and more, the obligation of criticism to accomodate it. Precisely because the syllogism compliments, the fallacy mocks, and precisely to that extent. Isolate the logic and the syllogism compliments as form. It frames and points the argument more rigorously than tradition requires or readers expect. It lifts the conventional plea to a high level of rational discourse. Rather than appeal on emotional grounds alone, the speaker turns schoolman, creating in his choice of form a mistress who will listen to reason. Rather than plead that his suit should be granted, he claims it must, crediting the mistress with a mind that will bow to demonstration. But all is false: the fallacy vitiates the formal compliment. While the syllogism appeals to her rational soul, the fallacy betrays his vegetable love. The form honors the mistress, the fallacy makes the honor quaint.

For the mistress is not supposed to see how the argument works. It's possible to suspect as much on presumptive evidence alone, since fraud is the ordinary purpose of fallacies. But in this case the victim is particularly vulnerable. Smith's interpretation shows that much depends on how we perceive the character of the speaker in the evoked dramatic setting. The same is true for the mistress. Will she catch the fallacy? No. Or yes and no. But not yes. It's not that three centuries of criticism missed the logic, what matters is that—strictly on form—a typical woman of Marvell's time would not be expected to catch it. We know the mistress only as the poem allows her to be construed. As a woman—coy, emblazoned, typically Petrarchan in her low definition, not further individualized in this respect—she would have no access to university education, would lack formal training in the trivium, would not have studied logic, its forms and their fallacies. Even among women of class and standing, education in Stuart and Commonwealth Britain rarely proceeded much past the feminine accomplishments. As one historian writes, "there was little likelihood of much education beyond the elementary stage, except in such subjects and refinements as music and dancing, needlework, drawing and French."[15] To such a mistress the speaker presents and seals his pointed conditional syllogism with a logical *imprimatur* that might as well be Latin. The mistress is being bullied.

Thus Legouis says of the speaker that "he means to triumph over this female reluctance through the male vigour of his intellect."[16] There's something right with this analysis. Missing the fallacy, Legouis nevertheless catches a certain tone. Insofar as the logic of the poem is a male prerogative, the fallacy patronizes. But if male vigour triumphs over female reluctance, it's due less to intellect than injury, and what Legouis calls intellect might better be called advantage, a proprietary mode of presentation here demonstrably abused. In this light the fallacy transforms the mistress from a real if fictitious person to a foil, from persona to sex object. She becomes a victim of mystification, of dialectical violence.

This is not to say that she is deceived. Allow the mistress some natural instinct or common sense, and well might she doubt or deny the conclusion. Particularly if she were bright and sensitive, as the poem gives us reason to believe, she would certainly feel that it's false, know from intuition and experience that it just can't follow. But unless the mistress were exceptional, some finely tutored Maria Fairfax perhaps, she would be hard put to formulate the feeling—to abstract the syllogism from its rhetorical development, break it down, find the fallacy, and explain why the argument fails. The mistress, who still exists only as the poem addresses her, lacks practice, for instance, at such basic exercises as converting the first sentence into the standard conditional form. She lacks the skill to draw from the enthymeme the implied conclusion that bridges the premises and the injunctions. She lacks the experience in dialectic to recognize and refute the fallacy in the same terms and with the same technical punctilio that its witty academic formulation demands. This is the sense in which the argument offers "no opportunity for debate, much less response." The Nymph's reply to Marlowe's Shepherd proceeded from the discovery of buried premises: "*if* all the world and love were young." But here no Raleigh steps forward to school the mistress in dialectic and challenge the speaker's fallacy. A master of logical subterfuge, the speaker is safe as Safire from analysis and prompt reproof.

At this point morality raises its many heads. In his initial premise, the speaker may have excluded moral issues from the argument, but insofar as the poem imitates life, he cannot exempt the argument itself. The speaker stands open to praise and blame. If he manipulates and mocks the mistress, the reader is put in a delicate position. For he is asked to respond in circumstances where he would least care to, in a poem governed by the conventions of genre and the spirit of play. Allen Tate put the case against the moral reading in such terms.

> The Platonist ... might decide that Marvell's "To His Coy Mistress" recommends immoral behavior to young men, in whose behalf he would try to suppress the poem. That, of course, would be one "true" meaning of "To His Coy Mistress," but it is a meaning that the full tension of the poem will not allow us to entertain exclusively.[17]

Criticism rightly finds such a moral reading inadequate, so the reader who makes a moral response runs the risk of seeming to condemn sex or seduction when the pertinent issue is deceit. The speaker works a fraud upon the mistress. By specious means, he gains power over her, or at least he seeks to exercise a power of casuistry upon her mind. If the sophist makes the worse argument seem the better, the speaker makes a worthless argument seem definitive—to his own profit and at her intellectual expense. Whether or not the advantage he takes is sexually privileged, the speaker's argument misrepresents and misleads. In this respect, for good or bad, though particularly apropos "that moral seriousness" in Marvell which "pervades almost everything that he wrote,"[18] the poem grows all the more complex. Character becomes qualified, action questionable. A distance opens between Marvell and his speaker.

★   ★   ★

The fallacy led me at first to suspect that Marvell created a speaker whose deceit was a measure of his character. Marvell drew a portrait of an artful speaker who takes the reader into his confidence as though "Coy Mistress" were a scene from Henry James by way of Wayne Booth. As the fallacy dawns on Marvell's ideal, male, educated reader—himself a character no less contrived if somewhat less complex—the speaker winks at this reader, to the reader's embarrassment, if not indignation or horror. While many an actual reader may be imagined winking back, the ideal response may be suggested by imagining the speaker many years later, grown coarse, as Browning's Duke in "My Last Duchess."

It seems to me now that some of this supposing is necessary, much of it wrong, none of it sufficient. It makes sense of the fallacy all right, gives it a dramatic function that respects the speaker's witty, ironic control. Read this way, the poem grows in dimension and reverberative energy. But Marvell has designed "Coy Mistress" so as to demand a further turn. For in response to the charge of fraud the poem itself now protests. Too much remains, too much has been ignored. All the elements that are separable from the logic create a common reader who for three hundred years has found himself in sympathy with a moral speaker, or who (Tate's Platonist apart) at least has found no cause for moral complaint. This reader may have missed the syllogism and the fallacy, but that doesn't mean he missed the poem, or misheard its tone, not to the extent of taking hero for villain. Criticism needs to reconcile a pertinent fallacy with a responsible pleader, a deliberate fallacy with a sympathetic lover. It needs to restore the problematically invigorated poem to a reader who finds the speaker blameless, morally and rhetorically admirable.

I think the poem will sustain a third interpretation that saves the first two from their contradictions. It finds the logic relevant. It finds the speaker aware. But it supposes that he commits the fallacy not to deceive the mistress but to challenge and tease her. He still frames the argument badly on purposes, which condescension would indeed disparage the mistress, were it not for her compliance, even her complicity. She holds still for this nonsense precisely because she recognizes it for nonsense, grand ingenious nonsense, transparently delivered as such. The speaker is devious, but he is not deceitful. Include the mistress in the knowledge that his argument doesn't follow and the conflict between logic and feeling is resolved.

In this interpretation the speaker's tone credits the mistress with sense enough to dismiss the conclusion, sensibility enough to find the form intriguing, to want to solve it. His tone continues to assume that she will be unable to do so. Thus the argument has the force not of fraud but of gambit in a game, and the game is forfeits. When the speaker proposes his challenge, daring the mistress to entertain the argument and attempt refutation, he anticipates that her entanglement will let him claim triumph and prize. As he further anticipates her wary hesitation, syllogism turns dilemma, which only laughter can dissolve.

The speaker's argument is not real but pretended, or the plea is real, the proof is sheer pretense. The actual compliment the speaker pays the mistress is his assumption that she will recognize the difference between serious and simulated demand, recognize his ironic detachment from his own false position, recognize that position as pose. A shared understanding to such effect is their open secret. Postulate such a tone, let the speaker impersonate a character who treats love as logical inference, and he will argue speciously but deserve no blame, swagger but raise no resentment. More positively, in this act of tacit inclusion, the speaker will accomplish his rhetorical purpose, to move two minds, two persons, closer together. This interpretation grants the poem its demonstrated logical complexity but returns it to the common reader with the speaker's honor no less intact than his mistress's. The reader gets a different poem, none the worse and by some standards better, and more importantly he gets a poem consistent with his perennial good opinion of the speaker.

This interpretation continues to see the logic as proprietary, but not oppressive. If speaker and mistress share the knowledge that the syllogism is frankly spurious, the charge of fraud can be thrown out, and with it the charge of privilege abused. Clearly now, the speaker does not dissemble, he simulates dissembling; the mistress knows this, and the speaker knows she knows. The sophist's trick in want of a philosopher's reproof should rather be seen as the lover's playful challenge, as in a stage magic whose audience recognizes the effect for illusion but wonders at the mechansim. In the portrait of the mistress that such inferences paint, she listens with amused frustration because the speaker has mischief, not malice, in mind. While the rules of the game require a sexual penalty for intellectual failure, both players are well aware that any such forfeit can only be free. Validity apart, neither believes that seduction could be plausibly induced by deductive constraint. Both realize that the speaker uses the argument not to deceive but to dazzle. Both realize that he expects the mistress to be pleased by his performance, pleased in spite of the advantage that he takes, indeed because of it. To a reluctantly appreciative mistress, the speaker presents his argument like a display of male plumage.

Subordinate to rhetoric, Marvell's logic works as structural conceit. The process by which the fallacy contradicts the feeling, only to elicit it, makes the conceit metaphysical, at least by a broad definition, and this proposed resolution of the paradoxical argument fits with the virtually universal judgment that its tone is tense, witty, vexed, and generally ironic. The discovery that the logic won't hold puts rhetorical design in a different light. It complicates and clarifies the relations that bind speaker and mistress, poet and reader. Permit the idea that in "Coy Mistress" the logic is patiently ludicrous, and those four persons stand each revealed in more elaborate roles. Clearly enough, the speaker assumes new responsibilities. He steps from the shadows of a stock role—for however complex his language of love and death, the role has always been simple as to motive and purpose—and takes on dramatic character that requires greater psychological range. To a lesser extent, but from a distance still deeper in stereotype, the mistress too steps forward into character, taking on a stature worthy of her title role. And so does the ideal reader, whose part grows until he is almost drawn into the poem, at least in the sense that he finds himself forming not just critical but dramatic attitudes: male and matriculate, such a reader is the man behind the arras, a character to whom (as in asides) the speaker also plays, the fellow student of syllogisms who can appreciate the technical shape of the argument.

Marvell himself remain. Permit the idea that fallacy is gambit, the mistress teased by peacock sophistry, and the distance that had opened between the poet and his speaker draws close again. Thus when Marvell creates a mistress equal to that speaker, she may likewise approach some ideal of Marvell's own. For she is very much the speaker's match. As the mistress is coy, so does the speaker prove coy. As he is playful and tender, so too is she, and modest and witty as well, a woman so in sympathy not only with the speaker but also with the poet's subtle powers that she looks suspiciously like a projection, Fair Lady to the poet as Pygmalion. Was she as real and live as Legouis believed? Coy in that sense too, reluctant to be found in Marvell's sublunary world, she offers him this inferable glimpse. Amused, she glances from her silence in the poem.

Notes

1. Herbert Grierson, *Metaphysical Lyrics and Poems* (London: Oxford University Press, 1921), pp. xxxvii–xxxviii; Douglas Bush, *English Literature in the Earlier Seventeenth Century* (London: Oxford University Press, 1945), p. 173; Pierre Legouis, *Andrew Marvell, Poet, Puritan, Patriot* (Oxford, 1965), p. 34.

2. Wilfred L. Guerin, Earle G. Labor, Lee Morgan, and John R. Willingham, *A Handbook of Critical Approaches to Literature* (New York: Harper and Row, 1966), pp. 55, 57.

3. Anne E. Berthoff, *The Resolved Soul, a Study of Marvell's Major Poems* (Princeton: Princeton University Press, 1970), p. 111.

4. Guerin, et al., p. 57; Berthoff, ibid.

5. T.S. Eliot, "Andrew Marvell, *TLS*, 31 March 1921. reprinted in *Selected Essays*, new edition (New York: Harcourt, Brace, & World, 1950), and Andrew Marvell, *A Collection of Critical Essays*, ed. George de F. Lord (Englewood Cliffs: Prentice-Hall, 1967), p. 21.

6. J.V. Cunningham, p. 213ff.; Elizabeth Story Donno, ed., *Andrew Marvell, The Complete Poems* (Middlesex: Penguin, 1972), p. 233; J.B. Leishman, *The Art of Marvell's Poetry*, 2nd ed. (New York: Minerva Press, 1968), p. 70.

7. Conversely, if time, no crime; but no time; therefore, crime. The form of the syllogism depends in part but insignificantly on how the actual sentences are reduced to positive or negative propositions. It should be noticed that a logical signpost also introduces the final couplet. By this stage of the argument, the speaker is so confident of his case that he moves from subjunctive to indicative, leaves the conditions and foretells the future: "we will make him run." Once his mistress's logical obligation has been demonstrated, he can abandon the hypothetical argument. Prediction and predication both assume her unconditional surrender.

8. Allen Tate, in Ralph Ross, John Berryman, and Allen Tate, *The Arts of Reading* (New York: Apollo, 1960), p. 305–306.

9. Bruce E. Miller, *North Dakota Quarterly*, 1962, pp. 48–49. The reference is from a recent Marvell bibliography in *ELR* 5 (1975): 271–86. Barbara Herrnstein Smith, *Poetic Closure* (Chicago: University of Chicago Press, 1968), pp. 133–35.

10. J.C. Maxwell, "Marvell and Logic," *N & Q*, July 1970, p. 256a. The reference is from *The Poems and Letters of Andrew Marvell*, ed. H.M. Margoliouth, third ed., rev. Pierre Legouis with the collaboration of E.E. Duncan-Jones (Oxford, 1971), 1: 252. I take the force of "but" in line one to mean "if only," not "only if."

11. Schopenhauer is thus quoted without source in W. Ward Fearnside and William B. Holther, *Fallacy, the Counterfeit of Argument* (Englewood Cliffs: Prentice-Hall, 1959), frontpapers.

12. Eliot, "Andrew Marvell"; Cunningham, "Logic and Lyric," reprinted in his *Tradition and Poetic Structure* (Denver, 1960), pp. 40–58.

13. Barbara Herrnstein Smith, *Poetic Closure*, p. 134.

14. Ibid., p. 134. The next three quotes from Smith in this paragraph are from pp. 134–35.

15. T.L. Jarman, "Education," in *Life Under the Stuarts*, ed. J.E. Morpungo (London, 1950), p. 73, but several authors could be cited to similar effect.

16. Pierre Legouis, *Andrew Marvell*, p. 34.

17. Allen Tate, "Tension in Poetry," in his *Essays of Four Decades* (New York: Swallow, 1970), pp. 64–65.

18. John Press, *Andrew Marvell* (London: British Book Center, 1958), p. 18, but several authors could be cited to similar effect.

THE MOWER MOWN

Marvell's Dances of Death

KENNETH FRIEDENREICH

I

THE PHRASE I take from "Damon the Mower" for the title of my essay has been called by Geoffrey H. Hartman "the neatest example of the converse in Marvell's poetry."[1] As the compact phrase turns back on itself, it suggests to Hartman "the emblem of apocalypse, a figure of divine ironies, of unpredictable reversals."[2] The phrase dances on the waves of the imagination; it conjures a distinct, vivid picture of Death brandishing his scythe for whom Damon is but another blade of grass, while it simultaneously describes the irony of Damon's act of cutting himself down and then mocking at the "poetic justice" of the accident: "For Death thou art a Mower too" (l. 88). "The Mower mown" makes a picture, but the phrase itself provides the gloss that transforms the picture into an emblem that also can be interpreted variously: Is it an emblem of unrequited love? Or self-destructive passion? Of human mortality? Or human clumsiness? The proximity in the phrase of the subject to the predicate supports in a variety of ways Damon's ironic reversal: the subject in the syntax of the phrase, (the Mower) is also the subject (Damon) of the poem. The closeness of the act to the actor is in turn reinforced by the quickly falling alliteration of the m-sounds. This recalls that the occupation and here, the identity, of the protagonist (*mower*) derive from the verb *to mow* (OED, v.[1]). In addition, another meaning of the verb *to mow* and also *mower*, now obsolete, is "to make mouths," to jest (OED, v.,[3] [2], n.,[2]). In the eyes of the narrator, Damon may well be a "Mower" in both senses. To this double sense we must add the woeful assonance of the long "o" sound—it prolongs where the consonants suggest the rapidity with which Damon is hewn down. There is also the pun, *mown-moan*, that taken with these other elements, expresses Damon's unhappy disposition as he acts out his sexual frustration in the meadow. This compact phrase thus generates much through associative imagery and through elaborate wordplay: Damon is victimized by his love for Juliana; in his furor he accidentally victimizes himself by cutting his own ankle. He tries to be lord of the field, but the narrator who remarks that he was "By his own Sythe, the Mower mown," makes mouths at Damon's folly. And, beyond all of this, Hartman points out a biblical allusion in the phrase (I Cor. 15:54–55).[3]

The phrase, "the Mower mown" is, then, a *locus classicus* in showing what the experience of reading and responding to Marvell's poetry can be like. A smooth line that at first appears to be so comprehensible and so neat soon betrays us into the apprehension of multiform possibilities. This particular phrase exhibits Marvell's talent for crowding infinite riches (well, almost) into little space.

The phrase is also a *locus classicus* in another sense, inasmuch as it shows that Marvell's treatment of Death is playful, detached, and ironic. The themes of death and mortality in Marvell are handled much differently than in those poets with whom he is most often and closely associated—Donne, Herbert, Crashaw, Vaughan, Browne, and Traherne—which is not to say that they are less witty or more obtuse than he.[4] Marvell treats death with insouciance, and a consideration of some of the lyrics published in the 1681 *Miscellaneous Poems* will show that he sounds and often resolves the theme of human mortality in a way which makes him unique among his Metaphysical compeers, so that the triumph of death is diminished, it seems, as in "Damon the Mower," by aesthetic invention rather than by doctrinal or philosophical allegiances.

Death and last things, after all, are what so many Metaphysical poems are about:

Webster was much possessed by death
And saw the skull beneath the skin;
And breastless creatures under ground
Leaned backwards with a lipless grin.

★   ★   ★   ★

Donne, I suppose was such another
Who found no substitute for sense,
To seize and clutch and penetrate;
Expert beyond experience,

He knew the anguish of the marrow
The ague of the skeleton;
No contact possible to flesh
Allayed the fever of the bone.[5]

The attitude that Eliot celebrated in the Jacobean dramatists and the Metaphysical poets was reiterated by numerous critics. With abiding certainty, Ruth Wallerstein says "No theme takes us more deeply into the temper of the seventeenth century than its attitude towards death."[6] Likewise, Louis L. Martz supposes that the meditation on death was a "most widely and intensely cultivated" habit of the poets of the age, adding that "The most striking aspect of all such meditations, ... is the full self-awareness of the vision: the eye of truth cuts aside all cant, looking with a grim satirical humor upon all the follies of the world, seeing the worst of life and death with the poise of a detached, judicious intellect: the very poise of Hamlet in the gravediggers' scene."[7] J.M. Cohen writes that the whole century "saw the menace of the death's head" everywhere, and that this obsession with dying was the symptom "of reaction against a profound disillusionment ... the seventeenth [century] saw the Renaissance's hopes of a civilized society ruined by civil and religious strife."[8] These views are critical commonplaces: death and dying in seventeenth-century poetry, both in a spiritual and licentious context, are expected. How, then, does Marvell play upon expectations!

II

Unlike Donne or Browne, Marvell usually does not escort his reader through the morgue, the charnel house, the cemetery, although in his best-known lyric, "To His Coy Mistress" (pp. 27–28), the urgency of the persona's situation leads Marvell, in a rare instance, to do so:

> Thy Beauty shall no more be found;
> Nor, in thy marble Vault, shall sound
> My ecchoing Song: then Worms shall try
> That long preserv'd Virginity:
> And your quaint Honour turn to dust;
> And into ashes all my Lust.
>
> (ll. 25–30)

Stanley Stewart has considered this poem in the context of the medieval tradition of the *memento mori* in order to show Marvell's expansion, by means of a Christian topos, of his Catullian model.[9] But all the terror of the grave, its inevitable permanence, its stillness, are here undercut by the pun on "quaint." In ribald, Chaucerian terms, it suggests that the "Honour" upheld by the female genitalia is, like Falstaff says, just a word, very insubstantial indeed, mere dust. At the same time, almost as an addendum, the persona views the tomb where, finally, his own passion will have burned itself out. The picture of human mortality is not serious. It engenders laughter instead. Certainly, all of the horrors of the grave and the mortification dissipate utterly in the closing couplet of the second stanza:

> The Grave's a fine and private place,
> But none I think do there embrace.
>
> (ll. 31–32)

"Embrace": the speaker has never lost sight of his objective throughout his description of the underworld!

Marvell's description of worms crawling about the decomposing genitalia of his coy mistress may be graphic, vivid, and lewd, but he does not feel compelled as Donne so often does to stir bones, as in "The Relique"; indeed, unlike Donne, Marvell's projection of the grave essentially describes what happens to the woman, not to him. Unlike Donne, Marvell displaces the terror of the body's dissolution in death by fixing it on someone else. Donne feasts on this self-dissolution:

> When my grave is broke up againe
> Some second ghest to entertaine,
> (For graves have learn'd that woman-head
>   To be to more then one a Bed)
>   And he that digs it, spies
> A bracelet of bright haire about the bone,
>   Will he not let'us alone, . . .
>
> ("The Relique" ll. 1–7)[10]

Donne's obsession with his own death is quite well-documented, and it is manifest in his poetry.[11] The lifeless corpse—his own—is a subject of continuing fascination:

> Who ever comes to shroud me, do not harme
>   Nor question much
> That subtile wreath of haire, which crowns my arme; . . .
>
> ("The Funerall")

> When I am dead, and Doctors know not why,
>   And my friends curiositie
> Will have me cut up to survay each part, . . .
>
> ("The Dampe")

> If th'unborne
> Must learne, by my being cut up, and torne;
> Kill, and dissect me, Love; for this
> Torture against thine owne end is,
> Rack't carcasses make ill Anatomies.
>
> ("Loves exchange")

> Before I sigh my last gaspe, let me breath,
> Great love, some Legacies; Here I bequeath
> Mine eyes to *Argus*, if mine eyes can see,
> If they be blinde, then Love, I give them thee; . . .
>
> ("The Will")

Death and dismemberment, sickness and decay, make Donne's amorous poetry extremely *physical*; these obsessive concerns carry over into his religious poetry as well, where they intensify his personal feelings of moral debility and sinfulness.

In *Religio Medici*, Sir Thomas Browne contemplates the fact of his own mortality in most clinical terms. Although his expressed detachment might make Browne closer in spirit to Marvell than to Donne, the terms of the description are more akin to those of the death-obsessed personae of the *Songs and Sonets*:

> This is that dismall conquest we all deplore, that makes us so often cry (O) *Adam, quid fecisti*? I thanke God I have not those strait ligaments or narrow obligations to the world, as to dote on life, or to be convulst and tremble at the name of death: Not that I am insensible of the dread and horrour thereof, or by raking into the bowells of the deceased, [or the] continual sight of Anatomies, Skeletons, or Cadaverous reliques, like Vespilloes or Grave-makers, I am become stupid, or have forgot the apprehension of mortality; but that marshalling all the horrours, and contemplating the extremities thereof, I finde not any thing therein able to daunt the courage of a man, much lesse a well resolved Christian.[12]

Browne's description reminds us of Donne in its details; in both, the reader is never too far from the anatomy lesson, the spittle ward, the freshly-digged grave. Death's dreary presence is ever at hand. In contrast, even when Marvell does, as in "To His Coy Mistress," open the tomb, it is more for rhetorical effect than for our studied gaze. His persona is not dismembered, his bones aren't disturbed. He dies a "poetic" death—a Petrarchan lover's death—consumed by his own lust. So do, of course, Donne's personae in the *Songs and Sonets*, but Marvell does not dwell on the physical aspects of the man's death in the way that his predecessor does. Rather, it is the coy mistress who is envisaged amid the "Cadaverous reliques." Obviously, within the argumentative structure of "To His Coy Mistress," the idea of the grave's terror is introduced by the speaker in order to move the woman to capitulate to his desires. If this is, then, one of Marvell's strongest and most graphic passages about dying, in my judgement it is relatively tame in contrast to the mortifying settings and descriptions of Donne and Browne. After all, Marvell's idea that "The grave's a fine and private place" has little in common with either Donne's overcrowded urban cemetery or Browne's hospital morgue.

III

Some of Marvell's most interesting treatments of the subject of death occur in those lyrics that have been called pastorals or semi-pastorals.[13] I would like to single out "The Picture of little T.C. in a Prospect of Flowers" (pp. 40–41), and "A Dialogue between Thyrsis and Dorinda" (pp. 19–21).

In one sense the pastoral world excludes death. There are an abundance of pastoral poems, especially in the sixteenth and seventeenth centuries, that depict life in the countryside as being outside time. The day is passed joking or lamenting about lovers, or in song contests, or in admiring the virtues of the pastoral life-style. The only "dying" is Petrarchan, if at all. On the other hand, the traditions of pastoral have contained since their origins (Theocritus's First Idyll is a lament for Daphnis, the dead shepherd) the elegiac impulse. These two kinds of pastoral writing are usually very well delineated, and only rarely do authors subvert the pristine world of the former by introducing into it real disease and real death—Spenser, of course, introduces time into the timeless pastoral world in *The Shepheards Calendar* (1579), and in Book 6 of *The Faerie Queene* he describes how brigands murder Meliboe and abduct Pastorella. He shatters the tranquility and the inviolability of the pastoral paradise he creates. Likewise, although he is less drastic—i.e., no brigands— Marvell quietly undermines the inviolability of his pastoral artifice.

"The Picture of Little T.C. in a Prospect of Flowers" fits into the rubric of semipastoral as Miner defines that term because the virtues and values of pastoral life are made implicit in the poem's first five lines:

> See with what simplicity
> This Nimph begins her golden daies!
> In the green Grass she loves to lie,
> And there with her fair Aspect tames
> The Wilder flow'rs, and gives them names:

The terms are loaded—"simplicity," "Nimph," "golden daies"— within the first two lines the impression of pastoralism is secured. The girl behaves with simplicity; innocence and simplicity often go hand in hand in pastoral. T.C. is called nymph, a sobriquet that links her to a pagan past of sweetness; she begins her life in the golden age. Furthermore, as she reclines on the grass, she exemplifies the qualities of freedom and *otium* (ease) that characterize pastoral existence. She dwells in a world of pristine beauty, and Marvell additionally suggests that the world is prelapsarian. She names flowers as Adam, prior to the Fall in the Garden of Eden, occupied himself by naming God's creatures.

As the persona gazes upon T.C., he wonders what her future will be (stanza 2), whether she will conquer Cupid, and is led to exclaim in admiration: "Happy, who can / Appease this virtuous Enemy of Man!" (ll. 15–16). Suddenly the rug has been pulled out from under our feet. Into the prelapsarian scene of rural innocence intrudes the serpent, the "Enemy of Man." Marvell's irony in diction is overwhelming, and the paradox of the combination of the adjective "virtuous" with the phrase "Enemy of Man," which no reader would not recognize as Satan, displays the confused emotions of the persona. Satan entered Eden (and by analogy the prospect of flowers) and brought death into the world. Contemplating the exterior beauty of little T.C., the persona has taken for granted that it reflects her soul, and that she is virtuous. But imagining how she will steal away men's hearts, she becomes mankind's adversary, and the language of the persona causes him to betray himself. His perspective is not only spatially different from T.C.'s—he is outside the prospect looking in; his perspective is also different *temporally*—he looks back on her innocence from his fallen state, after his "golden daies" have long faded, after he has lost his innocence and been expelled from the garden.

His own feelings towards T.C. contaminate the pastoral *otium* suggested in the opening stanza. The artifice of pastoral is thus undermined; and in stanza 3, the confused desires of the speaker make this fall out of innocence into mortality more explicit. At the beginning of the stanza, he wants to "in time compound," which is to say, he wants to bargain with Time, come to terms with it (*OED*, v. 10–11), in order to attempt to match his skills as a lover against T.C.'s "conquering Eyes" (ll. 16–17). He wants her, in short, to grow up fast. But, while he relishes that prospect, he is also afraid of what T.C. might do to him, and at the close of the stanza decides that it would be safer merely to observe, as he is doing at the moment,

to "be laid, / Where I may see thy Glories from some Shade" (l. 24).
If he is so confused by watching the young girl, we can only imagine
how men will react to T.C.'s charms when she matures! Thus, the
third stanza transports us further away from the pristine condition
described in stanza 1.

The displacement continues in the final two stanzas; the impassioned perception of T.C. by the persona actually effects the change
that brings on T.C.'s own decline from her "golden daies". His
reactions are exactly those that he predicts other men will have when
T.C. matures. He therefore decides to wait:

> Mean time, whilst every verdant thing
> It self does at thy Beauty charm,
> Reform the errours of the Spring;
> Make that the Tulips may have share
> Of sweetness, seeing they are fair;
>
> (ll. 25–29)

Like Maria Fairfax in *Upon Appleton House*, T.C. possesses the power
to order and regulate Nature because of her beauty and innocence—
this is a feeling carried over from stanza 1, where T.C. was seen
naming the flowers. But suddenly we are aware that something is
altered: the spring has committed mistakes, the tulips are fair and
should be sweet, but they are not. By implication, the persona hopes
T.C.'s outward beauty conceals grace but not deformity. He hopes
that she can accomplish reform in the *mean time*. She has already been
placed into time by the speaker; she is no longer just a sweet nymph
frolicking about in a pastoral *pleasance*. As her beauty waxes and
matures, she will paradoxically move further and further away from
her "golden daies" and her admirable "simplicity."

Yet there is another twist, another displacement to take us
further away from T.C.'s first world. Having decided to watch
and wait, the persona hopes that T.C. will survive into womanhood,
so that his curiosity may finally be satisfied as to how she'll turn out.

But O young beauty of the Woods,
Whom Nature courts with fruits and flow'rs,
Gather the Flow'rs, but spare the Buds;
Lest *Flora* angry at thy crime,
To kill her Infants in their prime,
Do quickly make th'example Yours;
    And, ere we see,
Nip in the blossome all our hopes and Thee.

(ll. 33–40)

At one level the persona's advice is typical of a parent or adult's advice to a child to respect the handiwork of Nature: in plucking flowers, be sure to only take those that are ready to plucked, and let the buds have their chance to grow. But on the level of confused passion that the persona displays, he cannot see himself perishing. If death is going to deprive him of the opportunity to see how T.C. "turns out," it will be because she dies, not he. As in "Young Love" the possible death of the innocent highlights the infatuation of their detached admirers. The male observer in each poem seems immune from disaster. Fate will take the girl away in "Young Love," here, "*Flora* . . . Do quickly make th' Example Yours" [i.e., T.C.]. This particular dislocation, the inability of the considerably older male observer to contemplate his own extinction, further demonstrates how in the passing of time, each has long before lost his innocence.

    The purity and permanence of the pastoral world are subverted by the interplay between the persona's detached contemplation of T.C. and his emotional responses to her. He calls her "virtuous" because her outward demeanor (a Platonic commonplace) reflects what he feels must be inner purity. However, she proves to be "Enemy to Man," too; in deranging the persona by her behavior, T.C. actually suffers a fall and decline because of the feelings she elicits from the persona. It is almost as if she knows she is being observed; her "golden daies" in stanza I are forgotten as the observer talks of T.C.'s "crimes" against Flora. She is already practicing on the flowers, plucking them one by one, how to take away the hearts of men. The penultimate dimeter line—"And, ere we see"— suggests not only how frail the flesh truly is, how quickly perishable it is, but also indicates how quickly the *picture* of little T.C. in the prospect of flowers can change from the innocent nymph to the "young beauty of the Woods." T.C. falls, so to speak, not because of what she does initially, but because of how her actions are perceived and experienced by the observer. Her behavior will be determined by male responses to her, and the instance of the persona's complex reactions are the index of her fall from innocence. What she now does ingenuously she will one day accomplish with skill. It is the effrontery of the speaker to hope that she will survive her decline from innocence, projecting on to her all of the stigma of mortality that he cannot face as he realizes that he will always be too old for her. The lyric that began by establishing "simplicity" and Edenic innocence ends on a death threat; but Death intrudes not as a monster skull to intimidate T.C. (who has intimidated the persona), but as the last resort of an angry goddess, the projection of the feelings of an infatuated man who knows he should know better.

In "A Dialogue between Thyrsis and Dorinda" Marvell considers mortality within a more elaborate facade of pastoral machinery, fusing the idealized pagan landscape with a vision of Heaven.[14] The point of the dialogue is to utter a death wish. Dorinda, having heard from Thyrsis about the joys of Heaven, would like to experience them at once. She declares, "How I my future state / By silent thinking, Antedate" (ll. 27–28). Before too much longer she is convinced: "I'm sick, I'm sick, and fain would dye: / Convince me now that this is true; / By bidding, with mee, all adieu" (ll. 40–42). Dorinda tempts Thyrsis like Eva tempts Adam; neither can be anything without the other. Thyrsis, in declaring his feelings, is almost comically glib:

> I cannot live without thee, I
> Will for thee, much more with thee dye.
>
> (ll. 43–44)

There is no moment's pause, no long rationalization. Thyrsis has convinced Dorinda, and that is also good enough reason for him to die. I think this poem shows Marvell at one of his most playful occupations, the reversal of expectations in a poetic genre. Considering the long account of heavenly joys in pastoral terms (ll. 9–38), one could expect an exemplum or moral to conclude the dialogue, where Thyrsis and Dorinda might declare their desires to live upright until such time as they pass out of the world they inhabit.

But Marvell doesn't do this: there is no plea for simplicity or humility, no statement that the idealized pastoral life can be taken as a type for a blessed Christian life. In order to reach Elysium, Thyrsis and Dorinda decide to kill themselves. This is not a Christian resolution at all. In fact, the death they plan for themselves is completely pagan; it is a philosopher's suicide:

> Then let us give *Carillo* charge o'th' Sheep,
> And thou and I'le pick poppies and them steep
> In wine, and drink on't even till we weep,
> So shall we smoothly pass away in sleep.
>
> (ll. 46–49)

"A Dialogue" raises the question of the limits of Christian pastoral, something which Henry Vaughan also does, albeit much differently, in "Vanity of Spirit."[15] By extending the conceptual analogy between the pastoral *pleasance* and Heaven as far as possible, the two merge in a kind of amoral and relativistic perfection. Distinctions break down. If one can imagine total innocence on both sides of the grave, then it really matters little, as Thyrsis and Dorinda conclude, to help oneself over to the other side. They are not frightened by death, but actually welcome it as a passing sleep, a drug-induced stupor. Marvell thus demonstrates that by extending the implications of the fusion of the pagan pastoral and the Christian *ad absurdum*, one can even allow for suicide. The Christianized pastoral, Marvell seems to say, can be reduced to sugar candy, literally, the opium of the people. Why might he show this? Perhaps because the "naivete with which Dorinda faces her new knowledge throws us back to what is *not* said in the poem: the all-too-real differences of holy living and holy dying.... The simplicities of Christian teaching are in both cases called into question: there are no home remedies for life or for death."[16]

In "The Picture of little T.C." the pastoral insulation against death is subtly undermined by the feelings of the speaker and his projection of his own fears of mortality onto the innocent girl he observes. In "A Dialogue," death is announced as a theme from the very opening of poem. This in itself is interesting because traditionally there is rarely a sense of mortality in pastoral poems, unless, of course, they are elegiac eclogues. The title does not, I think, prepare us for

When Death, shall part us from these Kids,
And shut up our divided Lids,
Tell me *Thyrsis*, prethee do,
Whither thou and I must go.

(ll. 1–4)

The ingenuous tone of Dorinda's query is perfectly suited for the pastoral mode, but her subject, which admits death into the pastoral settings, is not. But the ensuing discussion avoids the physical details of death, and instead concentrates on the parallels between Elysium and Thyrsis and Dorinda's pastoral refuge. The kind of death agreed upon, as we have already seen, is dreamt away in a drug. What then is at issue here is not a remonstrance that we are mortal, but a demonstration in ludicrous terms of how we can in fact neutralize all of our fears of death and of the accountability of the human soul by merely inventing a poetic subterfuge. In this sense, the poem itself produces the same kind of response to these issues as the mixture of wine and poppies. While I quite clearly concur with Colie's assessment of Marvell's ironic intent in this dialogue, I do not think that we ought therefore presuppose that simply because the poet is capable of criticizing blithe formulae and homilies, he would in fact subsequently confront the subject of mortality and death more directly in other poems. Were the matter that simple, Marvell would have hardly been compelled to keep his personal distance from the matter through the artifices of his poems, as in "A Dialogue between Thyrsis and Dorinda," behind an elaborate pastoral facade, or as in "A Picture of little T.C. in a Prospect of Flowers," through the complex persona of the observer who projects his fear of death onto the young girl he finds so attractive.

IV

What does Marvell do with a mode of writing where mortification is the rule rather than the exception, like "A Dialogue between the Soul and Body" (pp. 21–23)? Elsewhere in this collection, Professor Pequigney shows this poem's relationship to the rhetorical traditions of academic debating. Leishman has suggested that the poem is fashioned after the *Dialogus inter Corpus et Animum*, which originated in the twelfth century.[17] These dialogues were often exercises in self-mortification, with Soul getting the better of Body. Themes of death and decay are hardly understated in them. Here is a portion of a thirteenth century lyric found in the Trinity College, Cambridge ms 323 [f. 27a], in which the soul scores its point against the sinful body:

> Thenne sait the soule to the licam,
> ' Wey! that ic ever in thee com.
> Thu noldes, Friday, festen to non,
> No, the Setterday, almesse don,
> No, then Sonneday, gon to churche,
> Ne Christene werkes wurche.
> Neir thu never so prud,
> Of hude and of hewe ikud,
> Thu shalt in othre wonien and wormes thee tochewen,
> And of alle ben lot that her thee were ilewe'.[18]

Soul indicts Body for laxity and pride, conjuring up its punishment in the grave, like Marvell's coy mistress, devoured by worms. This mortification is the crucial point of the lyric, and the poet builds to it by depicting the sins of the flesh in the first twenty lines.

Marvell defeats conventional expectations—as Professor Pequigney suggests, Body actually scores a point in the debate—also, Marvell's dialogue is remarkably free from mortification. As Colie supposes, Marvell exhausts the genre: "The poet not only overturns the usual expectation of any well-read reader by making the soul and the body into whining complainers instead of aggressive advocates for exclusive programs of life, but also presents them so that their traditional independence are seen to be illusory."[19] Colie believes that Marvell's theme is the call for a new formulation of religious values to replace outmoded ones (thus parallel to "A Dialogue between Thyrsis and Dorinda"). Hers is a persuasive reading of a lyric that may have been left incomplete.[20] For my purposes, however, Marvell's dialogue is unique because of the minimal attention he pays to mortality. The horror of the grave—the climax of the medieval lyric—is left out of Marvell's dialogue altogether. The most damaging charges Soul levels at the body are made in the opening stanza. It mocks the body in terms of new science; the bones rotting in the charnel house are supplanted by the infernal machine.

The Mower Mown

> O who shall, from this Dungeon, raise
> A Soul inslav'd so many wayes?
> With bolts of Bones, that fetter'd stands
> In Feet; and manacled in Hands.
> Here blinded with an Eye; and there
> Deaf with the drumming of an Ear.
> A Soul hung up, as'twere, in Chains
> Of Nerves, and Arteries, and Veins.
> Tortur'd, besides each other part,
> In a vain Head, and double Heart.
>
> (ll. 1–10)

Clearly the opening speech of Soul is conceived according to the traditional metaphor of anima imprisoned in the prison of corpus. Soul is "fetter'd," "manacled," "hung up, as twere, in Chains"—Soul is tortured by blinding and like Bosola's traducing of the Duchess of Malfi is subjected to drumming noise. Yet the lament is almost too strong; the exaggeration of Soul's incarceration makes me think of Charlie Chaplin in "Modern Times," hung up in the gears of a huge machine. The soul is somehow strung up in a network of "Nerves, and Arteries, and Veins." Bolts can mean fetters, of course (*OED*, n. 6), but the meaning also current in Marvell's day was "A stout metal pin with a head, used for holding things fast together" (*OED*, n. 7). There is a comic picture of enforced mechanization in the opening stanza. What replaces mortification here is a sense of frustration compunded in exasperation.

In a type of poem where decay and death are usually prominent, Marvell mentions the verb, "to die," but once (l. 18). And, within the context of the final four lines of the speech of Body where it occurs, death becomes an object of annoyance instead of fear. It accuses Soul:

> . . . wanting where its spight to try,
> Has made me live to let me dye.
> A Body that could never rest,
> Since this ill Spirit it possesst.
>
> (ll. 17–20)

The body actually sees death as an example of intentionally bad planning and workmanship by Soul; it is an inconvenience to be put up with. This metaphor of mechanical construction seems to me borne out in the body's final complaint in terms of design and building:

> What but a Soul could have the wit
> To build me up for Sin so fit?
> So Architects do square and hew,
> Green Trees that in the Forest grew.

> (ll. 41–44)

On one hand we have Body, a "bolt of Bones" that like a machine out of the best science fiction is continuously repairing itself (ll. 27–30), and on the other hand we have Soul, caught by its own animus in a machine "that could never rest." Instead of the mortifying lesson of medieval body/soul dialogues, Marvell invents a microdrama that I think could have been composed by Ionesco or by Beckett. Its context is absurd; both Soul and Body take an inventory that looks less like a contest in rhetorical skill than an exploded parts diagram for a household appliance. In this context, death is not the object of terror designed to convert remiss Christians. It is but an inconvenience to be endured. Marvell's mechanization of the functions of Body and Soul further remove death from Donne's charnel house or Browne's anatomy lesson; where they give us dank odors and disintegrating organs, Marvell gives us the grinding of gears and a sense that emotionally, all of the signals and circuitry are shorted out:

> Joy's chearful Madness does perplex:
> Or Sorrow's other Madness vex.
> Which Knowledge forces me to know;
> And Memory will not foregoe.

> (ll. 37–40)

By discussing the poetic impulse to praise God in "The Coronet" (pp. 14–15), Marvell touches on a theme dealt with by Herbert in his "Jordan" poems and Vaughan in his "Mount of Olives" poems. In form, Marvell's lyric corresponds closely to Herbert's "The Wreath," and its title recalls, of course, Donne's cycle of interlocking sonnets, "La Corona." But as a rare instance in Marvell's lyrics of a poem dealing with his own fall, it does not suggest the sense of personal sin and guilt in physical terms we find expressly in Donne or Herbert's religious verses, where the poet-persona's shortcomings are manifested by corruption and death:

> And gluttonous death, will instantly unjoynt
> My body, and soule, . . .
>
> ("Holy Sonnet" 6)

> So my devout fitts come and go away
> Like a fantastique Ague: . . .
>
> ("Holy Sonnet" 19)

> O thinke mee worth thine anger, punish mee,
> Burne off my rusts, and my deformity,
> Restore thine Image, so much, by thy grace,
> That thou may'st know mee, and I'll turne my face.
>
> ("Good Friday, 1613. Riding Westward")

> That wee may change to evennesse
> This intermitting aguish Pietie;
> That snatching cramps of wickednesse
> And Apoplexies of fast sin, may die;
>
> ("The Litanie," 24)

> A Wreathed garland of deserved praise,
> Of praise deserved, unto thee I give,
> I give to thee, who knowest all my wayes,
> My crooked winding wayes, wherein I live,
> Wherein I die, not live: . . .
>
> ("A Wreath")

> Death, thou wast once an uncouth hideous thing,
> Nothing but bones,
> The sad effect of sadder grones:
> Thy mouth was open, but thou couldst not sing.
> For we consider'd thee as at some six
> Or ten yeares hence,
> After the losse of life and sense,
> Flesh being turn'd to dust, and bones to sticks.
>
> ("Death")[21]

In Donne's poems we see again what was seen in the *Songs and Sonets*—he rivets his attention on corrupt and decaying flesh. Death dissects the speaker, or the speaker is infected by agues of impiety; he is deformed in the Good Friday poem. In Herbert's *The Temple*, "Death" follows immediately after "The Wreath." Writing about "The Wreath," Arnold Stein contends that "The form of the poem does not merely turn back on itself; it has been turning the whole time, the verbal device being conceptual, a winding with a purpose, and the purpose is to transform."[22] Stein supposes a transformation from the speaker's erroneous ways to his acceptance of God's (ll. 3 and 10). There is a demonstrable parallel in Marvell's "The Coronet," but with a twist created by Marvell's attitude towards his own death in the poem. Marvell's garland, like Herbert's disingenuous wreath, is inspired by a desire for fame and recognition as a sacred poet. In Marvell's poem, his flawed state is revealed in his discovery of the serpent in his garland; like Herbert he begins to question his own motivations about composing such verse. But here is where, I think, the two poets go separately.

Herbert recognizes that his vanity and pride, hidden by poetic invention, will actually lead him not to life, but death. The repetition of the preposition "Wherein" towards the end of line four and then immediately again at the beginning of the fifth line shows how Herbert cannot deceive himself from his true motivations for attaining recognition for his poetic ingenuity—he would like the lyric to be an indicator to the reader that because he composes pious verse, he is saved—"Wherein I live." But Herbert also sees behind this facade—in praising God in his poem, he wants the reader to praise the poet, not God. The self-recognition of sin is almost immediate: "Wherein I die, not live."

Marvell comes essentially to the same realization as Herbert, but he displaces the deadly implications of the discovery on to Satan:

> Alas I find the Serpent old
> That, twining in his speckled breast,
> About the flow'rs disguis'd does fold,
> With wreaths of Fame and Interest.

> (ll. 13–16)

But he does not come face to face, like Herbert, with the prospect of his own physical and spiritual death and request God show him a new and simple and straight way. Instead he asks God to untie his pride from his poem by destroying the Serpent, but if necessary

> . . . shatter too with him my curious frame:
> And let these wither, so that he may die,
> Though set with skill and chosen out with Care.

(ll. 22–24)

Now, it is quite possible to interpret these lines as the poet's prayer that God destroy *him* if that is the only remedy for the sin of pride— if God can kill Satan by shattering the poet's curious frame (i.e., his body), he is ready. But is he? The demonstrative pronoun "these" must refer to the leaves (= lines) of the poem, not to the poet's physical being. He furthermore expresses a bit of remorse for the necessary destruction of the poem, advertising, *even as he asks that it be destroyed*, that it is "set with Skill and chosen out with Care." It is an oblique recognition that he is still very much a victim of his own vanity and pride. For me, physical death in this passage is unambiguously subsumed by the persona's concession to destroy the poem (which, of course, he doesn't do). Let me explain.

If Marvell is trying to say, as Colie believes, that "poetry bends to the spiritual discipline of the soul," or, as Pequigney says, that a perfect crown of praise by a poet would place moral values preeminently above aesthetic ones, we might think that Marvell would follow Herbert in making the fact of his own physical and spiritual deaths more explicit.[23] Herbert says unequivocally, *I die*. But Marvell doesn't; he cushions the deathblow by being at two removes from it —one, the victory of Christ over the Serpent, and two, the destruction of the poem itself.

I quoted above from "Death" because it demonstrates that Herbert's first impressions of death were as a gaping devourer whose inevitability he put away from his mind in his "crooked" (cf. "The Wreath") days. But the subsequent poem goes on to show that, having been transformed (cf. "The Wreath" again), death holds no terror for him. The new attitude pervades the following poems in *The Temple*; it ends on a note of resolution, purpose, self-awareness.

Marvell does not even begin to hint at such a resolution in "The Coronet," although he does seem to replicate Herbert's motions from the crooked to the straight and the complex to the simple. As Colie indicates, there is an apparent change in syntax

between the first sixteen and concluding ten lines of "The Coronet,"
but that this change is more apparent than real. She says the final lines
"*seem* to assert simplicity," but that in essence Marvell's poem shows
"the impossibility, in the fallen world, of personal sincerity [through]
conventions of frankness."[24] By "conventions of frankness" Colie
means the sequence of feelings and actions which the poem actually
reproduces—Marvell's decision to write a poem praising God, his
discovery of his selfish motives, his plea to exorcise the devil from
his impulses, his alteration of syntax from elaborate to flat. Unlike
"The Wreath," which resolves into simplicity, Marvell recognizes
that such simplicity is itself an artifice; in other words, in the fallen
world, he is essentially helpless, short of a miracle through God's
intervention, of ever excluding feelings of pride.

It is in this striking context that Marvell avoids the possibility
of confronting his own death directly. In a world so far removed
from ingenuous and sincere behavior, Marvell finds it hard to wish
for his own death or believe, as Donne or Herbert appear to in their
religious lyrics, that what he truly wishes for is his own death as
punishment for and release from his sinful nature. If Marvell in "A
Dialogue between the Soul and Body" exhausts a genre, perhaps
"The Coronet" does so as well. He admits in this second poem that
man is incapable of composing a proper religious poem so long as
he is unable to divorce from the poetic impulse his desire for fame,
recognition, and personal satisfaction; in turn, this discovery implies
that no matter how vocally a man protests to desire death to free him
from his mortal frailty, it is difficult to convince oneself, let alone
anyone else, that the experience of death is what one truly wants.
Marvell's displacement of the death issue in "The Coronet" instructs
us that survival is instinctive in devout as well as in secular times.
His pose in this poem is not that of Hamlet in the gravediggers'
scene, but rather that in the famous third act soliloquy:

> ay, there's the rub,
> For in that sleep of death what dreams may come,
> When we have shuffled off this mortal coil,
> Must give us pause.

V

I wish to conclude my discussion by looking at "The Garden" (pp. 51–53), and Marvell's handling of mortality there. The order of events in the poem apparently follows the Platonic ladder in moving from body to mind and mind to soul.[25] But the conventional expectations are not fulfilled. Instead, the real star of the show is the mind. Indeed, through the first five stanzas, Marvell builds a lavish *locus amoenus*, in which the persona finally finds himself "Insnar'd by Flowers" and falling down into the grass (l. 40). He has stumbled, been ensnared, and fallen, but—as in "The Picture of little T.C." where the phrase "Enemy of Man" is considered outside its usual religious context—these verbs actually describe physical actions in the garden, and are divorced from specific religious associations.[26] On the other hand, though, the fall onto grass could possibly be seen as a reminder of mutability and the transitory nature of things in the world. For the moment the body reclines pleasantly, and then the mind "Withdraws into his own happiness," first, by finding its semblance in the beautiful objects that compose the garden setting and then, moving beyond:

> Yet it creates, transcending these,
> Far other Worlds, and other Seas;
> Annihilating all that's made
> To a green Thought in a green Shade.
>
> (ll. 45–48)

There has been no end to exegesis of this last couplet. Legouis retains Margoliouth's paraphrases, that the lines "may be taken as meaning either 'reducing the whole world to nothing material, i.e., to a green thought,' or 'considering the whole material world as of no value compared to a green thought.'"[27] These interpretations imply stasis, where I think we should be looking for its opposite. The mind, I said, is the star of the show in "The Garden"; it holds together the human entity—the body, whose pull is downwards, and the soul, which alights on a tree like bird, aspiring to its "longer flight" (l. 56).

Rather than entering a static or ecstatic moment, the mind is busy. It creates other worlds—like the poetic imagination which Theseus and Hippolyta discuss in *A Midsummer Night's Dream*, the mind creates something more real than the material world. In creating other worlds, the mind imitates God, the first Creator, the first poet. But in creating these other worlds, and certainly the mind's act of creation includes the "other world" of the poem itself, the mind figuratively destroys the actual, material world by substituting for it one of its own manufacture, which is, of course, "The Garden" itself. Whatever is annihilated and reduced to "a green Thought in a green Shade" is presented by the poem itself. So the mind is at once a source of creation and destruction, it murders and creates, it gives form to chaos and reduces all from to chaos if it wishes. Marvell provides simultaneously the machinations of the artistic impulse—creation and annihilation.

This whole process, as Berthoff reminds us, takes place in time and also takes time.[28] The body reclines in the mutable grass and the soul waits for the future time of its ascent. The present belongs to the mind. In coming down from the moment of the mind's apotheosis, we reenter time, although, of course, we have never really left it. What we have participated in is the mind's activities of annihilating the material world and replacing it with its own—the poem—in which the illusion of stasis has been maintained in the time it takes to read the poem. The comparison in stanza 8 of this little garden to Eden reminds us that not only has a great deal of time passed, but that there has also been a great falling off. Adam lost both his solitude and innocence to Eve: "But 'twas beyond a Mortal's share / To wander solitary there" (ll. 61–62). We notice how Marvell telescopes time: he calls Adam a mortal even before he has fallen. And suddenly, death has been brought into the world as the token of our fall from primal innocence, "that happy Garden-state."

The reader figuratively enters that golden past through the act of reading the poem; the mind escorts us into its moment of supreme artistic process, and it escorts us out again. It has not been illusion or fantasy—in essence we have been transported in the real experience of reading the poem and have touched something of great constancy. Like the persona, too, we are apt to mutter that this moment is too good too last.

The last stanza settles us back completely into the mortal world. The "skilful Gardner" is at once the poet, who has set flowers and herbs in his poem, the man employed to landscape and garden, and God, who first created gardens. Their works, however, exist on a plane above which the Sun "Does through a fragrant Zodiack run" (l. 68).[29] Time is really moving along rapidly. As it does, the bee labors incessantly to bring forth enough honey to carry him through the death of the years, the winter. The bee's instincts are its hedge against mortality; likewise, the poet's work of the mind is his. Both creatures compute time. In such a beautiful setting, a man could offset somewhat the depressing fact of his own mortality: "How could such sweet and wholesome Hours / Be reckon'd but with herbs and flow'rs!" (ll. 71–72). In contemplative solitude, the mind has the power to leave time, to be suspended outside of a world in which all things perish. But in man's fallen state, he is at best only capable of this motion for a few short moments: "To this extent, the poem is a paradoxical but unmistakable *carpe diem*, the more breathtaking because its argument leads us in the direction opposite to the traditional lyric persuasion's *carpere*, back to the simple morality of the phrase. The day we are to pluck is the garden-day of solitude; . . . in which 'creating' and 'annihilating' prove to be two aspects of the same operation."[30]

"The Garden" is typical of Marvell's atypical attitude towards death. Death is in our world, and the movement of the sun declares that time never ceases. But there is no guilt or self-laceration in the persona's recognition that he is mortal. I know of no lyric in the period in which Marvell wrote where the fall of man is comprehended in a manner so free of pain and remorse and longing. This does not mean that what has been lost is taken casually or lightly. To the contrary, the preciousness of the hours spent in the garden only intensifies the sense of loss. The poem tells us that art possesses the potential to create and to annihilate, to transcend death-bearing time, but the activities of the mind are also a somber reminder of "the observable fact that human experience and human understanding are finite."[31] In this sense, "The Garden" may be a most excellent gloss for the theme announced in the opening lines of *Paradise Lost*.

VI

This discussion of Marvell's treatment of the death's head theme which so fascinated his Metaphysical counterparts asserts, I think, his uniqueness among them. Space does not permit me to consider other poems, such as the mowing sequence in *Upon Appleton House*, or regrettably, "Damon the Mower," in which my curiosity about this entire subject was initially aroused, to mention but two. What I hope this analysis has demonstrated is that Marvell is not morbidly fascinated by his own death the way other Metaphysical writers seem to be; in his eschatological pursuits, the fact that Marvell is going to die does not seem overstated or obsessive. Does the fact that it is subsumed in other matters, such as the complex emotions of the observer in "The Picture of little T.C.," or the artifices of humility in "The Coronet," indicate that Marvell was fearful of his death, so much so that he could never discuss it directly like Donne or Herbert? I do not know, and cannot presume to anatomize his psyche. Perhaps we can catch the steps in Marvell's *Totentanz* by looking elsewhere, to the work of an other time and place. One of the great moments in Thomas Mann's novel, *The Magic Mountain* is when Hans Castorp awakes from his dream about humanity. He speaks:

> I will let death have no mastery over my thoughts. For therein lies goodness and love of humankind, and in nothing else. Death is a great power. One takes off one's hat to him, and goes weavingly on tiptoe. He wears the stately ruff of the departed and we do him honour in solemn black. Reason stands simple before him, for reason is only virtue, while death is release, immensity, abandon, desire. Desire, says my dream. Lust, not love. Death and love— no, I cannot make a poem of them, they don't go together. Love stands opposed to death. It is love, not reason, that is strong. Only love, not reason, gives sweet thoughts. And from love and sweetness alone can form come: form and civilization, friendly, enlightened, beautiful human intercourse—always in silent recognition of the blood sacrifice. Ah, yes, it is well and truly dreamed. I have taken stock. I will remember. I will keep faith with death in my heart, yet well remember that faith with death and the dead is evil, is hostile to humankind, so soon as we give it power over thought and action. *For the sake of goodness and love, man shall let death have no sovereignty over his thoughts.*[32]

In Mann's own gloss of the passage from his novel he says that his protagonist "arrives at an understanding of humanity that does not, indeed, rationalistically ignore death, nor scorn the dark, mysterious side of life, but takes account of it, without letting it get control over his mind."[33] Marvell, like Mann's Castorp, is aware of the death's head, but one feels that through the artifices of his lyrics he is capable of distancing himself from mortality without averting or denying death's existence. His is the response of a very self-conscious, very resolved creative faculty; the response of a man quite tough and reasonable.

Notes

1. "Marvell, St. Paul, and the Body of Hope," *ELH* 31 (1964): 175–94, reprinted in George deF. Lord, ed., *Andrew Marvell: A Selection of Critical Essays* (Englewood Cliffs, N.J.: Prentice-Hall, 1968), pp. 101–19. I quote here from p. 115.

2. Hartman, p. 115.

3. Hartman, p. 115, n. 26.

4. Little notice of death per se has been taken in Marvell's poetry, although Anne E. Berthoff touches on it, *"The Resolved Soul": A Study of Marvell's Major Poems* (Princeton: Princeton University Press, 1970), pp. 1–35, 134–39.

5. T.S. Eliot, "Whispers of Immortality" (ll. 1–4, 9–16), quoted from *The Complete Poetry & Plays, 1909–1950* (New York: Harcourt Brace & World, 1962), pp. 32–33.

6. Ruth Wallerstein, *Studies in Seventeenth Century Poetic* (1950; reprint ed., Madison: University of Wisconsin Press, 1965), p. 5.

7. Louis L. Martz, *The Poetry of Meditation* (1954; reprint ed., New Haven: Yale University Press, 1965), pp. 135, 137.

8. J.M. Cohen, *The Baroque Lyric* (London: Hutchinson, 1963), p. 32.

9. Stanley Stewart, "Marvell and the *Ars Moriendi*," in Earl Miner, ed., *Seventeenth Century Imagery: Essays on the Uses of Figurative Language from Donne to Farquhar* (Berkeley and Los Angeles: University of California Press, 1971), pp. 133–50.

10. Sir Herbert Grierson, ed., *Donne: Poetical Works* (1933; reprint ed., London: Oxford University Press, 1968), pp. 55–56. All subsequent references to Donne are taken from this edition.

11. R.C. Bald, *John Donne: A Life* (New York: Oxford University Press, 1970), especially pp. 509–36.

12. Sir Geoffrey Keynes, ed., *Sir Thomas Browne: Selected Writings* (Chicago: University of Chicago Press, 1968), pp. 44–45.

13. J.B. Leishman, *The Art of Marvell's Poetry* (New York: Minerva Press, 1968) uses these terms as a title for his third chapter, pp. 101–92, but does not define them, particularly the latter. I refer the reader to Earl R. Miner, *The Cavalier Mode from Jonson to Cotton* (Princeton: Princeton University Press, 1971), pp. 232–38, for a discussion of semipastoral, and my own forthcoming study of *Henry Vaughan* in the Twayne's English Authors Series. Basically, semipastoral is the term for those poems that will often mention a pastoral detail or two, such as a name like Lucasta or Corydon, or mention of fields or meadows or cots to imply a pastoral perspective operating throughout the whole poem.

14. Edward William Tayler, *Nature and Art in Renaissance Literature* (New York: Columbia University Press, 1964), pp. 99–100.

15. Rosalie Colie, *"My Ecchoing Song": Andrew Marvell's Poetry of Criticism* (Princeton: Princeton University Press, 1970), p. 129. In "Vanity of Spirit" Vaughan's persona is a hermit, a favorite character in sixteenth- and particularly seventeenth-century retirement poems or praises of solitary living (cf. Milton's "Il Penseroso"). In his lyric, Vaughan questions the presumption that the "retiree" makes, that he is, because of his retirement, able to fathom the mysteries of God's creation.

16. Colie, p. 129.

17. Leishman, pp. 210–12.

18. T.R. Davies, ed., *Medieval English Lyrics* (1963; reprint ed., Chicago: Northwestern University Press, 1964), pp. 73–74. Also see Carleton Brown, ed., *English Lyrics of the Thirteenth Century* (1932; reprint ed., Oxford: Clarendon Press, 1965), p. 31. Here is Davies's modern version of the lines: "Then says the soul to the body, 'Alas! that I ever entered you. You would not on Fridays fast until noon, nor on Saturdays give alms, nor on Sundays go to church, nor do Christian works. Never mind how proud you were, famous for your skin and complexion, you shall dwell in earth and worms shall chew you thoroughly, and you shall be loathesome to all who were dear to you here.'"

19. Colie, p. 57.

20. Legouis, *Commentary*, I:249: "the anonymous corrector of *T2* has drawn his pen through the last four lines of the fourth stanza and has written below: '*Desunt multa.*' The poem may originally have continued through several more ten-line stanzas, of which only the last four lines of the poem in its present condition survive."

21. Quoted from F.E. Hutchinson, ed., *The Works of George Herbert* (1941; reprint ed., Oxford: Clarendon Press, 1957), pp. 185–86. Donne's verses are again quoted from Grierson, pp. 295, 302, 308, and 316, respectively.

22. *George Herbert's Lyrics* (Baltimore: Johns Hopkins Press, 1968), p. 145.

23. Colie, p. 43. Pequigney's comment was made during a seminar meeting on Marvell at the State University of New York at Stony Brook in 1973.

24. Colie, p. 82.

25. Legouis, *Commentary*, I:270.

26. See Legouis's reference to A.H. King, *Commentary*, I:268.

27. Legouis, *Commentary*, I:268–69.

28. Berthoff, pp. 152–53.

29. The implication here is that such activity as the mind performs is the best

way to make use of our limited time; see Frank Kermode, "The Argument of Marvell's 'Garden'," *EIC* 2 (1952): 241.

30. Colie, p. 170.

31. Colie, p. 177.

32. Thomas Mann, *The Magic Mountain*, trans., H.T. Lowe-Porter (1927; reprint ed., New York: Vintage Books, 1969), pp. 494–95. Marvell, however, is not as naive as Mann's character—fortunately.

33. Mann, "The Making of the Magic Mountain," reprinted in the Vintage edition, p. 724.

Some Apocalyptic Strains in Marvell's Poetry

Joseph H. Summers

We should beware of supposing that whenever in the study of Christian politics we meet with apocalyptic, eschatological and even millennial concepts, we are necessarily dealing with those chiliastic "religions of the oppressed" which are so much and so rightly studied. Concepts of this order formed a vital and powerful element in the vocabulary of Christian society, one just as likely to be employed by members of the established power structure as by rebels against it; they were used to explain events and justify claims too dramatic and unprecedented to be dealt with in any other way, and the powerful as well as the powerless might find themselves needing to do this.

But the language of apocalyptic was thus widely employed because only a dramatised providence seemed capable of explaining secular and particular happenings when their particularity was so marked as to assume the character of sudden change

J.G.A. Pocock, "Civic Humanism and its Role in Anglo-American Thought."[1]

SOME YEARS AGO Rosalie Colie remarked that "It is often difficult to remember that Andrew Marvell the poet was also a polemical Puritan and practical politican, so little do his surviving poems reflect his public activity," and she went on to note the relations between

"Marvell's 'Bermudas' and the Puritan Paradise." [2] Most of Marvell's poems are still usually read as if they were composed outside of time, lyrics of a poet with general sensitivity and a wonderful ear who was concerned with myth and pastoral and literary and religious traditions. I would not question that account of Marvell's gifts and concerns, but a number of the poems show also the poet's sensitive and particular responses to his own time and place, the importance of which it is easy to underestimate or to miss.

Marvell's classicism is sometimes thought to indicate his deepest allegiances and to be largely responsible for his playful uses of multiple genres and stances. A wide acquaintance with classical history and texts, in addition to a knowledge of changes in expression, taste, and assumptions, might be expected to lead to a relatively static or cyclical view of history: the more it changes the more it is the same. If one knows what happened and what was said in the past, one must often experience the sense of déja vu as one looks at the events and statements of the present. But such an expectation is likely to be perfectly fulfilled only in times of social and political stability. Augustine, after all, was a "classicist" convinced of literally earth-shaking changes in human and divine history and life, and something of his attitude could appear in almost any later classicist. Before Augustine, of course, there were tragedies and epics and Virgil's "Messianic Eclogue" which focused precisely on moments of extraordinary change, events which made the future seem forever different from the past: the Trojan War, the founding of Rome, the curse on the house of Cadmus or Atreus. For many Christians in the Middle Ages, the world might, in comparison with such classical perspectives, have seemed relatively static: the most important transforming event had occurred once for all time, and the fluctuations of events while Nature gradually decayed (or even gradually improved) in expectation of the final Judgment could seem relatively unimportant, particularly if the divine revelation was thought to be complete, and no further enlightenment concerning ethics, society, or history to be expected. After the Reformation, that position became increasingly difficult to maintain, I believe, particularly for Protestants. However strongly the Reformers clung to the notion that they were only attempting to restore the church to its primitive condition, the attempt itself implied that sudden and radical changes were possible, and the assumptions of a static or "traditional" society which appeals to established justice and law were rendered problematic. Change could be conceived not as a decline from an ideal or timeless realm of justice or truth but as a necessary, even if cataclysmic, effort to recover lost truth—or even to discover new truths in a continuing revelation.

One of the most difficult tasks for a certain type of classicistic mind is to accommodate its timeless geometric or "spatial" structures to the vicissitudes of time without relapsing into a meaningless relativism or into nihilism. To imagine and to come to terms with fundamental change is always difficult. But the effort was almost inevitable, I believe, for some of the sensitive poets who survived and responded to the extraordinary changes in English society and religion during the mid-seventeenth century. What if tomorrow should be truly different from today—or yesterday? What if rights and duties and possibilities should be utterly transformed? What if men should begin to live and to love in new fashions and with new senses of purpose?

Christopher Hill is one of the few who have been concerned both with placing Marvell's poetry within its time and with Marvell's imaginative response to the possibility of profound or revolutionary change. In his provocative essay, "Society and Andrew Marvell,"[3] he remarked, quite justly, that most of the critics have misinterpreted Marvell's retrospective account of the Civil War included in *The Rehearsal Transpros'd*, 1672, an account which gives fascinating evidence of Marvell's openness to the possibility that "Nature" (or Providence) may work extraordinarily within history. Since they have been frequently misunderstood, I quote the crucial paragraphs complete and within their contexts. Marvell has been analyzing the doctrines and motives of the innovating "Arminians":

> So that those who were of understanding in those days tell
> me, that a man would wonder to have heard their kind of preachings. How in stead of the practical Doctrine which tends to the
> reforming of Mens Lives and Manners, all their Sermons were
> a very Mash of *Arminian* Subtilties, of Ceremonies, and Decency,
> and of *Manwaring*, and *Sibthorpianism* brew'd together; besides
> that in their conversation they thought fit to take some more
> licence the better to *dis-Ghibelene* themselves from the *Puritans*.
> And though there needed nothing more to make them unacceptable

to the sober part of the Nation, yet moreover they were so exceeding
pragmatical, so intolerably ambitious, and so desperately proud,
that scarce any Gentleman might come near the Tayle of their
Mules. And many things I perceive of that nature do even yet stick
upon the stomacks of the *Old Gentlemen* of those times. For the
English have been always very tender of their Religion, their
Liberty, their Propriety, and (I was going to say) no less of their
Reputation. Neither yet do I speak of these things with passion,
considering at more distance how natural it is for men to desire
to be in Office; and the less a Clergyman is so, the more he deserves
to be commended. But these things before mentioned, grew yet
higher, after that Bishop *Laud* was once not only exalted to the
See of *Canterbury*, but to be chief Minister. Happy had it been for
the King, happy for the Nation, and happy for himself, had he
never climbed that Pinacle. For whether it be or no, that the
Clergy are not so well fitted by Education, as others for Political
Affairs, I know not; though I should rather think they have advantage above others, and even if they would but keep to their
Bibles, might make the best Ministers of State in the world; yet
it is generally observed that things miscarry under their government.
If there be any Counsel more precipitate, more violent, more
rigorous, more extreme than other, that is theirs. Truly I think
the reason that God does not bless them in Affairs of State, is,
because he never intended them for that imployment. Or if
Government, and the preaching of the Gospel, may well concur
in the same person, God therefore frustrates him, because though
knowing better, he seeks and manages his greatness by the lesser
and meaner *Maxims*. I am confident the Bishop studied to do both
God and his Majesty good service, but alas how utterly was he
mistaken. Though so learned, so pious, so wise a Man, he seem'd
to know nothing beyond *Ceremonies*, *Arminianism*, and *Manwaring*.
With that he begun, and with that ended, and thereby deform'd
the whole reign of the best Prince that ever wielded the *English*
Sceptor.

For his late Majesty being a Prince truly Pious and Religious,
was thereby the more inclined to esteem and favour the Clergy.
And thence, though himself of a most exquisite understanding,
yet thought he could not trust it better than in their keeping.

Whereas every man is best in his own Post, and so the Preacher in the Pulpit. But he that will do the Clergyes drudgery, must look for his reward in another World. For they having gained this Ascendent upon him, resolv'd whatever became on't to make their best of him; and having made the whole business of State their *Arminian* Jangles, and the persecution for Ceremonies, did for recompence assign him that imaginary absolute Government, upon which Rock we all ruined.

For now was come the last part of the *Archbishops* indiscretion; who having strained those strings so high here, and all at the same time, which no wise man ever did; he moreover had a mind to try the same dangerous Experiment in *Scotland*, and sent thither the Book of the *English Liturgy*, to be imposed upon them. What followed thereupon, is yet within the compass of most Mens memories. And how the War broke out, and then to be sure Hell's broke loose. Whether it were a War of Religion, or of Liberty, is not worth the labour to enquire. Whichsoever was at the top, the other was at the bottom; but upon considering all, I think the Cause was too good to have been fought for. Men ought to have trusted God; they ought and might have trusted the King with that whole matter. *The Arms of the Church are Prayers and Tears*, the Arms of the Subjects are Patience and Petitions. The King himself being of so accurate and piercing a judgment, would soon have felt where it stuck. For men may spare their pains where Nature is at work, and the world will not go the faster for our driving. Even as his present Majesties happy Restauration did it self, so all things else happen in their best and proper time, without any need of our officiousness.

But after all the fatal consequences of that Rebellion, which can only serve as Sea-marks unto wise Princes to avoid the Causes, shall this sort of Men still vindicate themselves as the most zealous Assertors of the Rights of Princes? They are but at the best *well-meaning Zealots*.[4]

Marvell writes as one who was too young to experience the causes of the war, but who has heard (and read) a great deal about them, and who is witnessing something like a repetition of them in the efforts of Samuel Parker and his kind to convince Charles II that he should abandon religious toleration and rule absolutely. According to his account, the original troubles came exclusively from the innovations and the intolerance and arrogance of the "Arminian" clergy. Charles I innocently and piously submitted himself to Laud's policy and was destroyed for his pains. Even Laud is not presented as at all evil (his relative innocence is obviously contrasted with Parker's malice), but as a pious man who was led astray by a few theological issues and who had no sense of politics. There is no ambiguity whatsoever about the "rightness" of the two sides. What can be seen now, if not before, is that the "Good Old Cause" was "too good to have been fought for" because the anti-Laudians were both right and had the people and history as well as God on their side; and Charles was "of so accurate and piercing a judgment" that he would eventually have perceived those facts and would have dismissed his mistaken and foolish councillors: religious toleration and the establishment of a relatively "low" or "broad" Anglicanism would have triumphed without a war. It would probably have been difficult for Marvell to argue in a work intended to influence Charles II that the war *was* good or necessary; but the chief import of the passage is the underlying agrument that Charles II should not allow himself to be led astray by venal clergymen who argue for intolerance and absolutism, officiously attempting to deflect the English government from its proper course. They are at best *"well-meaning Zealots,"* who would, if followed, lead another Charles into a position which might give rise to a new civil war. But this Charles, surely, warned in time, will resist such evil councillors and will learn to act in accordance with social reality and the new moment in history. One may be tempted to read some irony into the sentence about "his present Majesties happy Restauration," but in addition to echoing the common phrase, the sentence both serves as a reminder that the Restoration was not achieved by aggressive or innovative behavior on the part of Charles and paraphrases the biblical reminder that "all things work together for good to them that love God" (Rom. 8:28).

The chief differences between the view of Charles I here and that in *An Horatian Ode* are largely accounted for by the differing perspectives taken and the differing audiences addressed. The pretended audience of *The Rehearsal Transpros'd* is anyone who has read Samuel Parker's *A Discourse of Ecclesiastical Poliie, wherein the authority of the Civil Magistrate over the Consciences of Subjects in matters of Religion is asserted; the Mischiefs and Inconveniences of Toleration are represented, and all Pretenses pleaded in behalf of Liberty of Conscience are fully answered* (1669) and Parker's subsequent works (*A Defence and Continuation of the Ecclesiastical Policie* [1671] and *A Preface Shewing what grounds there are of Fears and Jealousies of Popery*, published with Bishop Bramhall's *Vindication of himself and the Episcopal Church from the Presbyterian Charge of Popery* in 1672), and who might be influenced by them; but the assumed audience for much of it, and particularly the passages I have quoted, seems to be Charles II himself, appealed to, both as a wit and as a man of intelligent self-interest, to avoid the kinds of attitudes and actions which had led to his father's death. Many of the basic problems of the past still exist, but they can be endured or resolved by enlightened behavior, without tragedies or cataclysmic events or revolutions. *An Horatian Ode upon Cromwell's Return from Ireland* addresses chiefly potential critics and supporters of Cromwell and, after line 113, Cromwell directly, concerning the situation in the early summer of 1650.[5] The astonishing change has recently occurred: Charles has been beheaded and has acted properly the part of a king on the scaffold if not before. Cromwell is viewed as the "force of angry Heavens flame," a providential figure whose natural and personal worth made his victory as a "greater Spirit" inevitable, and who is worthy of support so long as he remains "still in the *Republick's* hand" and so long as he continues a victorious military leader. Cromwell's actions have transformed the "Kingdom old" in a manner for which Roman rather than English or Hebrew history provides the closest analogies. The "present" at this moment differs from the past to a degree previously almost unimaginable. It is the business of Cromwell, his soldiers, and English citizens to understand and to respond to present reality rather than hopelessly to mourn for what has gone.

Although Marvell is probably best known today as the poet of gardens, persuasions, dialogues, and perhaps "The Definition of Love," it is remarkable how many of his poems assume, consider, plea for, or even imitate moments of significant choices which change or seem to change everything: the soul's "resolution," Damon's meeting with "Pan," Juliana's coming into the world of the Mower, Chloe's rejection of Daphnis, the poet's attempt to make a garland for Christ, his persuasion of his mistress to consummate their love or his acknowledgment that their love cannot be consummated, Fairfax's retirement, Cromwell's military victories and assumption of power—even the notion of permanent retirement to a garden. In the pages which follow I wish to consider a few poems which, rather than concentrating on past choices, contemplate future possibilities that may transform the presents that the speakers know.

The ordinary language of praise in the seventeenth century often anticipated such developments: as panegyric approached closer to the language of apotheosis, the new god or goddess could be expected to manifest divinity through changes in the governance of our earthly realm. But ordinarily such poems used the language of extravagant compliment decoratively or playfully—no other light dares show where Cynthia shines, trees crowd into a shade where e'er she walks. At most perhaps there is a masquelike sense of perfection restored or achieved, but usually with little sense of the particularities of the transformation in ordinary life or in future history. The language of metamorphosis, which Odette de Mourges has shown to prevail throughout the century,[6] also envisaged extraordinary changes and transformations. It often retained, I believe, some of its original Ovidian usage: the metamorphosis tended to be from the human and changeable to the inanimate or symbolic and abstract, girl to tree or swain to daffodil—the metamorphosis from the living world of love and change in time to a world of art and meaning without change. Marvell, like Milton, usually transmuted the traditions which he used.

In "The Picture of Little T.C. in a Prospect of Flowers" (pp. 40–41) as in the vision of Maria Fairfax at the end of *Upon Appleton House*, Marvell envisions the possibility that a young girl might, in her mature triumph, transform both nature and the life of man.[7] The way in which those future triumphs are imagined probably owes a good deal to the fact that the poet had recently lived through political and military events that seemed to change the past ("the world turned upside down" as more than a metaphor of disorder) and to promise a new society, still unfixed in details, which might surpass past dreams of individual and social possibilities. In "The Picture of Little T.C.," the vision is presented as one which no living man could welcome in absolute assurance that he might share in its glories:

Who can foretel for what high cause
This Darling of the Gods was born!
Yet this is She whose chaster Laws
The wanton Love shall one day fear,
And, under her command severe,
See his Bow broke and Ensigns torn.
   Happy, who can
Appease this virtuous Enemy of Man!

O then let me in time compound,
And parly with those conquering Eyes;
Ere they have try'd their force to wound,
Ere, with their glancing wheels, they drive
In Triumph over Hearts that strive,
And them that yield but more despise.
   Let me be laid,
Where I may see thy Glories from some shade

             (ll. 9–24)

Certainly, the vision is in part playful,[8] but it is also deliberately and imaginatively entertained. The possibility of a new reign so virtuous and beautiful that we might not be able to survive its perfections gives rise not only to some sense of willed "distancing," but also to the warning concerning the difficulties of such astonishing transformations of nature and to the caution that even transcendent mortals should undertake their attempts at reforms and new orders with care and a proper sense of danger:

Mean time, whilst every verdant thing
It self does at thy Beauty charm,
Reform the errours of the Spring;
Make that the Tulips may have share
Of sweetness, seeing they are fair;
And Roses of their thorns disarm:
   But most procure
That Violets may a longer Age endure.

> But O young beauty of the Woods,
> Whom Nature courts with fruits and flow'rs,
> Gather the Flow'rs, but spare the Buds;
> Lest *Flora* angry at thy crime,
> To kill her Infants in their prime,
> Do quickly make th' Example Yours;
>   And, ere we see,
> Nip in the blossome all our hopes and Thee.
>
> (ll. 25–40)

I do not believe the speaker here simply patronizes youthful notions that the "errors" of nature can be reformed nearer to the heart's desires; but he certainly wanrs that even a "Darling of the Gods" must recognize some limitations—the chief, that the reformations must not be such that they lead to the death of new life and the end of further promises of other, newer transformations.

Before Maria's appearance at the end of *Upon Appleton House* the poem has introduced us to the house and its history, the gardens, the meadows (grown, mowing, mown, and in flood) with all their images of man's active engagement in sacred and profane history, the woods and their multiple perspectives on retirement and the contemplative life. Along the way there have been numerous occasions when individuals acted decisively to change or try to change the course of history. The "*Suttle Nunns*" (l. 94) seduced Isabel Thwaites and attempted to "intercept" the destined "great Race" of the Fairfaxes (l. 248), but Sir William acted justly and bravely and his strength won the lady and assured the succeeding race of military heroes. The description of the gardens constructed as a five-bastioned fort provides the occasion for an apostrophe to England as the destroyed garden, an earthy paradise wasted by the Civil War:

> Oh Thou, that dear and happy Isle
> The Garden of the World ere while,
> Thou *Paradise* of four Seas,
> Which *Heaven* planted us to please,
> But, to exclude the World, did guard
> With watry if not flaming Sword;
> What luckless Apple did we tast,
> To make us Mortal, and Thee[9] Wast?
>
> (41:321–28)

In the former age,

> The *Gardiner* had the *Souldiers* place,
> And his more gentle Forts did trace.
> The Nursery of all things green
> Was then the only *Magazeen*.
> The *Winter Quarters* were the Stoves,
> Where he the tender Plants removes.
> But War all this doth overgrow:
> We Ord'nance Plant and Powder sow.

(43:338–44)

The description of the desolation of the world outside the estate at Appleton House contrasts sharply with the various delightful perspectives which the poem has developed for us within those bounds. It is more than understandable that a number of readers have read the lines that follow as covertly (or even openly) critical of the Lord General Fairfax for retiring from military and political life just at the moment when he could have restored England to something resembling its original garden state: doesn't anyone who could do so have the duty to do so? The position is sympathetic and seems almost unchallengeable, except that it ignores the limitation and the mystery concerning Fairfax's power which Marvell is careful to note in this poem of praise addressed to his patron: the restoration of England, like all other revolutionary or transforming historical events, depends not merely upon the abilities and will of the hero but also upon the will of God:

> And yet their walks one on the Sod
> Who, had it pleased him and *God*,
> Might once have made our Gardens spring
> Fresh as his own and flourishing.
> But he preferr'd to the *Cinque Ports*
> These five imaginary Forts:
> And, in those half-dry Trenches, spann'd
> Pow'r which the Ocean might command.

> For he did, with his utmost Skill,
> *Ambition* weed, but *Conscience* till.
> *Conscience*, that Heaven-nursed Plant,
> Which most our Earthly Gardens want.
> A prickling leaf it bears, and such
> As that which shrinks at ev'ry touch;
> But Flowrs eternal, and divine,
> That in the Crowns of Saints do shine.
>
> The sight does from these *Bastions* ply,
> Th' invisible *Artilery*;
> And at proud *Cawood Castle* seems
> To point the *Battery* of its Beams.
> As if it quarrell'd in the Seat
> Th' Ambition of its *Prelate* great.
> But ore the Meads below it plays,
> Or innocently seems to gaze.

(44-46:345-68)

In retiring in 1650 from the service of a government whose policy he could no longer support, Fairfax made a difficult choice of conscience: his "pleasure," the poem implies, was also God's. He will now engage in uprooting ambition and cultivating conscience in a life which may lead to sanctity as well as contemplative wisdom. The time for the new "deliverance" is not at hand, but Fairfax's garden fortress, symbol both of his political retirement and continuing moral warfare, seems to reprimand and threaten Cawood Castle, symbol of the Archbishop of York's misplaced (and now defeated) ambition: the *quality* of Fairfax still possesses the potentiality for intervention in history and for defeat of the powers of this world.

Only after the speaker's retreat from the meadows in flood into the woods and their intimations of allegories, "*mystick*" revelations, and ecstasy, does he return, at evening, after the flood, for relaxation and lazy fishing. But at the approach of Maria, he hides "Pleasures slight," thinking it a shame that such "judicious Eyes" as Maria's should surprise "a Man" with "such Toyes" as "Hooks," "Quills," and "Angles" (ll. 649-54):

> *She* that already is the *Law*
> Of all her *Sex*, her *Ages Aw*.

(82:655-56)

But his efforts at reformation are minor in comparison with those of Nature and the Sun, who act much as they do when confronted with divine transformation (or destruction) of their reigns in Milton's "Upon the Morning of Christ's Nativity":[10]

> See how loose Nature, in respect
> To her, it self doth recollect;
> And every thing so whisht and fine,
> Starts forth with to its *Bonne Mine*.
> The *Sun* himself, of *Her* aware,
> Seems to descend with greater Care;
> And lest *She* see him go to Bed;
> In blushing Clouds conceales his Head.
>
> (83:657–64)

It is possible to read these lines, as J.B. Leishman seems to in comparing them with Cleveland's "Upon Phyllis walking in a morning before sun-rising,"[11] merely as the usual pastoral hyperbole of the mistress as the civilizing reorderer of nature, playfully applied to a very young girl. But both the earlier descriptions of the occasions when Fairfaxes have or might have transformed the historical moment and the following elaborate simile of the magic moment when the vision of the kingfisher transforms nature make it difficult to do so:

> So when the Shadows laid asleep
> From underneath these Banks do creep,
> And on the River as it flows
> With *Eben Shuts* begin to close;
> The modest *Halcyon* comes in sight,
> Flying betwixt the Day and Night;
> And such an horror calm and dumb,
> *Admiring Nature* does benum.
>
> The viscous Air, wheres'ere She fly,
> Follows and sucks her Azure dy;
> The gellying Stream compacts below,
> If it might fix her shadow so;
> The stupid Fishes hang, as plain
> As *Flies* in *Chrystal* overt'ane;
> And Men the silent *Scene* assist,
> Charm'd with the *Saphir-winged Mist*.

Maria such, and so doth hush
The World, and through the *Ev'ning* rush.
No new-born *Comet* such a Train
Draws through the Skie, nor Star new-slain.
For streight those giddy Rockets fail,
Which from the putrid Earth exhale,
But by her *Flames*, in *Heaven* try'd,
Nature is wholly *vitrifi'd*.

(84–86:665–88)

The American reader may need to be reminded that the large kingfisher of eastern North America is quite unlike the small, brilliantly colored European kingfisher which Marvell describes so accurately and evocatively. The moment "betwixt the Day and Night" suggests the same light as that which Vaughan saw on "this hill" "After the Sun's remove" in "They are all gone into the world of light!" [12] the moment of afterglow which bathes everything in a new yellow intensity—pinks raised to salmons—a light that truly "tramples on" our days. The visionary light transforms the halcyon's metallic blue green to azure and sapphire. Before this vision nature's every benumbed element aspires to a condition of greater stability, men are charmed by the "*Saphir-winged Mist*," and time itself tries to stop as in anticipation of the ultimate purification and transformation of the universe we know.

These lines have moved rapidly from elaborate compliment to apocalyptic vision. Those that follow envision Maria more personally and familiarly, in this place and within a possible human future. She is the source of the virtues of Appleton House (she gave the gardens their beauty, the woods their "streightness," the meadow its sweetness, the river its purity), and the estate gratefully returns the gifts as a proper scenic frame for her. She aspires to "higher Beauties" and has learned languages "for the *Wisdome*, not the Noyse" (l. 710), since wisdom is "*Heavens Dialect*." Her wisdom extends to knowledge of how to "prevent" all the usual masculine methods of sexual siege—wisdom assisted by her training

In a *Domestick Heaven* nurst,
Under the *Discipline* severe
Of Fairfax, and the starry Vere.

(91:722–24)

She lives a reprimand to women who have placed all their "useless Study" on their faces and never dared "knit" their brows at vice for fear of causing wrinkles; Maria shows that only knowledge and virtue can fill all the furrows tilled by time. But ultimately, with maturity, her talismanic powers must leave Appleton House for the world of time and history outside:

> Hence *She* with Graces more divine
> Supplies beyond her *Sex* the *Line*;
> And, like a *sprig of Misleto*,
> On the *Fairfacian Oak* does grow;
> Whence, for some universal good,
> The *Priest* shall cut the sacred Bud;
> While her *glad Parents* most rejoice,
> And make their *Destiny* their *Choice*.
>
> (93:737–44)

Since there are no male heirs, there will be no more heroes named Fairfax who enter into the active life and change English history. But Maria will supply "beyond her *Sex* the *Line*" when "Fate her worthily translates, / And find[s] a *Fairfax* for our *Thwaites*." (ll. 747–48). The passage is a compliment both to Maria and to her family, and since it concerns the future, it is necessarily vague in its details. But I think the "*sprig of Misleto*" and the phrase "for some universal good" evoke the possibilities of future heroes whose destined interventions into and transformations of history may resemble those of Aeneas; such possibilities are supported not only by the past manifestations of Fairfacian virtue within the poem but also by the usual Marvellian expectations that the perfections of the retired or contemplative life will eventually be manifested in the active sphere. Despite the darkness of the final stanzas, the poem ends with openness to the possible promise of significant action, change, transformation. Marvell could not have anticipated that numbers of later readers, with hindsight of the fact that Maria Fairfax's politic marriage to George Villiers, second Duke of Buckingham, resulted in unhappiness and no legitimate issue, find it difficult to respond to the hopes as anything but ironic.

The First Anniversary of the Government under O.C. (pp. 108–19) (published originally, and anonymously, in 1655 as *The First Anniversary of the Government under His Highness* The Lord Protector)

celebrates more fully than *An Horatian Ode* astonishing past political
and social change, and it looks forward to apocalyptic possibilities.
Cromwell has now demonstrated that he differs from "Man":

> Like the vain Curlings of the Watry maze,
> Which in smooth streams a sinking Weight does raise;
> So Man, declining alwayes, disappears
> In the weak Circles of increasing Years;
> And his short Tumults of themselves Compose,
> While flowing Time above his Head does close.
> *Cromwell* alone with greater Vigour runs,
> (Sun-like) the Stages of succeeding Suns;
> And still the Day which he doth next restore,
> Is the just Wonder of the Day before.
> *Cromwell* alone doth with new Lustre spring,
> And shines the Jewel of the yearly Ring.
>
> (ll. 1–12)

He has accomplished more in one year than monarchs in platonic
years. While monarchs contribute as little to the music of history
as images that "with vain Scepter, strike the hourly Bell" (l. 41)
or as "wooden Heads unto the Viols strings" (l. 44), Cromwell is
the master musician who has outdone Amphion by charming not
only all the recalcitrant elements of nature for the building of
"Th'harmonious City", but the even more difficult material of the
"Minds of stubborn Men" for the construction of the miraculous
Commonwealth:

> The Commonwealth does through their Centers all
> Draw the Circumf'rence of the publique Wall;
> The crossest Spirits here do take their part,
> Fast'ning the Contignation which they thwart;
> And they, whose Nature leads them to divide,
> Uphold, this one, and that the other Side;
> But the most Equal still sustein the Height,
> And they as Pillars keep the Work upright;
> While the resistance of opposed Minds,
> The Fabrick as with Arches stronger binds,
> Which on the Basis of a Senate free,
> Knit by the Roofs Protecting weight agree.
>
> (ll. 87–98)

From that basis, Cromwell has become the new Archimedes who "hurles e'r since the World about him round." (l. 100).

This astonishing achievement, this apparently supernatural intervention in the ordinary workings of nature and the social forms and traditions of the past, is not the end of time—although it may prove to be the prelude to that end. It is impossible to determine to what degree the details of the biblical Apocalypse reflect Marvell's private convictions or hopes and to what degree they are introduced as a method of undercutting and redirecting the attacks which the more radical groups to whom the poem alludes hostilely (Fifth Monarchists, Quakers, Ranters, and Anabaptists) were making against Cromwell at the time. At any rate the poem argues, "If these the Times, then this must be the Man" (l. 144). Cromwell has demonstrated almost divine capacities for leadership; not knowing (as no one can know) "where Heavens choice may light," he, like Milton's unfallen angels, "Girds yet his Sword, and ready stands to fight" (ll. 147–48). If the people of England and foreign leaders as well will follow Cromwell, and *if* it is heaven's will, then Cromwell may begin the millennial kingdom.

The poem stands open to that extraordinary possibility. But the human elements—the opposition of the foreign princes, hostility at home, chance (as in Cromwell's nearly fatal carriage accident in Hyde Park on 29 September 1654), and the very fact of Cromwell's human mortality—all seem to foreshadow, in the midst of the celebration of the anniversary, that the divine possibilities will not be fulfilled, that heaven has not willed that this should be the time. The foreign princes care nothing for the "great Designes":

> But mad with Reason, so miscall'd, of State
> They know them not, and what they know not, hate.
> Hence still they sing Hosanna to the Whore,
> And her whom they should Massacre adore:[13]
> But Indians whom they should convert, subdue;
> Nor teach, but traffique with, or burn the Jew.
>
> (ll. 111–16)

The ultimate argument against the immediate establishment of the kingdom of God is that sin itself (the poem develops at length the sins of the radical opposition, "Accursed Locusts, whom your

King does spit / Out of the Center of th'unbottom'd Pit" ll. 311–11)
will necessarily delay it:

> But Men alas, as if they nothing car'd,
> Look on, all unconcern'd, or unprepar'd;
> And Stars still fall, and still the Dragons Tail
> Swinges the Volumes of its horrid Flail.[14]
> For the great Justice that did first suspend
> The World by Sin, does by the same extend.
> Hence that blest Day still counterpoysed wastes,
> The Ill delaying, what th'Elected hastes;
> Hence landing Nature to new Seas is tost,
> And good Designes still with their Authors lost.
>
> (ll. 149–58)

Divine justice seems likely to determine that "we" have deserved
neither our heroic leader nor the sight of ultimate perfection.

The last part of the poem defines and defends Cromwell's
actions in the past and present and attacks his enemies. At the time
of the accident in Hyde Park, when the rumor circulated that
Cromwell had been killed, "we" first despaired, like the first man
who searched mournfully all night in the west for the departed sun;

> When streight the Sun behind him he descry'd,
> Smiling serenely from the further side.
>
> (ll. 341–42)

The hostile foreign princes provide the climactic tribute to the
miracle of Charles's and England's revivals. The poet's final direct
address to Cromwell balances delicately the greatness of the present
achievement with the fragility of its complete dependence upon
Cromwell's life:

> Pardon, great Prince, if thus their Fear or Spight
> More then our Love and Duty do thee Right.
> I yield, nor further will the Prize contend;
> So that we both alike may miss our End:
> While thou thy venerable Head dost raise
> As far above their Malice as my Praise.
> And as the *Angel* of our Commonweal,
> Troubling the Waters, yearly mak'st them Heal.
>
> (ll. 395–402)

Cromwell, the great disturber who ruined "the great Work of Time,/And cast the Kingdome old/Into another Mold," has proved to be the divine agent of healing as well as change.[15] In the vision of the poem, no more than stagnant waters is a static, traditional society likely to provide such healing. The last line clearly implies that without Cromwell, an "untroubled" England will lose its participation in God's "healing" and continuing revelations of divine purpose within historical change.

Not many readers have found "Bermudas" (pp. 17–18) seriously concerned with historical or political matters. Sometimes dismissed as a charming if rather odd trifle, it has also been read as a difficult if not baffling poem and even as a covert attack on its Puritan singers as hypocritical and theologically unsound—primarily, it seems, on the assumption that Puritans should not repond to the sensuous pleasures of an earthly paradise.[16] A number of years ago however, Rosalie Colie remarked on the importance of the historical religious and political elements of the poem:

> over and over again in this literature [concerning the early settlement of Bermuda] we read the colonists' fear of Spanish attack and their hatred of Catholicism, together with their self-consciousness of the peculiar grace granted them and their island. So Marvell's singing oarsmen too exalt God's praise to "Heavens Vault" in the hope that it "perhaps rebounding may/Echho beyond the *Mexique Bay*," proclaiming the English God and his territories on the sea-winds of the New World.[17]

Later, in *"My Ecchoing Song": Andrew Marvell's Poetry of Criticism*, Colie stated succinctly the thematic complexities of the poem:

> "Bermudas" entwines the Exodus theme with the language of earthly paradise and of the psalms of praise, enclosing its ecphrastic vignette in a frame intelligible to contemporaries, who knew about the pieties expressed by the Virginia Company in offering a haven to exiles "Safe from the Storm, and Prelat's Rage" and were aware of the challenge from idolators "beyond the *Mexique Bay*." An exemplum-poem, its message clear in spite of its spotty explication and indefinite application, "Bermudas" compresses many traditions

into small space, and enlarges the spectacle of earthly paradise to include thematic considerations generally foreign to that ideal, encapsulated space.[18]

Later in the volume she described the way this poem, like "The Garden," shares a certain mysteriousness with some of Marvell's other lyrics, so that "it seems to hold 'more'" at each reading:

> We know a great deal about the poem and its content, perhaps even its occasion. . . . What we do not know, though, is what is going on in this poem. What are the people up to, in that "small Boat, that row'd along?" . . . We seem, like the "list'ning Winds," simply to overhear the oarsmen's psalm of praise about the island's supernatural wonders. Though in this poem the themes of withdrawal and emergence, characteristic of so much of Marvell's poetry, are clear enough, and we think we know something of the specific reasons for withdrawal ("the Storms, and Prelat's rage"), the reasons for and the direction of emergence remain concealed. These singing oarsmen go about their business, perhaps also about their Father's, but they do not tell us just what their errand is.[19]

If we read the poem in the light of those poems which celebrate and anticipate astonishing, near apocalyptic change, we will still find it wonderfully resonant and suggestive, but the "mysteries" may no longer seem so puzzling or disturbing. The central hymn is clearly placed by the framing introduction and conclusion which suggest solutions to many of the problems:

> Where the remote *Bermudas* ride
> In th' Oceans boome unespy'd,
> From a small Boat, that row'd along,
> The listning Winds receiv'd this Song.

(ll. 1–4)

> Thus sung they, in the *English* boat,
> An holy and a chearful Note,
> And all the way, to guide their Chime,
> With falling Oars they kept the time.

(ll. 37–40)

With such an authoritative evaluation in the conclusion, it would seem misplaced ingenuity which would try to prove that the "note" of the hymn is neither holy nor cheerful. The opening lines establish our distance both from the experience and the song of these singers: we can only imaginatively "overhear" what, after their remarkable deliverance and in their new paradise distant from England, they sing. Despite some readers' impressions, they have not just arrived on the islands (so far as I know, no colonists rowed across the Atlantic); they now live in the Bermudas and they know them well. Since we are not told why they are in the "small Boat, that row'd along," it surely does not much matter—although rowing must have been the most common way of going from one settlement along the coast to another, from one island to another, or simply of going out to fish.

The hymn itself begins with the inevitability, for these people, of praise to God:

> What should we do but sing his Praise
> That led us through the watry Maze,
> Unto an Isle so long unknown,
> And yet far kinder than our own?
>
> (ll. 5–8)

Where "Sea-Monsters" are wrecked, they have been delivered, safe both from "Storms and Prelat's rage." The line, "He lands us on a grassy Stage" (II), does not pretend to describe literally the nature of the Bermuda coast, but the pastoral "stage" on which may be played a new scene in the masque of the unfolding of the divine will in history—remarkably different from the "*Tragick Scaffold*" of Charles I's last scene, but perhaps of ultimately greater significance. The central lines, 13 to 28, describe magically the wonders of the "eternal Spring" of this earthly paradise which has been provided as their refuge: fowls and fruit and beauty surpassing the artifices of man. Those lines are climaxed by the reference to the gift of the "pearl of great price," the Gospel (Matt. 13:46):

He cast (of which we rather boast)
The Gospels Pearl upon our Coast.
And in these Rocks for us did frame
A Temple, where to sound his Name.
Oh let our Voice his Praise exalt,
Till it arrive at Heavens Vault:
Which thence (perhaps) rebounding, may
Eccho beyond the *Mexique Bay*.

(ll. 29–36)

There is no question here of giving "that which is holy unto the dogs" or casting "pearls before swine."[20] These singers fully value the preciousness of the "Pearl." Grateful for their blessings, they end their hymn with a return to its opening: "What should we do but sing his Praise?" With the gift of the Gospel and the "Temple" (a *place* where they may worship), they will praise until their version of Magnificat reaches "Heavens Vault." The "perhaps" in the final lines represents neither their nor Marvell's "scepticism" or "irony," but the proper diffidence concerning the precise ways in which their moment of beatitude and triumphant delivery may be reflected back upon the larger world of God's actions and purposes in history. The playful physicality of "From thence (perhaps) rebounding, may / Eccho beyond the *Mexique Bay*" shadows clearly the possibility that the praise of this new center of "purified" protestant worship may give rise to revolutionary religious and political changes both in the Spanish and Portuguese centers of Catholic power in the New World and even beyond them.

The last lines are extraordinary. Rather than merely singing in order to make the work go faster in the way that most people use chanties, these oarsmen seem to row in order to "guide the Chime" of their song. A bit like both Milton's good angels and the Cromwell of the *First Anniversary*, these singers remain alert to the possibility that they will be chosen as instruments for God's plans. They carefully and deliberately subordinate their labor to their song; but their labor has provided the means by which "they kept the time," not only of this hymn of praise and of this moment of history, but of a present open to unknown future possibilities.

Most poets, like most other people, either imagine that they live in relatively stable worlds where the future will be very much like the past (the changes that do occur will follow the recurrent rhythms of the seasons), or, if they do imagine (or even experience) radical changes, they respond to them either with horror or with fanatical devotion to a sacred cause. Seventeenth-century Englishmen, knew that their world was not stable. Part of Marvell's distinction is not only that he responded fully and imaginatively to the signal public events of his time (the Civil War, the regicide, Cromwell's military victories, Fairfax's retirement, the Protectorate, the colonial ventures, the death of Cromwell, the Restoration), but also that he remained both sensitively and realistically alert to notions of future radical or ideal change, the gains as well as losses of both their fulfillment and their failure. Marvell envisaged man as achieving at least part of his humanity within social and political life, and he seems to have thought that the mysterious and providential human possibilities were not yet exhausted.

Notes

1. *Politics, Language and Time, Essays in Political Thought and History* (London; Atheneum, 1972), pp. 83–84.

2. *Renaissance News* 10 (1957): 75–79.

3. *Puritanism and Revolution: Studies in Interpretation of the English Revolution of the 17th Century* (London: Secker and Warburg, 1958), pp. 337–66. The essay was first published in *Modern Quarterly*, no. 4 (1946): 6–31.

4. *The Rehearsal Transpros'd and The Rehearsal Transpros'd The Second Part*, ed. D.I.B. Smith (Oxford: Oxford University Press, 1971), pp. 133–35.

5. I find largely persuasive John M. Wallace's analysis of the rhetorical audience of the poem in *Destiny His Choice: The Loyalism of Andrew Marvell* (Cambridge: Cambridge University Press, 1968), pp. 69–105. While less concerned with audience, Donald M. Friedman's *Marvell's Pastoral Art* (Beckeley and Los Angeles: University of California Press, 1970), pp. 153–75, gives a sensitive and politically alert reading of the poem. I wrote a few pages on the poem in *The Heirs of Donne and Jonson* (London: Oxford University Press, 1970), pp. 167–71.

6. *Metaphysical, Baroque and Precieux Poetry* (Oxford: Oxford University Press, 1953).

7. Friedman remarked on the relationship between the poem in *Marvell's Pastoral Art*, p. 241. I attempted a fairly deatailed reading of "Little T.C." in "Marvell's 'Nature,'" *ELH* 20 (1953): 121–35.

8. Cf. Frank J. Warnke, *Versions of Baroque: European Literature in the Seven-*

teenth Century (New Haven: Yale University Press, 1972), pp. 108–22, on the sense of "play" throughout Marvell's poetry.

9. Margoliouth reads *The.* I print the reading of Wilkinson's copy of *1681,* noted by Legouis, 1:72.

10. The parallels are noted by E.E. Duncan-Jones, *Poems and Letters,* 1:291.

11. *The Art of Marvell's Poetry* (London: Hutchiuson University Library, 1966), pp. 80–82, 224–25.

12. Henry Vaughan, *The Works,* ed. L.C. Martin, 2nd ed., (London: Oxford University Press, 1957), pp. 483–84.

13. "Her whom they should Massacre" is the Whore of Babylon, the Antichrist. In *Antichrist in Seventeenth Century England* (London: Oxford University Press, 1971), pp. 100–107, 128–31, Christopher Hill notes the manner in which many Protestants in midcentury moved from the earlier identification of the Antichrist with Rome to its identification with other centers of corruption or persecution. Here, the poet promises that his "Muse shall hollow far behind / Angelique *Cromwell*" as he "Pursues the Monster thorough every Throne: / Which shrinking to her *Roman* Den impure, / Gnashes her Goary teeth; nor there secure" (ll. 125–30) Rome's is the ultimate "Den," but "thorough every Throne" may imply that she has a number of others, not necessarily limited to the thrones of Catholic princes.

14. I find it difficult to remember exactly Milton's line when I read Marvell's: it is, "Swinges the scaly horror of his folded tail" ("On the Morning of Christ's Nativity," l. 172).

15. Legouis's note (1:328) that "Cromwell troubles the waters when he takes great decisions, alone," seems to limit too precisely the implications of the final lines.

16. See R.M. Cummings, "The Difficulty of Marvell's 'Bermudas,'" *MP* 67 (1970): 331–40, and Tay Fitzdale, *ELH* 43 (1975): 203–13. Toshihiko Kawasaki, by contrast, thinks the "flaws" are the poet's: "It seems that he indulged his inveterate regressive dream and built his own island paradise in the air" ("Marvell's 'Bermudas'—A Little World, or a New World?" *ELH* 43 [1976]: 43). Kawassaki admits (p. 44) a minimal historical concern: "This last line, if any, testifies to Marvell's indebtedness to Oxenbridge's evangelism, or, at least, to some aspects of the general expansionist tendency rampant in the Protestant England of the mid-seventeenth century."

17. *Renaissance News* 10 (1957): 78.

18. (Princeton; Princeton University Press, 1970), p. 22.

19. Ibid., 141.

20. Matt. 7:6. That there *were* swine in Bermuda may be interesting, but the fact is not mentioned in the poem.

MARVELL AND THE MASQUE

MURIEL C. BRADBROOK

THROUGHOUT THE sixteenth and seventeenth centuries, different poetic forms moved into the foreground or receded into the background, not only according to the practice of poets but according to the social influences and pressures that worked, now through one poetic channel, now through another. Between the flowering of Elizabethan poetry and the arrival of the Augustan city, the shift from lyric and narrative to dramatic poetry and its reversal follow the ebb and flow of popular sympathy and concern. Dramatic poetry was at first deeply influenced by the rhetorical patterns of Senecan lament and Petrarchan sonnet; when in mid-Jacobean times power ebbed from this great form and the poetry of meditation developed, lyric became the exploratory and sensitive tool. With the deepening of social conflict, poets turned to "the paradise within," each evolving his own blend of themes and images.[1] In the reign of Charles I, particularly that part known as "the eleven years' Tyranny," when he ruled without a Parliament (1629–40), the political effects of courtly poetry were achieved through pastoral and masque.

The masque, an expansion of language beyond that customary in the public theater, depended on song, dance, spectacle, company and occasion. Inigo Jones had triumphed over the rejected Jonson, so that spectacle and variety, rapidly changing and elaborate scenes provided a nonverbal language of ambiguity, while the actual words were "frozen" in set patterns of praise. Ancient ruins and modern architecture, grotesque antimasques in great profusion leading by vistas to the great transformation scene were used by the architect and engineer to convey all the wonder, elevation, and rapture which the poets had termed "delight." The power and glory of the masque lay in its costumes, its whirling light effects, its rapid shifts of scene, its ever more complicated cloud machines, bringing heaven down to earth.[2]

The king's Arcadia, almost a little Versailles before Louis XIV, was presided over by Charles and his queen (who attended Black-friars and even, with her French ladies, enacted *The Shepherd's Paradise*). However, the more refined their courtly games, the more Charles and his circle cut themselves off from ambitious young men who renounced court ambitions—like George Herbert, who built a temple to which in later years Crashaw added the steps, Knivet the gallery and Christopher Harvey an adjacent synagogue.

Among the products of Herbert's university and of his college, Trinity, was Andrew Marvell, whose roots were in the Puritan north, but who, as an undergraduate, ran away to join the Jesuits (from whom he was recovered by his father). Marvell, who saw the case for both sides in the growing conflict, was to remain a patient builder of bridges, a moderate thinker in an age when moderation was an active notion unrelated to neutrality. He drew the narrow elegance of Caroline courtly life back into poetry of much wider scope, if of more inward and solitary concern.

Marvell's lyrics, the best of which tend to be about retirement, apply the Arcadianism of Charles' court to the situation created by its collapse. When on 6 November 1632, Gustavus Adolphus was killed in Germany, one writer of court masques wrote a lament, only to be answered by another:

> Tourneyes, Masques, Theaters better become
> Our *Halcyon* dayes; what though the German Drum
> Bellow for freedome and revenge, the noyse
> Concerns us not, nor should divert our joyes;
> Nor ought the thunder of their Carabins
> Drowne the sweet Ayres of our tun'd Violins;[3]

Marvell wrote when the thunder of Carabins had been heard in England, when another king had been killed, in circumstances unparalleled, by his own subjects. From a Yorkshire garden, among haymakers and neatherds, he addressed his country:

O Thou, that dear and happy Isle,
The Garden of the World erewhile,
Thou *Paradise* of four Seas,
Which *Heaven* planted us to please,
But to exclude the World, did guard
With watry if not flaming Sword,
What luckless Apple did we tast,
To make us Mortal, and the Wast?

Upon Appleton House 41:321–28

The court masque has amply shewn itself to be the predominant dramatic form of the reign of Charles I.[4] In spite of the previous efforts of Ben Jonson, it was no longer literary, but a ritual of dance, song, and display—"Power conceived as art"—in which the king and queen, appearing in person, enacted the harmony they claimed to dispense over their kingdom. For this, the disguise of a shepherd or shepherdess (in costly robes), as representing the humblest level of their subjects, enabled the central figures to create a suggestion of unity—even if we are reminded by Henrietta Maria not so much of the old Shepherds' Play as of the Petit Trianon. The two central figures dispensed a godlike power; to be efficacious, the monarchy must be the center of the rite.

But *Ceres* corn, and *Flora* is the Spring,
   Bacchus is wine, the country is the *King*.
      (*The Last Instructions to a* Painter ll. 974–75)

wrote Marvell many years later, uniting in this couplet the chief figures of Nabbes's masque, *The Glory of the Spring*.[5]

Charles would present a Christmas masque to his queen, she would return him one at Shrovetide. Their marital felicity and irradiating virtue as "Hymen's twin, the Mary-Charles,"[6] constituted a political act; "to control the way the people saw the monarch was to control their response to the royal policy as well." Unfortunately these politics of display were confined to the court and the visiting ambassadors. Moreover, this celebration of cosmic harmony often gave occasion to great disorder—maneuvering for places and precedence, pilfering and pillaging, although Charles himself, unlike his father, remained a model of decorum. He was intensely concerned with his own image; his role modulates, no doubt at his own dictation, from heroic lover to triumphant emperor, to the stellified successor to Jove, to the ruler of the ocean (and imposer of ship money), finally to the patient, long-suffering, Christlike Philogenes of the last masque, danced when war with the Scots had already begun.[7]

The courtiers were in turn offered homage by their servants, the musicians and the players in the antimasques. These latter might be critical—those in *The Masque of Peace*, for instance, criticize Charles's licensing of "projectors"—but all such dissidence was "purged" before the dazzling epiphany of the finale.

Charles was a small man, but at the centre of *Salmacida Spolia*, at the apex of a throne was "his Majesty highest in a seat of gold" which had the effect of giving him physical predominance. The scene might be diminished to scale, the torchbearers might be children. The costumes, costly but fantastic, gave, as it were, a new identity to the masquers. To move out of the frame into the dancing place was itself a wonder, a sort of incarnational descent of the god.

Thomas Carew's *Coelum Brittanicum* (Shrovetide, 1633) displaces all the heavenly deities, in their bestial forms of the zodiac, to replace them by the British monarch.[8] It opens with the impresa of the Lion and the Lily, for the king and queen. Various claimants to divine rule, including Pleasure and Five Senses, are banished before the masquers emerge from a hill which grows out the earth. After the masquers' dance

> the scaene againe is varied into a new and pleasant prospect cleane differing from all the other, the nearest part shewing a delicious garden with severall walks and perterra's set round with low trees, and on the sides against these walkes, were fountains and grots, and in the furthest part a Palace, from which went high walkes upon Arches, and above them open Tarraces planted with Cypresse trees, and all this together was composed of such Ornaments as might expresse a Princely Villa.
>
> (*Poems*, p. 181)

The final scene, in which the gods were displaced, showed Windsor Castle and the new stars, of which one, more great and eminent than all the rest, figured His Majesty.

Here can be seen the sort of images that Marvell was to use in "A Dialogue Between the Resolved Soul and Created Pleasure," for different ends, and in "Upon the Hill and Grove at Billborough," to ends quite opposed to those of the masque.

Carew's pastoral dialogues in miniature form develop the roles of individual masquers; they transform the social rite into a more personal one. *An Hymeneall Dialogue between Bride and Groom* (with Chorus) opens:

> *Groom:* Tell me (my love) since Hymen ty'de
> The holy knot, hast thou not felt
> A new infused spirit slide
> Into thy brest, whilst thine did melt?
>
> *Bride:* First tell me (sweet) whose words were those?
> For though your voyce the ayre did break
> Yet did my soul the sence compose
> And through your lips my heart did speake.
>
> (*Poems*, p. 66, ll. 1–8)

The two pastoral dialogues present shepherd and nymphs enjoying each other, but each within a little frame of dramatic situation—the intruding Thyrsis, or the singers who present the aubade of parting lovers. These lyrics were set by Walter Porter or Henry Lawes (he gave one of the pastoral dialogues to two tenors or trebles, with thorough bass).

The mention of Lawes is sufficient to recall that it was his brother William who published Milton's *Comus*, as well as supplying the music and apparently playing in the original performance, at which those experienced masquers, the youthful Lady Alice Egerton (who had danced in *Tempe Restored* at court), and her two brothers took the leading parts. Milton's masque against masquing, his plea for temperance in a form traditionally used for extravagant display, appropriated the convention against which the masque at Ludlow Castle exerts its force. The chariot of Sabrina—the deity who resolves all enchantments, goddess of chastity, of the River Severn —rises out of the fresh stream adorned with gems, for Sabrina is the daughter of a king. She is summoned by a song and she appears singing in reply. That she may represent the ancient British church, sprinkling sacred and baptismal drops, is suggested by the prayer for her prosperity with which the episode concludes—a prayer which no goddess should need. "Sprung of old Anchises' line," she rises from the waters and as she sinks back, the Lady herself rises from the enchanted chair, and the action moves forward.

Milton was writing after the attack of Prynne had made clear Puritan hostility to the masque, but this hostility was sporadic. When Cromwell came to full power he himself commissioned a masque from James Shirley for the entertainment of the French ambassador, and for the wedding of his daughter Mary, Andrew Marvell composed a pair of songs in the tradition of the masque-pastoral, where the lady appears first by proxy in duet as a goddess, Cynthia, then in a more equal match, celebrated by the common people, as Marina, bride of "the Northern Shepherd's son."

A number of Marvell's poems were set to music—"A Dialogue between Thyrsis and Dorinda" by John Gamble and by Matthew Locke, and also by William Lawes, who modified it (see Legovis' Commentary in *Poems*, p. 248). Lawes was killed when Marvell was but twenty-three, so that the poem is placed among the works of his youth. Carew, who was twenty-seven years older than Marvell, died when Marvell was only nineteen, but the poems were printed the same year (1640). Marvell was eight years later to write commendatory verses for Lovelace's *Lucasta*. The elegies on Lord Hastings (who died 24 June 1649) and the son of the great lord of earlier masquing, Francis Villiers (killed 7 July 1648) employ the imagery of a "great Turnament" followed by a masque in which the gods are revealed by the drawing of a "veil" (or "traverse"):[9]

> Onely they drooping *Hymenaeus* note
> Who for sad *Purple*, tears his *Saffron*-coat
> And trails his *Torches* th'row the Starry Hall
> Reversed, at his *Darlings* Funeral

(ll. 43–46)

and by a "serious imitation" of fight, which ends in the hero constructing a "pyramid" of bodies for his sepulcher, so that his death really sounds like some kind of martial game between Love and Death. It was part of Marvell's wit to use the conventions of emblematic art in new and startling contexts as, later, he was to use the ritual of the masque for Puritanical sentiments.

Two pictorial companion pieces, "The Unfortunate Lover"

and "The Gallery," are conceived in action as a series of transformation scenes: the first opening with "a masque of quarrelling elements," the second presenting contrasting pairs of humours— Clora the murderess, Clora as the dawn goddess; Clora as a witch, and Clora as Venus. All these pictures furnish the lover's mind, his interior palace, but his favorite is that of the simple shepherdess "with which I first was took." In each poem the scenes depict energetic action; so too, "The Picture of Little T.C. in a Prospect of Flowers" follows the lively activities of the child, and looks forward to the even livelier activities of her girlhood.

Carew could combine masque writing with lyric as two equally acceptable forms of courtly exercise, for he was naturally in the circuit of the court, son of Sir Matthew Carew, of the old Cornish family, and cousin to Raleigh; his friend Aurelian Townshend came from the gentry of Norfolk (the seat was at Dereham). Milton, son of the City of London, could by use of paradox, exercise himself in the masque form; but Marvell, son of a Yorkshire vicarage, and Milton's junior by more than a decade, could not directly employ all that vanished with the outbreak of civil war. He could, however, through the force of its images transmute and use this obsolete political rite to add depth and energy, to give to his lyric that special drive and momentum which characterizes it, while within the poems the social consequences of the breaking of old patterns produced tragic ironies. The perplexed and troubled conscience, the divided loyalties of the men who lived through so many changes of government in church and state, could be reunited only by toil within "the quick forge and working house of thought." Marvell's handful of lyrics, produced as prologue to a long and active political career, represent, in the most concentrated form, this search for a new stability in a "shattered frame."

The use of masque and pastoral as suppressed or as undersong can be discerned in such lyrics as "The Coronet," or the pastoral "Dialogue between Thyris and Dorinda," a poem of unexpected obscurity (it was printed in the Folio between two political poems and, as we note above had wide success with a musical setting). The persona in "The Coronet," (pp. 14–15), who openly rejects earthly for Christian worship, also subsequently recognizes that even the second is corrupted with worldliness. The argument of the poem moved through thesis and antithesis to synthesis. The first verse "dismantles" the "towers" that adorned the shepherdess's head, but within the new crown

> Alas I find the Serpent old
> That, twining in his speckled breast,
> About the flow'rs disguis'd does fold
> With wreaths of Fame and Interest.
>
> (ll. 13–16)

The serpent in Eden is fatal; but in terms of earthly wisdom the serpent in chaplet form was a symbol of eternity. As such, he appeared as the scepter or emblem of that power in the final tableau of *Coelum Britannicum*:

> ... the great Cloud began to breake open, out of which stroke beames of light; in the midst, suspended in the Ayre, sate Eternity on a Globe, his Garment was of a light blue, wrought all over with Stars of gold, and bearing in his hand a Serpent bent into a circle, with his taile in his mouth. (ll. 1075–80)
>
> (*Poems*, p. 182)

In the final verse, Marvell appeals to the Lord whom he had designed to honour, "But thou, who only could's the Serpent tame ..." either to pluck out the Serpent, or trample on both him and the poet's offering, so that the "broken frame" may "crown thy Feet, that could not crown thy Head." Chapman and Donne had appropriated the coronet to pious uses, but this renunciation ends with a new image that might well have featured in the galleries of the Most Catholic Majesty.

The "Dialogue between Thyrsis and Dorinda" (pp. 19–21) begins with praise of an Elysium where the lovers may, after death, "pass Eternity away":

> Oh, ther's, neither hope nor fear
> There's no Wolf, no Fox, nor Bear.
> . . . .
> No Oat-pipe's needfull, there thine Ears
> May feast with Musick of the Spheres.
>
> (ll. 21–22, 25–26)

That shepherd's paradise, which Henrietta Maria had brought down to earth, had been sadly recognized by the great Elizabethan pastoralist, Drayton, in his latest work, *The Muses Elysium* (1630) as only a "paradise within":

> That faire Felicia which was but of late,
> Earth's Paradice, that never had her peere,
> Stands now in that most lamentable state
> . . . .
> The little infant on the mothers lap
> for want of fire shall be so sore distrest,
> That while it draws the lank and empty pap,
> The tender lips shall freeze unto the breast;
> The quaking cattle which their warmstall want . . .
> The hungry crows shall with their caryon feast.
>   ("The Tenth Nymphall" ll. 65–67, 93–97.)[10]

The last and greatest crime is that of the men who fell all the trees till the land "stands disrob'd of all her rich attire," so that any wanting timber to build are constrained to dig caves in the ground. Drayton, now an old man, presents himself as the satyr who has strayed over the mountains into the Muses' country; this piteous renunciation of all that he had sung as a pastoralist must itself be put in pastoral terms, as the welcoming shepherds promise him vengeance:

> Here live in blisse, till thou shalt see those slaves
> Who thus set vertue and desert at nought;
> Some sacrific'd upon their grandsires graves,
> And some like beasts in markets sold and bought
> . . . .
> Until those base Felicians thou shalt heare,
> By that vile nation captived again,
> That many a glorious age their captives were.
>   ("The Tenth Nymphall" ll. 137–40, 146–48)

Marvell then had precedent for the ironic use of pastoral; the Elysium that Thyrsis and Dorinda seek is very like Drayton's:

> There, sheep are full
> Of sweetest grass and softest wooll
> . . . .
> Shepherds there, bear equal sway,
> And every Nimph's a Queen of *May*
>
> (ll. 31–32, 37–38)

They depart to drink wine mingled with poppy, "so shall we smoothly pass away in sleep."

This apparent sanction of suicide gives an accurate if mordant view of successful court pastoralism, at the same time, of course, as it suggests (if the religious interpretation is favored) a "life beyond the grave." For at all events, this is not the life of middle earth. The implicit rejection of pastoral and the serene realms of the masquers' Arcadia gives sharpness to this lyric, and it makes it, like *Lycidas*, an indictment of the "blind mouths." The soothing, too innocent set of questions and answers suggests (in their tone and movement) an unconvincing ignorance. Of course, those who can never resist the pun on "die" will take another meaning, but this lyric, to my mind, carries a political as well as a personal dimension; its Bower of Bliss no longer offers the harmless play of Arcadia.

An Horatian Ode may be placed between Cromwell's return from Ireland and his departure for Scotland, that is, between May and July 1650. In the opening lines, Caesar's crossing of the Rubicon is recalled in a reference to Lucan; but Cromwell urges his "active Star" to a more than Caesarean birth, in violence beyond that of the Unfortunate Lover. He cut his way through his own party (he was soon to supersede Fairfax as Commander-in-Chief), went burning through the air

> And *Caesar's* head at last
> Did through his Laurels blast.
>
> (ll. 23–24)

This triumph, however, is also a "ruin"; and the royal actor on his tragic scaffold still carried a "helpless right."

Here Marvell was accurately reflecting the ironies of the moment when Charles stepped out from under the great painted ceiling of the Banqueting Hall, with its apotheosis of James I. He was beheaded at

the door of his own theater; his world of fragile images had been smashed by Cromwell's "Trust in God and keep your powder dry."

The building that has been begun is Capitoline, but the two rivals for the chief part in this tragic masque have discerned divided roles. It has been observed that "there are two Cromwells in the poem, the scourge of God and the leader of His chosen people."[11] The Royalists themselves had derived the king's right from ancient conquest till the war went against them; Cromwell tried to persuade Charles that trial by battle registered the judgment of God.[12]

The strength and anguish of the images breaks through the calm frame of Horatian verse. It has been remarked that if the poem shows poise and urbanity, it is the poise and urbanity of a man on the rack. The degree of shock which the execution sent through all England can still be traced in the poems written at Nunappleton, where Marvell resided for two years from early in 1651 to early in 1653 in company with Fairfax, the man of conscience who would not lead an expedition against the Scots, from which the poet soon emerged resolved to spend his time in the public cause. Nunappleton was for Marvell what, centuries later, Coole Park became for Yeats.

In celebrating Nunappleton, Marvell drew upon the Horatian tradition of the country house poem,[13] to which Jonson had contributed in *To Penshurst*, his poem to Sir R. Wroth, Carew in his poems on Saxham and Wrest, Herrick in his panegyric to Sir Lewis Pemberton.[14] In all these, the modest, useful center of hospitality is contrasted with more ostentatious buildings. Nunappleton House was finished only in 1649, but it was a traditional place, except indeed for its elaborate garden. Marvell is able therefore to praise Fairfax in terms of his modesty, his sobriety, and his preference for good human relationships:

> A stately *Frontispiece of Poor*
> Adorns without the open Door;
> Nor less the Rooms within commends
> Daily new *Furniture of Friends*.
>
> (9:65–68)

At a time when most architecture was designed for ostentation more than use, this house which had been designed so that "things greater are in less contain'd" expands to admit the greatness of the Lord General,

> But where he comes the swelling Hall
> Stirs, and the *Square* grows *Spherical*;
>
> (7:50–51)

Alteration of scale, like that of the masque, enlarges the central figure; Marvell is giving to Fairfax the kind of praise that the masquers gave to royalty, but he is paradoxically giving it in praise of an abdication of power. An ancestor had burst through the walls of another house of retirement, a nunnery, to claim his bride; Fairfax has built in the gardens a mimic fort with five bastions, but "as aiming one for every sense." His endeavor, like that in the struggle between the resolved soul and created pleasure, mounts by humility.

The playful development of floral salutes and parades may recall the pastoral world of Henrietta Maria as Chloris[15] or the gallantries of Lovelace's *Amarantha, a Pastoral* where the flowers salute the heroine in her country retreat with equal alacrity (but where the struggles of the Civil War are reduced to romantic monstrosities, mere bugaboos). Here, the jests are poignant; even then Fairfax, had he not chosen retirement, "might have made our Gardens spring / Fresh as his own and flourishing." But Paradise is now a waste land. Though Fairfax cultivates the trees of his own fields and groves, the desolate Felicia of Drayton had become still more desolate.

Moving on from the house to the garden and thence to the meadows, Marvell himself undergoes a kind of transformation or alteration of perspective, which reflects the larger social transformations of "the Garden of the World." This he describes in terms of the changing scenes in a masque. "Marvell is looking not at things but images."[16] Now men grow small, and grasshoppers huge; now the flowers seem fathoms deep in a sea of grass.

Fairfax's tenants are mowing the hay; after which they dance, set up haycocks, turn out the cattle to graze, and finally, as the meadows are flooded, the cattle, already diminished to the size of fleas in the huge expanse, but moving like constellations, become transformed with everything else, and we enter a world where glowworms could be comets.[17] All this is described in symbols of warfare, and of masque.

> No Scene that turns with Engines strange
> Does oftener then these Meadows change.
>
> (49:385–86)

The scenes that turned were Inigo Jones's invention, first seen in *The Masque of Queens*, 1609.

Changing scenes are revealed by a "Traverse" or stage curtain, first used in public theaters, but (as shutters) introduced for *The Masque of Oberon* (1611). That this is what is meant, is made plain in stanza 56:

> This Scene again withdrawing brings
> A new and empty Face of things;
> A levell'd space as smooth and plain
> As Clothes for *Lilly* stretcht to stain.

The great painter Lely and the painted scene recall Davenant in "the painted world" of *Gondibert* presenting the six days of Creation —Davenant, author of the last masque, and chief transmitter of scenic art to the next age. Davenant's *Gondibert*, an epic often compared by him, in his celebrated preface, to a palace, was perhaps the subject of parody here; but its huge extent brings a flickering between pygmy and giant scales, a "blink" by means of which appalling events can be surveyed, calmly.

Here the only "massacre" is that of the small birds hidden in the long grass, yet the words which Marvell uses are brutally accurate.[18] Women tossing the hay "represent the pillaging," the revolting aftermath of battle. Yet somehow it has become a matter for fancy. The last fancy is that a second Flood is obliterating all Creation.

The poet finally retreats to the wood itself, the "Ark," and in those depths meets new transformations, for he seems to have entered a fifth element

> Dark all without it knits; within
> It opens passable and thin;
>
> (64:505–506)

The effect of these changes is not unlike that which Eliot recorded at the outbreak of another war:

> As, in a theatre,
> The lights are extinguished for the scene to be changed,
> With a hollow rumble of wings, with a movement of darkness on
>   darkness,
> And we know that the hills and the trees, the distant panorama,
> And the bold imposing façade are all being rolled away—
>
> (Four Quartets, "East Coker," 3)[19]

while "they all go into the dark"—the captains, merchant bankers, eminent men of letters...."

The wood is not only dark, but strange; prophecies consume all history; all learning can be discovered in its "light Mosaic"; and suddenly Marvell too has passed through the looking glass, and appears in full masquing costume, curiously embroidered:

> And see how Chance's better *wit*
> Could with a Mask my studies hit!
> The Oak-Leaves me embroyder all,...
> Under this *antick Cope* I move
> Like some great *Prelate of the Grove*,
>
> (74:585–92)

Prelates, like Abbesses, are not serious figures here (though the Archbishop of York's Cawood Castle lay within sight). Reading in "Nature's Mystick Book," the poet becomes mentally calmed, and the excitement which had heated his brow and sent ideas spinning abates. Indeed, the lavish recall of Marvell's wide reading almost suggests the lavish bejewelling of the last masques, were it not so well compounded. Neo-Platonism and contemporaries like Benlowes, Cleveland, St. Amant, Davenant, have each supplied Marvell's imagination with ingredients; the flight of the mind, working at top speed, is too quick for each to be identified. The poet, utterly secure from the world's "shot," can "gaul its horseman all the day"; can even plead to be imprisoned and chained in the wood, "that I may never leave this place." The magic wood tempts as the cloister might tempt. With evening he emerges only to fish, a solitary sport indeed in a place that makes Thessalian Tempe obsolete.[20] In the final scene, his child pupil, running past, with her beauty charms the whole world into harmony and stillness. Representative of study and of the future, she rescues the poet from an indulgence which like that of Thyrsis and Dorinda, threatens to become too passive. She is compared with a comet—how different from earlier alarming comets!—and she portends action.

At an earlier entrance to the realm of eternity, in Carew's masque, a chorus of Druids, prelates of the grove, had seen their darkened sphere lightened by the starry look of the Queen Henrietta Maria

> ... *let thy Divine*
> *Aspects (Bright Deity) with faire*
> *And Halcyon beames becalme the aire.*
>
> (Third Song ll. 1027–29, *Poems*, p. 181)

Now Mary Fairfax is also the halcyon, and with her appearance the theater's "shuts" begin to close in. The masque is ended; as strange looking fishermen carry off their upturned coracles, these offer an image of the whole darkening hemisphere above.

> So when the Shadows laid asleep
> From underneath these Banks do creep
> And on the River as it flows
> With *Eben Shuts* being to close,
> The modest *Halcyon* comes in sight,
> Flying between the Day and Night....
>
> (84:665–67.)

Resolutely the poet enters the house, to say his farewell, as he turns towards the world, turns from Fairfax to Cromwell, that fiercer star.

> 'Tis not what once it was, the *World*,
> But a rude heap together hurl'd;
> All negligently overthrown,
> Gulfes, Deserts, Precipices, Stone.
>
> (96:761–64)

But at Nunappleton, in the "square" stanzas of his own architecture, he has learnt to reedify from the work of Fairfax.[21]

> Your lesser *World* contains the same.
> But in more decent Order tame;
> You *Heaven's Center, Nature's Lap,*
> And *Paradice's only Map.*
>
> (96:765–68)

In the rural retreat, memory of the courtly revels and of the civil war can be harmonized, if only momentarily. The fantasy of garden and meadows (antimasque) is succeeded by the gorgeousness of the woods and by the final transformation, the three stages of a masque. The bewildering shift of images that created the tensions of *An Horatian Ode* are dissolved. The building of a house, here, as in "Music's Empire" is the work of the poet and his lyre, of Amphion or Orpheus, not of an Architect.[22] It seems that at this time of supreme difficulty the accompanying power of music had in fact helped the verbalizing of what seemed to elude even the poet's power to conceive in words; by the time Marvell was celebrating *The First Anniversary of the Government under O.C.*, (pp. 108–19), written for December 1654 and published anonymously next year, the musical builder of the new state had become Cromwell himself:

> While indefatigable Cromwell hyes,
> And cuts his way still nearer to the Skyes,
> Learning a Musique in the Region clear,
> To tune this lower to that higher Sphere.
>
> (ll. 45–48)

This is essentially a masque in which Cromwell plays the chief part (l. 49–66, 100–103). He made himself less by ruling:

> For to be *Cromwell* was a greater thing
> Than aught below, or yet above a King:
>
> (ll. 225–26)

whilst his enemies confess he seems a king "And yet the same to be a King does scorn" (l. 388). This is a ritual not of power but of moderation.

The poem on the death of Cromwell is more royalist in style; but after the Restoration, Marvell set to work decreating revived Stuart myths, for his last piece of masque writing is the ironic description of the Dutch fleet sailing up the Medway (*Last Instructions to a Painter*, ll. 523–26, 535–50) followed by a storm (ll. 551–60).

Marvell's poetic energy transformed a convention for the celebration of stability and assurance—although as Stephen Orgel has observed, it was usually invoked in times of conflict if not of actual war. The rapid changes of scene from grave to gay, from land to sea to the heavens which Shirley's description of 1631 made plain[23] might indeed in outline suggest the central sequence of *Upon Appleton House*, except that since the whole aim of the masque is an unquestioning state of rapturous social identification, Marvell's use of it to explore, test, and probe the inner conflicts of his solitude represents at the very least, after the masque's destruction, the introjection of this courtly rite. Damon the Mower recalls Death; he is a strangely unhappy figure.[24] It was just the impossibility of any court masque which distanced the dancing of the hey almost as fully as the revels of "East Coker":

> In that open field
> If you do not come too close, if you do not come too close,
> On a summer midnight, you can hear the music
> Of the weak pipe and the little drum,
> And see them dancing round the bonfire
> The association of man and woman
> In daunsinge, signifying matrimonie—
> . . . .
> Rustically solemn or in rustic laughter,
> Lifting heavy feet in clumsy shoes,
> Earth feet, loam feet, lifted in country mirth
> Mirth of those long since under the earth
> Nourishing the corn.[25]

In the words of Eliot, Marvell's wit "involves probably a recognition, implicit in the expression of every experience, of other kinds of experience which are possible." In withdrawing to the garden, his modest and impersonal virtue allows him to enter both a larger and a smaller world, where the floral dial supplies the cosmic emblem—the sun working alike on flowers and bees. Marvell's power of packing the universe into a little space depends on his capacity to pour new poetic wine into old wineskins. In the end he achieved poetry without even the support of music or other "languages," yet also without any lurking desire to make his verses public. It is astonishing that such a piece as *On the Victory Obtained by Blake* should not have been printed, yet but for an accident, as it seems, all the poems would have remained unknown. So far are they from the claims to sacramental power which underlay the ritual of the Caroline masque. They were the solace of a jealously guarded privacy.

Marvell had run down the scale of creation. He might become a forest bird, but equally might become a vegetable:

> Turn me but, and you shall see
> I was but an inverted Tree.
>
> (71:367–68)

Unlike other pastoralists, he does not locate Eden in the past, still less, however, in the present. It lies perhaps with the colonists in the Bermudas—or more securely within a green thought in a green shade. Poetry offered the shield of Perseus in which the unendurable and unthinkable might be transformed:

> How safe, methinks, and strong behind
> These Trees I have incamp'd my Mind.

Poetry turns retreat into measured advance, dominance, triumph; not by the social ritual of the old masque—too often an instrument for self-delusion—but by the "esemplastic power" of solitary meditation.

Notes

1. Some public functions of the national theater were taken over by news-letters. Players had been "the abstracts and brief chronicles of the time," even to the extent of staging recent murders and other crimes. As Professor D.M. McKenzie

pointed out in his recent Sanders Lectures at Cambridge (1976), Ben Jonson returned to the stage after ten years' absence in 1626 to castigate in *The Staple of News* the league of seven London printers who formed a syndicate for such letters, led by Nathaniel Butter (known to Shakespeareans as printer of the Quarto of *King Lear*). For Jonson, the critical commentary of the playwright was a truer index of the times than scraps of gossip.

2. The best known description of this aspect of the masque comes in one of Shirley's plays, *Love's Cruelty*, 2.1. "A masque prepared and music to charm Orpheus himself into a stone ... a scene to take your eyes with wonder, now to see a forest wave and the pride of summer brought into a walking wood; in the instant, as if the sea had swallowed the earth, to see the waves capering above tall ships, Arion upon a rock playing to the dolphin, the Tritons calling upon the sea nymphs to dance before you." This is followed by a storm, that by a heavenly transformation scene, with angels, stars and the music of the spheres "that you would wish to be drowned indeed in such a happiness."

3. Rhodes Dunlap, ed., *The Poems of Thomas Carew with his Masque Coelum Britannicum* (Oxford: Oxford University Press, 1949), p. 77. Hereafter, references to Carew appear in the text with page numbers given in parentheses.

4. The works of Roy Strong and Stephen Orgel on Ben Jonson and Inigo Jones, and on the masque in general, have established this predominance; I have myself attempted to show its social implications in *The Living Monument* (Cambridge: Cambridge University Press, 1976).

5. Nabbes's masque is reprinted in *A Book of Masques* presented to Allardyce Nicoll (Cambridge: Cambridge University Press, 1967). Marvell was also indebted to Nabbes's *Microcosmos* for a "masque of quarrelling elements" (see *Poems*, notes to "The Unfortunate Lover," p. 255).

6. From Aurelian Townshend, *Albion's Triumph* (1631) in *Poems*, ed. E.K. Chambers, (Oxford: Oxford University Press, 1912), p. 77.

7. This was *Salmacida Spolia* by Davenant, 1640; also reprinted in *A Book of Masques* (see n. 4 above). A reconstruction of all the social implications of the occasion has been provided by C.V. Wedgwood, "The Last Masque," in *Truth and Opinion: Historical Essays*, (London: Macmillan, 1960).

8. This masque is based on Bruno's *Spaccio de la Bestia Trionfante*, which dates from 1584; Townshend's *Tempe Restored* is similarly based on the Valois *Ballet Comique de la Reyne* of the same period.

9. It is notable that Marvell begins his poetic career with two elegies for dead youths, and that death obtrudes into his pastoral with the figure of the Mower ("Death, thou art a mower too"), and of course into his most famous love poem "To his Coy Mistress."

10. Quoted from John Buxton, ed., *Poems of Michael Drayton* (London: Routledge & Kegan Paul, 1953), 1:283–84, and below, 285.

11. John M. Wallace, *Destiny his Choice: the Loyalism of Andrew Marvell*, (Cambridge: Cambridge University Press, 1968), p. 70.

12. Ibid., p. 28.

13. See George Hibbard, "The Country House Poem in the Seventeenth Century," *Journal of the Warburg and Courtauld Institutes*, 19 (1956): 156–74.

14. To which might be added *The Hock Cart* addressed by Herrick to Mildmay

Fane, Earl of Westmorland and Fairfax's kinsman, with its reminder "Feed him ye must whose food fills you" addressed to the laborers. (See Raymond Williams, *The Country and the City* [London: Chatto and Windus, 1973], p. 33 for an analysis of pastoralism.)

15.   Who hath not heard of Chloris and her bower
                   Fair Iris' act, employed by Juno's power
                   To guard the Spring and prosper every flower
                   Whom jealousy and hell thought to devour? . . .
                   Chloris the Queen of the Flowers.

                                         (Ben Jonson, *Chloridia*, 1631)

The village May Queen was seated in a bower where she remained to preside over the May Day sports.

16. Wallace, *Destiny his Choice*, p. 253. Anne Berthoff, *The Resolved Soul: A Study of Marvell's Major Poems* (Princeton: Princeton University Press, 1970), pp. 171–97, deals with this part of the poem as "The Masque of Nature" but is not really concerned with the form of the original masques.

17. See "The Mower to the Glo-worms" (*Poems*, p. 47):

                   Ye Country Comets, that portend
                   No War, nor Princes' funeral,
                   Shining unto no higher end
                   Then to pressage the Grasses fall

18. "Massacre"—one recalls the battle cry "Jesus—and no quarter!"

19. Quoted from T.S. Eliot, *Four Quartets* (New York: Harcourt Brace & Co., 1943), p. 14.

20. *Tempe Restored* (1632), one of Townshend's masques for Henrietta Maria. Miss Scoular has identified his posture with emblem pictures of a River God. See her *Natural Magic: studies in The Presentation of Nature in English Poetry from Spener to Marvell* (Oxford: Oxford University Press, 1965).

21. John Wallace believes that "the very stanza form itself is an image of Fairfacian virtue" because it embodies the form described by Puttenham in the *Arte of English Poesie* of "the square or quadrangle equilater" (eight octosyllabic lines). Puttenham writes that "The square [is] for his inconcussable steadiness likened to the earth," so that Aristotle terms a constant-minded man "a square man" (*Destiny His Choice*, pp. 237–38).

22. "Loyalism was created from Chaos, in those moments of desperation when the only conceivable action is the performance of daily routine," Wallace, p. 41.

23. See 2 above. The vast quantity of literary reflection packed into Marvell's poem has also been mentioned.

24. Since mowing is essentially temporary harvest work, Marvell may imply that Damon is no true rustic; he could not, like a shepherd, follow this occupation all the year, and at harvest time everyone must help get in the crop.

25. Eliot, *Four Quartets*, pp. 11–12.

THE SCOPE OF IMAGINATION IN
Upon Appleton House

ISABEL G. MACCAFFREY

IN THE NINTH STANZA of *Upon Appleton House*, Marvell locates the subject of his poem in language of grave import:

> The House was built upon the Place
> Only as for *a Mark of Grace*;
> And for an *Inn* to entertain
> Its *Lord* a while, but not remain.

> (69–72)

Fairfax's attitude toward his house (confirmed by lines of his own composing which Marvell's echo or anticipate)[1] indicates an awareness of his own mortality. "Inns are not residences," as Marianne Moore observed; Fairfax's true home is elsewhere. Line 72 balances upon *a while*, precariously signaling the temporal limits of a human life. In the poem's opening stanzas, Marvell develops the idea of spatial limitation through a sequence of geometrical conceits that allude to the economy of Nature as a model. These first ten stanzas, therefore, establish the terms to be explored in the perambulation of the estate; the tenth names nature and art as rivals in landscape architecture.

> But Nature here hath been so free
> As if she said leave this to me.
> Art would more neatly have defac'd
> What she hath laid so sweetly wast;
> In fragrant Gardens, shaddy Woods,
> Deep Meadows, and transparent Floods.

(10:75–80)

Gardens, woods, meadows, floods: on these stages, where art and nature mingle, the speaking pictures of Marvell's philosophical poem will unfold. It opens and closes with emblems of humility: the spherical or hemispherical enclosures that define the limits accepted as legitimate and ineviatable by the poet and the master of the house he celebrates.

Marvell's imagination is characterized by its resistance to external limits, and its submissiveness to the symbolic limits that express the soul's sense of its own disabilities. Much of his poetry is devoted to the exploration of limit; and the dominance of the theme suggests why so many of the poems fall under the rubric of pastoral. The dream of a perfect congruence between man and nature is one of the great myths of mankind, and it offers contexts for considering the urgent epistemological questions that obsess so many postmedieval imaginations.

> From this the poem springs: that we live in a world
> That is not our own, and much more, not ourselves.

The pastoral paradigm provides an *as if* that negates this chilly aphorism: let us imagine a world that belongs to us, that mirrors ourselves. The belatedness of Marvell in the tradition meant that he came to pastoral with a deep sense of both its virtues and its dangers, and his pastoral lyrics reflect this ambivalence. His paradises seldom remain intact. The Mower Damon, boasting of his privileged position as nature's favorite son, is already the victim of an alienating love. The Mower in "To the Glo-Worms," his mind "displac'd" by love of Juliana, regards with the melancholy of an outsider the "courteous Lights" of a creaturely world from which he is now exiled. Inveighing against gardens, he attacks the propensity of fallen man, "that sov'raign thing and proud," to reverse the beneficent relationship, established in Eden, between himself and nature. Instead of gazing into the mirror of natural innocence, he narcissistically forces Nature to give him back his own image. This is a version of idolatry: "The Pink grew then as double as his Mind; . . . The Tulip, white, did for complexion seek."

Yet Fairfax makes a garden at Nunappleton, and is not rebuked. It is the vocation of Adam. The dilemmas confronting the makers of gardens in a fallen world are also the dilemmas of poetry-makers. In both cases, there is a problematic relationship between imagination and its materials; and that relation is a specialized version of a larger problem—the disjunction between the human mind and the world in which it finds itself. The issues raised by Sidney in the *Apology* two gnerations earlier are firmly joined in Marvell's poetry. Does the imagination outsoar nature, as Sidney claimed, voyaging through the zodiac of wit and concocting its golden worlds beyond the range of the too-much-loved, imperfect earth? Or does the infected will that we inherit from Adam force us to accept a humbler role, curbing the erected wit and, as Bacon recommended, bowing and buckling the mind to the nature of things? These are crudely formulated versions of questions considered with great subtlety within the limited but intense range of Marvell's lyrics. And *Upon Appleton House* is a "sober frame" for a meditation upon the claims of imagination, that presumptuous defier of limits.[2]

All truly sober frames exist in a symbolic dimension that acknowledges the transience and "lowness" of their makers. Hence the careful geometries, spatial and temporal, of the opening stanzas. Marvell's architectural conceits are complemented by allusions to emptiness and fullness that comment on the contrast between a self-regarding art detached from its true sources, and the art which respects purposes which lie beyond it. Nature's artfulness exhibits a perfect decorum of form and content.

> The low roof'd Tortoises do dwell
> In cases fit of Tortoise-shell:
> No Creature loves an empty space;
> Their Bodies measure out their Place.
>
> (2:13–16)

The only truly "empty space" is inside the skull of a presumptuous human being, represented by the comic hubris of the "Forrain

Architect." Launched upon strange voyages in the spaces of his own brain, he illustrates the extravagance of an "unrul'd" imagination:

> That unto Caves the Quarries drew,
> And Forrests did to Pastures hew;
> Who of his great Design in pain
> Did for a Model vault his Brain.
>
> (1:3–6)

The violence perpetrated upon the landscape manifests the architect's conceit, in two senses of the word. It is an extreme instance of imagination's metamorphosing power: caves become quarries, forests pastures, in the interests of a "great Design" which has forgotten its origin in the patterns of created nature, the divinely designed universe. The architect's swelled head, "vaulted" by the pressure of his own conceit, is a model for a "hollow Palace" (l. 19), the epithet looking back to the hollowing out of artificial caves in stanza 1, and the condemnation of "empty space" in 2.

In contrast, the sober frame of Nunappleton, and the poem that celebrates it, are modeled upon the true "great Design."

> all things are composed here
> Like Nature, orderly and near.
>
> (4:25–26)

Upon Appleton House is an example of what it explores; the poet's design and God's are concentric structures. Images of enclosure and fullness express this "orderly and near" composition, imitating "the Beasts [that] are by their Denns exprest" (l. 11): "*Romulus* his Bee-like Cell" (l. 40), and Nunappleton itself, based upon a "*holy Mathematicks*" (l. 47) whereby "Things greater are in less contain'd" (l. 44). The immortal soul lives within its temporary house; the inn entertains its lord but a while. Many stanzas later, the poem closes with a series of concentric spheres: tortoise shells, men beneath their boat-roofs, the globe of earth suggested by the reference to the Antipodes, and the "dark *Hemisphere*" (l. 775) of the vaulted heavens. Thus in the course of his argument Marvell moves from the admonitory image of the tortoises in their "cases fit" to the extravagantly reconfirmed vision of men accepting the injunction to imitate nature's humility; having "shod their *Heads* in their *Canoos*" (l. 772), they have truly become "*Tortoise* like" (l. 773). The second image mocks the first, and at the same time affirms it; the progress of Marvell's imagination as it moves from the simple relationships of the opening stanzas to the metamorphosed and reimagined conceits of the close provides the poem's plot.

It is not, of course, a narrative plot, but a circular, meditative expatiation upon a perambulation—a walk through the estate of Nunappleton, and through the human imagination, the state of man. In the process, Marvell is able to consider the history of human arts, which can be seen as efforts, most of them unsuccessful, to reconstruct or regain paradise. History is supplemented by geography and topography, and the experiences of the contemplative observer offer examples of the dangers and pleasures of imagination in the foreground of the poem's action.

Appleton House itself is the second edifice to have been built on its site, and Marvell's contrast between it and its "Quarries," the former nunnery buildings, gives him his first opportunity to consider man's efforts to make his own world. His purpose here, as throughout the poem, is to define the paradoxical human condition. The definition must ultimately refer to God, and man's creaturely dependence upon his maker is everywhere reiterated, most crucially and perilously in Marvell's exploration of the human urge to imitate God's making, to evade limits and draw a map of salvation. The nuns who enclose themselves from the world, like the gardeners in "The Mower against Gardens," attempt to remake Nature in a human image. "Like themselves they alter all" (l. 215). They also practice corrupting "arts" that pervert natural order in the interest of "curious tasts" (l. 182)—*curious* bearing, in this context, its full weight of theological portent. Marvell's language has a deliberate, suggestive duplicity; the nuns, "handling Natures finest Parts" (l. 178), prepare a banquet of sense that compares unfavorably with the sublter delights offered by Created Pleasure to the Resolved Soul. The lines in stanza 22 on the preserving of fruit work metaphorically in two directions: the nuns intend the preservation of "mortal fruit" as a parable for the salvation of souls, but to the narrator's severer contemplation it offers an instance of presumption and the perversion of art.

The nunnery is one of Marvell's false paradises: "Within this holy leisure we / Live innocently as you see" (ll. 97–98). That it should be also false art is predictable. The reference to virginity as an analogue of the retired life, unexamined and artfully composed, is familiar to us from "The Picture of little T.C." and "The Nymph complaining" and, in a different form, "To His Coy Mistress." It is inverted at the end of *Appleton House* in the prophecy of Maria Fairfax's marriage; she, like her ancestress Isabella, will abandon innocence for experience, acknowledging that paradise must be lost if it is to be regained. Time, as well as nature, is redeemed at Nunappleton because the Fairfaxes, submitting to the design of Providence, "make their *Destiny* their *Choice*" (l. 744). This submission is one of the conditions of living in a true paradise; the false paradise, on the other hand, is destroyed because the nuns work "against Fate" (l. 247), which means also against nature. History becomes romance to demonstrate the working of the divine artist; the scene recalls the destruction of those other sinister artifices, the Bower of Bliss and Busirane's castle.

> Thenceforth (as when th'Inchantment ends
> The Castle vanishes or rends)
> The wasting Cloister with the rest
> Was in one instant dispossest.
>
> (34:269–72)

Having demolished the dangerous structures of false art, Marvell explores and defines, in the central movements of the poem, the conditions of a true paradise. These conditions are founded upon delicate relationships between nature and imagination, model and imitation. Rosalie Colie's adjective for the poem, "shifty,"[3] is nowhere better illustrated than here, where tenors and vehicles, objects and their reflections, repeatedly change places. Critics have remarked upon Marvell's habit of literalizing his metaphors,[4] but an even more complicated process is visible in the stanzas about Fairfax's garden, which is laid out "In the just Figure of a Fort" (l. 286). Stanzas 37–40 elaborate the figure, the flowers imitating metaphorically (but also in the actual design of the garden) the military activities of volleying, marching, bivouacking. "These five imaginary Forts" (l. 352) allude to, and are innocently modeled upon, their maker's vocation in the "real" world. But the game played by the lord general in his garden becomes something more serious under the pressure of the narrator's imagination. The pivotal stanza on the "fall" of England into civil war (41) is followed by a renewal of the metaphor of "sweet *Militia*" (l. 330), but now inflected so that we contemplate the meaning of innocence in the true original garden which was the model for this one. There, "all the Garrisons were Flowers" (l. 332), and "The *Gardiner* had the *Souldiers* place" (l. 337). In Fairfax's figurative garden, flowers "are" garrisons; but originally garrisons "were" flowers. The shift in the direction of the correspondence registers the difference between a truly innocent world and a world of partly regained innocence which merely alludes to the true concept in the process of figuring its opposite.

In the final couplet of stanza 42, Marvell inflects the image once more:

> But War all this doth overgrow:
> We Ord'nance Plant and Powder sow.
>
> (43:343–44)

Whereas Fairfax now "shoots" only "fragrant Vollyes" (l. 298), he once "sowed" with artillery; the world is turned upside down along with the image, and England becomes a waste land, the overgrown garden described in Shakespeare's history plays, with reference to another war. Two aspects of "present" reality are defined in the two metaphors: the garden that is like a fort, the warfare that parodies gardening. Between them lies the original garden—whether unfallen England or unfallen Eden—where tulips *were* guards, because no other kind of guarding was known, or necessary. Reality had not yet split into tenors and vehicles; there are no metaphors in paradise.

In this triple-tiered exploration of the garden / warfare correspondence, Marvell defines the activities of the fallen imagination. It can, with Fairfax, attempt to create a mortal image expressing what the mind knows of innocence and virtue, though even here the created world will bear the marks of its fallen condition, as it does in the martial stance of flowers and bees. Imagination can also create diabolical parodies of its origins: the acts of destruction that terribly resemble those of creation—the "sowing" of ordinance. Finally, the human imagination can turn from the making of either earthly paradises or earthly hells, and assume the visionary power to represent the realm of eternal existence, what has been and one day may be again. Marvell touches only lightly this region, which is the home of Milton's imagination. But the historical and cosmological reach of *Upon Appleton House*, from chaos to apoc-alypse,[5] conveys indirectly the power of imagination to see what the eye cannot see, beyond the limits of space and time. This trans-cendence of limit is not presumption; it is, rather, the morality of imagination, corresponding to the virtue of Fairfax in regarding his house as a symbol of aspiration rather than a literalizing of heaven (the nuns, on the other hand, try to "draw *Heav'n* nearer" to them-selves [l. 162]). There is an invisible perfection which provides the standard for man's incomplete perfections and fallings off. Marvell goes on, in a final inflection of the garden image, to describe another "planting," this time of a paradise within.

> For he did, with his utmost Skill
> *Ambition* weed, but *Conscience* till.
> *Conscience*, that Heaven-nursed Plant,
> Which most our Earthly Gardens want.
> A prickling leaf it bears, and such
> As that which shrinks at ev'ry touch;
> But Flowers eternal, and divine,
> That in the Crowns of Saints do shine.
>
> (45 : 353–60)

The stanza is framed allegorically to define a concept, and the peculiar allegorical relationship between the visible image and its invisible counterpart is strongly marked. What is metaphorical on earth—conscience feigned to be a plant—becomes literal in Heaven—a flower in the crown of a saint. Conscience, which has taken the saint to Heaven, is totally identified, at last, with the shining blossoms that crown the whole endeavor. But such identification can occur only "then" and "there"; in the here and now, we must make do with metaphors and a paradise within. Marvell's stanza bears witness to the power of the resolved soul, and of the virtuous imagination, to apprehend invisible reality and retire to a garden of the mind that is the only true anticipation of Heaven.

An analysis of the resources of figurative language and of imagination's legitimate and illegitimate powers, the garden stanzas of *Upon Appleton House* provide the poem with its structural and thematic center. In the next movement, perspective and tone alter. The narrator, up to now only a voice, becomes an "I" (l. 369), and with his entry into the action there is introduced the special ambiguous tone of self-inflation and self-mockery that Marvell reserves for his portraits of the artist.[6] The self that is displayed here has a particularly crucial role. He is the contemplative, the visionary, the maker of sober or extravagant frames in poetry; he is the man of imagination, and insofar as he is celebrated, chastised, corrected, mocked, instructed, admired, so is imagination.

Although the design of *Appleton House* seems spontaneous and rambling, even haphazard, it is in fact a map of the contours of the imagining mind, and its parts do not follow one another at random. Having described imagination's powers in the course of perambulating the garden, Marvell turns to the world beyond it to seek for confirmation of the validity of imagining. The meadow section concerns metamorphosis, the central imaginative act; but these metamorphoses occur in nature, which thus reasserts its primacy as a model and source for human art, which must be rooted in "reality." The changes and doublings and identifications of a wonder-working imagination are here displayed before the innocently gazing observer, *in fact*; Nature has its fictions and its seemings too. Marvell at the outset asserts the congruence of nature and art in the cooperating lines of a couplet:

> No Scene that turns with Engines strange
> Does oftner then these Meadows change.
>
> (49:385–86)

Nature's above art; its changing scenes offer first the mock war of the mowers, then the mown field with its "*Pyramids* of Hay" in cocks, the "levell'd" space of the denuded meadow "polisht" into a pasture for the village cattle, and finally the "Sea" of the flooded river. Amid these changes, imagination plays its own descants, varying the angles from which we view reality, multiplying the mirrors in which vision catches what it regards.

Reality confirms these imaginings, sometimes disconcertingly. Stanza 50 begins with an apparently innocent, but ominously weighted, descritpion of the mowers:

> With whistling Sithe, and Elbow strong,
> These Massacre the Grass along.
>
> (393–94)

The violent verb seems merely conventional in this couplet, invoking expectations of affinity between mowing and the death of all flesh. But the violence springs to life in the following lines, actualized in the unwitting but detestable murder of the rail:

> The Edge all bloody from its Breast
> He draws, and does his stroke detest;
> Fearing the Flesh untimely mow'd
> To him a Fate as black forebode.

> (397–400)

Suddenly the blood is real, not metaphorical, The abrupt literalizing of images is one of Marvell's characteristic devices, symptomatic of the self-consciousness of his art. Its effect here is even more complex than usual, almost too complex for the clumsy makeshift of explication.

Every reader of the poem has found himself puzzled by this stanza, and its mock-heroic companion, stanza 53. The images function, as Rosalie Colie has said, "to keep the notion of war trembling behind this landscape of bucolic well-being."[7] They carry our attention outward to the "real" world of events in history, but the implications of this movement are metaphysical as well as political. The stanza reminds us that language, and the transformations of language in metaphor, have their roots in the way things are; their vitality depends upon facts that are not linguistic or imagined. Marvell's dead metaphor in *Massacre* is revived when the mower carves the rail, and the fancy that had so casually used the verb is recalled to its responsibilities. There is a real shock in this movement from the metaphorical to the actual, and the shock forces us to consider the seriousness of imagination's contrivances. They are at once more serious and less serious than we might be inclined to suppose. More serious—because if we regard them merely as a game our art loses touch with its models; but also less serious—because imagination has a tendency to press its insights further than actuality will tolerate. This second truth about imagination emerges as the stanza ends, in a couplet that teeters on the edge of absurdity. "The Flesh untimely mow'd" derives its resonance from the unexpected intrusion of fact into fiction, the bloody stroke actually observed. But the fact will not bear the superstructure that imagination builds on it in the last line: "To him a Fate as black forebode." In a way,

233

of course, it merely asserts the truth: the mower *will* suffer a fate as black, will himself be cut down—"For Death thou art a Mower too." But talk of Fate and untimely death is a little too weighty for this context, and the tone collapses, in the next stanza, into self-mockery, as if to warn us that a self-absorbed imagination can err in the direction of portentousness as well as frivolity.

The extraordinary intervention of "bloody *Thestylis*" into the poem's fabric at this point has interested many critics. It is another shift of perspective, another crowding of imagination by reality, another reminder of the limits of fiction, and of its dependence upon an only partly controllable world of fact. But the tone this time is remarkably genial, even hilarious. Murdered birds multiply comically:

> When on another quick She lights,
> And cryes, he call'd us *Israelites*;
> But now, to make his saying true,
> Rails rain for Quails, for Manna Dew.

(51:405–408)

"To make his saying true," reality once more presses upon the poet's innocent locutions and proves them less than innocent; he cannot call anyone an Israelite with impunity in this emblem-ridden world that constantly displays the artfulness of God. Thestylis "carries the poet's biblical metaphor to an area into which he had not planned to take it,"[8] and once again the determination of reality to cooperate in his fancies makes the poet seem a little irresponsible, or at least a little careless of his own premises.

Perhaps determined to evade a charge of fanciful foolishness, Marvell assumes in the next stanza an air of laborious spelling out. His argument has the explicitness of a demonstration, in contrast to the glancing allusiveness in the stanza just preceding it. The analogy between this field and a field of battle is explained point by point.

> In whose new Traverse seemeth wronght
> A Camp of Battail newly fought:
> Where, as the Meads with Hay, the Plain
> Lyes quilted ore with Bodies slain:
> The Women that with forks it fling,
> Do represent the Pillaging.

(53:419–24)

Seemeth, as nearly always in Marvell, is a warning to tread lightly. Then the *as . . . so* of the simile reinforces the cautious tone. Inflecting vehicle and tenor, Marvell suggests the two-way perspective on the nature / war comparison that was examined in the passage on the military garden. On the field of battle, the plain is "quilted" with bodies as a mown field is with bundles of hay. And this hayfield "seems" a battlefield. The rhetorical patterning of the lines insists upon the imagination's self-awareness. A simile makes us think about both similarities as differences in the terms; it holds them apart, analytically. The effect here is to make the speaker seem careful and responsible; the mowing of a field *is* like the mowing down of flesh on a battlefield, but at the same time it is reassuringly unlike. Its heroism is only mock, its innocence genuine. The stanza thus restores the balance in our view of the mowers; they are neither murderers nor heroes nor spoiled innocents, though their actions point in all these directions. Fiction and fact are firmly distinguished. The women making hay "Do *represent* the Pillaging," but they are not pillagers. The statement expresses an analogy, no more and no less; there is enactment, but no dangerous identification.

Imagination must learn to know its limits. On the other hand, it may be surprised to find its seemings echoed by reality, as in the massacre of the rail and the intervention of Thestylis. A third and climactic instance of countermetaphorical transformation is the flood which concludes this section of the poem. The river, released from the floodgates,

> make the Meadow truly be
> (What it but seem'd before) a Sea.
>
> (59:467–68)

Thirty lines before, the smooth meadow was said to surround the rocklike or pyramidal haycocks, "Like a calm Sea" (l. 434); now that sea becomes literally visible, moving from the world of mind to the world without. The flood allows Marvell to play with notions of boats sailing overhead, in another sequence of topsy-turvy paradoxes. The disorientation produced by the flood appropriately rounds off this section, which is dominated by bewildering shifts of perspective (as from microscope to telescope in stanza 58), and by oscillations between literal and figurative description.

The flood stanzas match the two stanzas which introduce the

section; together, they make a watery frame for the multiple reflecting glasses of the meadow. As the narrator moves into that
wilderness of mirrors, he enters "the Abbyss . . . Of that unfathomable
Grass" (ll. 369–70), a "sea" where men are lower than grasshoppers,
as later they are lower than boats and fish. These dislocations are
susceptible of many readings, and have kept many critics busy. In
terms of the poem's major themes, the whole meadow passage
represents, I think, Marvell's effort to describe the medium in which
a rational amphibium must lead his life. We are amphibious not
only between earth and heaven, but between the world within and
the world without. Imagination unites the two, mediates between
them; or, more accurately, imagination is the means whereby we
perceive the continuity between world and mind. Elements from
the two worlds can change places readily because these realms of
being are congruent and interdependent, though we must resist
the temptation to assimilate them completely to each other. "What
we see is what we think": this title of a poem by Stevens perfectly
catches the ambiguities where mirrors confront each other at the
center of *Appleton House*:

> Where all things gaze themselves, and doubt
> If they be in it or without.

> (80:637–38)

In a fine kinesthetic image, Marvell reminds us of how it feels to
live in our element.

> To see Men through this Meadow Dive,
> We wonder how they rise alive.
> As, under Water, none does know
> Whether he fall through it or go.

> (48:377–80)

The swimmer sinking through seas profound cannot tell whether
he moves as the result of his own efforts, or is merely passive in the
hands of gravity. Do we "go" or "fall," control our environment or
submit to it? And, of course, in this stanza the sea is not really a sea
anyway, but a meadow; the very element is ambiguous. But Marvell
will not allow priority to either side, so at the end the meadow is not
"really" a meadow, but a sea.

Upon Appleton House, beginning with a lecture on the misuse and abuse of imagination, proceeds, in its later stages, to its true subject, which is also Wordsworth's subject: the great consummation between mind and the world, in which perception and creation, mirror and lamp, are evenly balanced.[9] The nuns lock themselves away from their world, expressly denying the amphibiousness of human nature.

> 'These Walls restrain the World without,
> 'But hedge our Liberty about.
> 'These Bars inclose the wider Den
> 'Of those wild Creatures called Men.
>
> (13:99–102)

The human soul is split into an "interior" spiritual self, and a "wild" natural self. Breaking down bars and walls, the virtuous Fairfax reunites the two in his marriage to Isabella Thwaites. The decent order of Nunappleton, at once natural and artful, expresses this union. Though in other poems by Marvell the resolved soul confronts the creation as its antagonist, here there is a truce between them, uneasily maintained but satisfying to both.

The retreat of the poet to his "Sanctuary in the Wood" (l. 482) balances the episode of the nunnery. At first, there is admiration for the artfulness of nature's designs. A union of opposites, amicably interlocked, finds an *exemplum* in the marriage of Fairfax and Vere, and the wood itself:

> Dark all without it knits; within
> It opens passable and thin.
>
> (64:505–506)

In this passable world it is easy to be a philosopher. The tone of the passage suggests the spontaneity and ease of an imagination delighted by a wholly intelligible universe. What it sees and what it makes are indistinguishable; voice and echo vibrate to the same frequency. "And there I found myself more truly and more strange."

This is the subtlest of Marvell's paradises. The poet is restored to a state of innocence without losing his worldliness. The wisdom of the ages is condensed in the "light *Mosaick*" (l. 582); he wears this learning lightly. Like Adam, he speaks the "learned Original"

237

(l. 570) that is the language of Nature itself. Stockdoves, heron, stork, woodpecker, "Traitor-worm"—these creatures delightfully instruct the poet in the manner of the emblem books of the day. They are, in fact, living emblems, offering a final example of Marvell's countermetaphorical technique, the literalizing of the figurative. The pages of "*Natures mystick Book*" (l. 584) are animated before our eyes, as the poet turns their "Leaves." We are meant to notice also, of course, that the emblems almost all point a sad or sobering moral; this paradise remains postlapsarian, and the climactic emblem of the worm in the oak (stanza 70) speaks explicitly of our corrupt flesh.

We are, therefore, prepared for the denouement of this episode, and for its successor which will conclude the poem. The poet, ravished by his reunion with nature, revels in extravagant identifications.

> And little now to make me, wants
> Or of the *Fowles*, or of the *Plants*.
> Give me but Wings as they, and I
> Streight floating on the Air shall fly:
> Or turn me but, and you shall see
> I was but an inverted Tree.
>
> (71:563–68)

Embroidered with oak leaves, clasped by ivy, he can think of nothing more desirable than perpetual bondage in the arms of benevolent nature. Yet he is, after all, neither a fowl nor a plant; he has no wings, and he maintains, perforce, the upright posture of a man. The imagery of bondage in stanza 77, which has attracted critical notice for the violence of its tone, gives a clue to the wishes thus expressed:

> Bind me ye *Woodbines* in your 'twines,
> Curle me about ye gadding *Vines* . . .
>
> (609–10)

We may remember another kind of bondage, differently judged:

> Cease Tempter. None can chain a mind
> Whom this sweet Chordage cannot bind.
>
> ("A Dialogue . . . Resolved Soul,
> and Created Pleasure," ll. 43–44)

The resolved soul, immune to the charms of music, cannot now submit to the ministrations of vegetable loves. The narrator of *Upon Appleton House* has found a refuge more salubrious than the artificial Eden of the nunnery, but he has pressed too far the idea of nature as a model, soberly recommended in the poem's opening stanzas. And he, like the nuns, thinks of his sanctuary as shutting out rather than encompassing.

> How safe, methinks, and strong, behind
> These Trees have I incamp'd my Mind.
>
> (76:601–602)

But this is an illusion. The rail, too, had thought itself safe.

> Unhappy Birds! what does it boot
> To build below the Grasses Root;
> When Lowness is unsafe as Hight,
> And Chance o'retakes what scapeth spight?
>
> (52:409–12)

Chance may sometimes display "better Wit" (l. 585); but it can just as easily work in this destructive way. Nature may be designed, but history is not, and history, "the World," is where we live. Against it, imagination must provide its own sanctuaries, temporary though they may be; nature cannot do this for us. Marvell's curious image for his isolation from "the World" may strike us as precarious:

> But I on it securely play,
> And gaul its Horsemen all the Day.
>
> (76:607–608)

This is a dangerous sort of play; we remember the wanton troopers who, "riding by / Have shot my Faun and it will dye." The Nymph's paradise was invaded; this one may be too.

In fact, Marvell keeps it safe for the extent of this poem, but only by another metamorphosis, which entails the poet's breaking of nature's "Silken Bondage" and his submission to a new, more human enchantment.[10] One of the games played in the final section is to pretend that Mary Fairfax is wiser than her tutor; he becomes a "trifling Youth," fumbling away his fishing gear before her "judicious

Eyes" (ll. 652–53). She speaks all languages, the mistress of Babel. This complimentary conceit points more seriously, however, to the superiority of the ideal embodied in Maria over the return to Adamic innocence briefly indulged by the poet. The "vitrifi'd nature contemplated in these stanzas (83–88) is outside time; it is described in the same visionary, nonmetaphorical mode as the flowers of conscience, "That in the Crowns of Saints do shine" (l. 360). The stillness of the presented moment, "betwixt the Day and Night" (l. 670), is not natural, but supernatural, an intermittence of the heart when imagination takes wing. We see, for a moment, a new earth, replacing the one that will be consumed in the flames of time; it is a world redeemed, and in it the redeemed soul takes its central place, reassuming its forsaken command over nature.

> 'Tis *She* that to these Gardens gave
> That wondrous Beauty which they have;
> *She* streightness on the Woods bestows;
> To *Her* the Meadow sweetness owes;
> Nothing could make the River be
> So Chrystal-pure but only *She*.
>
> (87:689–94)

Nature "recollects" itself around Maria. The human figure is now the model, Nature legitimately the mirror which gives man back his own image.

> And for a Glass the limpid Brook,
> Where *She* may all *her* Beautyes look.
>
> (88:701–702)

This paradise exists within the visionary imagination, though it is composed of elements visible to the physical eye. It is the paradigm for the poem's other paradises, but we are not allowed to contemplate it long. In the end we must reenter time and history; so Marvell looks ahead to the moment when fate will "translate" Maria to another role, where she can extend the family "Line." The Fairfaxes, like their "double Wood," measure the generations of time, make destiny their choice, and, marrying into the family of "starry *Vere*," incorporate fortune's emblem in their arms (l. 724).[11] In three penultimate stanzas, Marvell returns to the actuality of Nunappleton and gives it a precise ontological location. He begins with one of his key terms: *Mean time*.

> Mean time ye Fields, Springs, Bushes, Flow'rs,
> Where yet She leads her studious Hours . . .
>
> (94:745–46)

It is like the pause in "Little T.C." before her entry into the arena of love: "Mean time, whilst every verdant thing / It self does at thy Beauty charm" (ll.25–26). In a reverse process, in "The Garden" the mind withdraws through the portal of "Mean while" into its happiness. Human beings may enjoy interludes outside time when they can play at recreating paradise. Some historical examples of such interludes, evoked and dismissed in stanza 95, witness to mankind's enduring preoccupation with this *topos*. Nunappleton overgoes them all, but there is an implication that it too may someday become "obsolete." For it is, after all, not paradise but *Paradice's only Map*" (l. 768)—a chart for a journey whose real goal lies elsewhere. It is a place that can "entertain / Its *Lord* a while, but not remain."

In the concluding stanzas, Marvell achieves a delicate balance between art and nature, and between imagination's strength and its weakness. As in his shorter complimentary poem to Fairfax, "Upon the Hill and Grove at Bilbrough," so more subtly here, he approves the virtuous soul's impression of its stamp upon nature. For the natural world is fallen too, full of "excrescences"—"a rude heap together hurl'd" (l. 762).

> Your lesser *World* contains the same.
> But in more decent Order tame.
>
> (96:765–66)

Yet the decent order of Nunappleton, though it may endure in the mind, or in a poem, is transient, because our experience will not sustain any sort of permanence. It exists "mean time," a containing microcosm that can provide the ground for self-contemplation and self-transcendence. So nostalgia becomes the appropriate note for the poem's last movement: nostalgia for all the lost paradises, and for the world "as once it was" (l. 761). We are not surprised to find in the final stanza of *Upon Appleton House* a last version of pastoral, the mode devised by humanity to contain all its nostalgias.

Stanza 97 provides a series of contexts, spatial and temporal, for the gardens of Nunappleton in the macrocosm. *But now* does not arrest time; rather, it acknowledges time's flow, which concludes in the corresponding *now* eight lines later.

> But now the *Salmon-Fishers* moist
> Their *Leathern Boats* begin to hoist;
> And, like *Antipodes* in Shoes,
> Have shod their *Heads* in their *Canoos.*
> How *Tortoise* like, but not so slow,
> These rational *Amphibii* go?
> Let's in: for the dark *Hemisphere*
> Does now like one of them appear.
>
> (97:769–76)

The stanza moves in a tiny perfect arch from the observed detail of the salmon fishers, back to the earth at nightfall. At the center, imagination revels in analogies to make a paradoxical definition of man. He is an amphibium, an earthdweller whose imagination can outsoar its limits, can travel to the ends of the earth, and turn upside down the fixities of quotidian reality while preserving a decorum of "natural" forms. Though he may be "*Tortoise* like," he is "not so slow"; he can solve Zeno's paradox. At the end, as the hemisphere darkens, he returns to contemplate the multiplied concentricities cooperatively generated by nature and his own mind. The sky "does now like one of them appear"; one of what? The salmon fishers carrying their boats, the Antipodes in shoes, the rational amphibii in their tortoiselike dwellings? One of them or all of them; all happily consent to shape themselves in the same form. In this magical conclusion, expansion of vision is accompanied by an awareness of finitude; the sense that nothing is ever finished coincides with the sense of an ending, appropriate and inevitable and satisfying, to this poem. Sweetness and wit, which Donne once declared irreconcilable, here become natural partners.

Marvell's most profound poems are those in which he is reconciled to his own imagination, that human faculty so disposed to exaggeration and self-serving delusion. For him it is admirable only when it consents to work within limits, growing thereby more strong and heroic. In "To His Coy Mistress" it splendidly rises to the challenge of temporality, and at the end of "The Garden," having tried its wings, it willingly binds the zodiac of wit into a fragrant zodiac of flowers. Imagination gracefully capitulates to the conditions of mortality, and so transforms and makes beautiful those very conditions. Marvell's skill at ending poems is itself an honoring of the claims of limit. *Upon Appleton House* ends, like *Lycidas* and its forerunners, with the end of the day, acknowledging our submission to diurnal revolutions and the poet's acceptance of a traditional genre. The poem's limit is the sun's limit; the allusion to other pastoral cadences reminds us of the union of art and nature that characterizes this mode. We are invited to reenter the sober frame that is Nunappleton and *Upon Appleton House*: "Let's in."

Notes

1. Fairfax's manuscript poem, *Upon the New-built House att Appleton*, is cited by most editors of Marvell, notably Margoliouth / Legouis, 1:282: "Thinke not ô Man that dwells herein / This House 's a stay but as an Inne." This pious notion was a commonplace, as witness, e.g., its appearance in Erasmus' *Colloquies*: "And yet I depart from this life as from an inn, not from a home. Nature gave us a lodging to stop at, not to settle down in." (*The Colloquies of Erasmus*, tr. Craig Thompson [Chicago, University of Chicago Press, 1965], p. 682.)

2. For comment on the "analogy between the building and the poem," see John M. Wallace, *Destiny His Choice: The Loyalism of Andrew Marvell* (Cambridge: Cambridge University Press, 1968), pp. 237–39.

3. *My Ecchoing Song: Andrew Marvell's Poetry of Criticism* (Princeton: Princeton University Press, 1970), p. 250.

4. Ann Berthoff, discussing the poem in *The Resolved Soul: A Study of Marvell's Major Poems* (Princeton: Princeton University Press, 1970), speaks of "Marvell's favorite device of converting a symbol . . . into its phenomenal form and then reconstituting it metaphorically" (p. 183). See also her note 1, pp. 201–204.

5. Discussed by Maren-Sofie Røstvig in "'Upon Appleton House' and the Universal History of Man," *English Studies* 42 (1961): 337–51.

6. Marvell's "I" is examined by Charles Molesworth in "Marvell's 'Upon Appleton House': The Persona as Historian, Philosopher, and Priest," *SEL* 13 (1973): 149–62; he claims that "Introducing a *persona* was Marvell's most radical

addition to the genre of the country-house poem" (p. 153).

7. *My Ecchoing Song*, p. 262.

8. Ibid., p. 213.

9. As Ann Berthoff rightly says, Marvell deals throughout the poem with "the grand and simple theme of correspondence" (*The Resolved Soul*, p. 166).

10. The implications of the movement from the "Wood" episode to the conclusion have been well analyzed by M.J.K. O'Loughlin, "This Sober Frame: A reading of 'Upon Appleton House,'" in *Andrew Marvell: A Collection of Critical Essays*, ed. George deF. Lord (Englewood Cliffs, N.J.: Prentice-Hall, 1968), pp. 137–39.

11. The arms of the de Verses are "Quarterly gules and or, in the first quarter a mullet argent." The mullet may represent "the rowel of a spur," but could also "be taken to represent a star, and . . . it appears originally to have been interchangeable with the *estoile*" (Henry Gough and James Parker, *A Glossary of Terms Used in Heraldry* [reprint, n.p., 1966], p. 419). See also E.E. Duncan-Jones, "Notes on Marvell's Poems," *N & Q* 198 (1953): 431.

In ordine di ruota

Circular Structure in "The unfortunate Lover" and Upon Appleton House

Maren-Sofie Røstvig

I

Giordano Bruno's *De gli heroici furori* (1585) concludes with a circular poem in nine stanzas recited by nine men while standing in a circle—*in ordine di routa*.[1] The form is appropriate because the song celebrates the many "wheels" which govern our lives: the wheels of nature, for example, of time, and of fortune. Bruno's prefatory argument dedicated "to the most illustratrious Sir Philip Sidney" explains that this "chorus is ordered according to the number of the nine spheres" (77), a number "which governs the universality of things and in a certain way informs everything" (73). The poem is also circular in the familiar manner whereby the last line of one stanza becomes the first of the next, while the conclusion returns to the beginning. The song summarizes both the structure and the contents of the work as a whole, the two being inseparable since the argument, crudely stated, is that life is governed by rising and falling movements in such a manner that the end of one extreme denotes the beginning of its opposite.

Like Marvell's "The unfortunate Lover" Bruno's sonnet sequence is about the irresistible power of love. As Bruno puts it, "not without reason is the heart's passion called an infinite sea" (2:3; p. 236), and in this sea his *infortunato amante* finds himself as tempest-tossed and tortured as Marvell's. His "happy days," so he complains, "were shattered by the power of one instant" which made of him "an unfortunate lover forever."[2] The similarities between the two are so many and so striking that neither chance nor commonly shared sources can be held responsible. Marvell must quite simply have been familiar with Bruno's collection of sonnets and accompanying philosophical dialogues.[3]

The fact that *The Heroic Frenzies* is a work closely associated with the English literary scene is not the only reason why it is such a likely source. I have argued, on earlier occasions, that Marvell must have been familiar with the Hermetic dialogues, and Bruno's work not only contains typically Hermetic ideas concerning creation and regeneration, but combines them with a theory of the reconciliation of opposites which owes a considerable debt to Nicholas Cusanus—the philosopher Marvell quotes in *The Rehearsal Transpros'd*.[4] It is likely, however, that readers of *The Heroic Frenzies* would have been most strongly struck by Bruno's advocacy of ideas which come very close indeed to Augustine's *De vera religione*, a treatise of decisive importance to Renaissance poetics.[5] Bruno's poetics coincide with Augustine's on important points, and especially with regard to the significance attributed to formal arrangements. Equally Augustinian in spirit is Bruno's allegorical technique of exposition, and his basic theme of the ascent from lower to higher levels of existence.

Bruno's obliqueness may have exerted a powerful attraction on Andrew Marvell. The two works Bruno dedicated to Sir Philip Sidney (*De gli heroici furori*, 1585 and *Spaccio de la bestia trionfante*, 1584) are markedly oblique, albeit in different ways. The one is allegorical in a serious manner, the other in a joco-serious style which so complicates the allegory that it virtually resists interpretation. Marvell was a cautious man; if we are to believe John Aubrey, he was cautious to the point of fastidiousness in his choice of friends, and he was equally cautious in his treatment of religious issues, largely, perhaps, to avoid "profaning and violating those things which are and ought to be most sacred," to use a telling phrase from *The Rehearsal Transpros'd*.[6] In his lines on *Paradise Lost* Marvell voices the fear he had originally entertained that the poet would ruin "The sacred Truths to Fable and old Song," and he may easily have felt that a joco-serious style combined with the added obliquity of allegory would afford a measure of protection for whatever "sacred Truths" he himself may have wished to incorporate in his lines.

Then, too, obliqueness will often heighten the impact, as Augustine well knew, since what is discovered with difficulty is more highly treasured.[7]

Excellent examples of joco-serious writing are found in Bruno's *Expulsion of the Triumphant Beast*,[8] where the author plays with his readers like a cat with not overly intelligent mice, reserving what he calls the heart of his discourse for those capable of penetrating "into the pith of the meaning" (73). The dialogues, so he says, may seem excellent or vile, learned or ignorant, elevated or low, profitable or useless, religious or profane, all according to the character of his readers. All his propositions, however, must be carefully studied regardless of whether they seem serious or in jest; the multitude may mock the comical Silenus figures found on the surface of his writing, but below the surface, hidden and secure, can be found a treasure house of goodness and truth (71). The best clue to this hidden sense is in the structuring of his ideas, their order and number; fundamental principles are expressed in their internal arrangement. This is why he can write that he presents to Sir Philip Sidney "the numbered and arranged seeds of his moral philosophy" (72); he has taken care to place everything "in a certain number and order" (74). And this is of course why he begins *The Heroic Frenzies* by stating that he considers his subject "in the order that has seemed to me most convenient" (80).

Although by no means joco-serious in style or approach, *The Heroic Frenzies* is sufficiently sophisticated. Poems that seem like innocuous Petrarchan sonnets are expounded so as to compel the reader to realize that despite their apparent concern with an earthly mistress they actually convey images of divine love. As Bruno explains, he had originally thought of calling his book *Canticle*, but in the end he decided against it, in part to avoid censure from obtuse readers and in part because his own writing seemed so different from the *Song of Solomon*, "even though the same appearance and psychic substance is concealed under the shadow of the one and the other" (62). Solomon's figurative writing presents itself as such "openly and manifestly," but "this poem does not show us a face which so keenly invites one to seek a latent and occult sense . . ." (63). If readers, therefore, should feel that his poems express only an "ordinary love," and that he has invented his ingenious comments afterwards to make them seem more interesting, then they must kindly permit the author to define his own intention. As author he is very much present and so must be allowed to gloss his "canticles" which have "their own names, succession, and modes which no one can explain better and understand than myself . . . " (63).

If Bruno's *infortunato amante* does not express an "ordinary love," neither does Andrew Marvell's. Marvell's images require a similar glossing in terms of a metaphysic of love, just as his textual structure too, reveals an undeniable concern with ordered arrangements. In urging this parallel one runs the danger of seeming to associate Marvell with an author whose bias was, if not occult, then certainly distinctly unorthodox. But Bruno's "unfortunate lover" connects with a religious tradition of such impeccable orthodoxy that there is no reason to feel uneasy: behind Bruno's Petrarchan metaphors is a familiar religious argument which may be illustrated here by a quotation from Augustine's medieval disciple, Hugh of Saint-Victor:

> . . . let a man return to his own heart, and he will find there a stormy ocean lashed by the fierce billows of overwhelming passions and desires, which swamp the soul as often as by consent they bring it into subjection. For there is this flood in every man, as long as he lives in this corruptible life, where the flesh lusts against the spirit. Or rather, every man is in this flood, but the good are in it as those borne in ships upon the sea, whereas the bad are in it as shipwrecked persons at the mercy of the waves.
>
> (*De Arca Noe Morali*, 4:16)[9]

But before I discuss Bruno's elaboration of this religions imagery, a brief survey of Marvell's poem will be useful.

II

Marvell's enigmatic stanzas present a tissue of contraries with such verbal economy that one must constantly pause to consider the implications. Within the universe of this lover the very elements "quarrel," while he himself is the object of conflicting forces or impulses as in the case of the cormorants, one of which provides sustenance, while the other "on his Heart did bill." As an "*Amphibium* of Life and Death" the lover is placed "betwixt the Flames and

Waves," but the strongest contrast of all is between his total situation and his reaction to it as expressed in the three last stanzas: not only is he completely indifferent, he positively rejoices in his fate. Although "Forced to live in Storms and Warrs," dying he "leaves a Perfume here, / And Musick within every Ear." These are strange statements, but the conclusion is stranger still. All we can say is that the heraldic image—"In a Field *Sable* a Lover *Gules*"—must be climactic and triumphant, coming as it does after these images of sweet perfume and music. It, too, must show that harmony somehow has been born from disaster and torment.

It is entirely in the spirit of Giordano Bruno that the body of the poem contains what we may call "numbered and arranged seeds" in the form of key concepts strategically placed so as to create a perfectly balanced symmetrical sequence ABCDEFFEDCBA. The pattern may be diagrammed as follows:

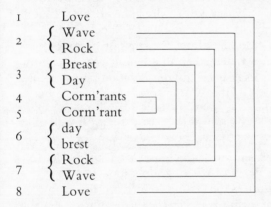

1	Love
2	{ Wave / Rock
3	{ Breast / Day
4	Corm'rants
5	Corm'rant
6	{ day / brest
7	{ Rock / Wave
8	Love

The placing of these words within the stanza can be extremely exact. *Cormorant* for example, is located in the third line in both stanzas, just as the chiastically arranged words *Breast-Day* and *day-brest* occupy the textual center of their respective stanzas. The poem, then, has a circular structure around a double center focused on the ambiguous "Guardians" of the "Orphan of the *Hurricane*." If the thematic movement were to reflect Bruno's philosophy of love, then it should indicate a cycle of descent and ascent, the descent being into a tumultuous passionate existence torn by contrary impulses and powers; at the textual center the conflict should reach its climax, thus releasing the energy to achieve the ascent to the ecstatic vision of absolute beauty (the Monad).

That there is a distinct change once the textual center has been passed is quite clear; the context becomes so different that the repetitions merely serve to point the contrast. Although Love personified occurs both in the first stanza and the last, in the first he is an "Infant Love" playing "By Fountains cool, and Shadows green," while in the last he is connected with wars and "Malignant Starrs." The images of stanza 2 similarly are repeated in the penultimate stanza but while in stanza 2 the attention focuses on the shipwreck and the "*Cesarian Section*" caused by the "master-Wave" and the "Rock," in stanza 7 the hostile environment is suddenly commanded in a manner we have not been led to expect: the lover grapples heroically with "the stubborn Rock," and he stands "nak'd and fierce," "Cuffing the Thunder with one hand." No Petrarchan lover ever braved a tempest in this peculiar way and in such a spirit of resolute endurance. All that this lover "drest / In his own Blood" attempts (*saies* interpreted as *says* or *assays*), he "does relish best."

As we approach the double center the contrast becomes more subtle. Stanza 6, like stanza 3, depicts an apocalyptic scene of extreme violence, and again one sees how careful the attention is to structure: the image of the "Fun'ral of the World" *concludes* stanza 3, but in stanza 6 the corresponding images have been placed *initially* when "angry Heaven" is said to desire "a spectacle of Blood" (lines 1–2). But in the earlier stanza a feeling of tenderness and pity prevails, and fear is very much present. In stanza 6, however, the reader feels like the spectator of a heroic action eliciting admiration, not pity.

The stanzas constituting the double center are linked by the repetition of the name of the birds and by the theme of irreconcilable opposites which nevertheless coexist: in stanza 4 the opposition is between the elements, in stanza 5 between the passions. The riddling quality is particularly marked in stanza 5 where the first thematic movement reaches its climactic conclusion. Here the lover is torn between hope and fear; he is famished and fed at the same time; he increases and is consumed, and he is both alive and dead. This is the centre around which the whole poem turns, and turns deliberately like a wheel to achieve a contrary state. The rock is as stubborn as ever, the tempest as mad, but the lover is no longer an "abject Heir." Instead he dominates the scene, using it for his own inscrutable purposes, and his refusal to acknowledge his torment reveals his kinship to Bruno's heroic of "frenzied" lover.

Lack of space prevents the detailed comparison between Marvell and Bruno which might substantiate my claim of indebtedness. Marvell's choice of title, however, is fairly conclusive, since the phrase occurs repeatedly both in Bruno's sonnet sequence and in his prose dialogues.[10] Indeed, Bruno's very point of departure is the observation (which on one occasion is referred back to Ficino's commentary on the *Symposium*) that the majority of men are incapable of assessing life truly, which is why heroic lovers are seen as "subjects of scorn, laughter, and vituperation" (92). But heroic love must needs be a torment "because it does not rejoice in the present, as animal love does, but in the future and absent ..." (99). As long as man is drawn both to inferior and superior objects of love he is "amphibious, divided, afflicted," but if the higher love prevails he becomes heroic—although in the eyes of the world he will seem "unfortunate" (203). Marvell's title, too, is ironically ambiguous at the expense of the world; through his supreme indifference to his condition Marvell's lover indicates that he has obtained the vision which transforms. The sonnet where Bruno celebrates the sudden transition and transformation abruptly changes the epithet from *unfortunate* to *fortunate*: "O fortunato amante!"[11] And he is fortunate because he has obtained his spouse in the sense attributed to the *Song of Solomon*.

Another link between Bruno and Marvell is that in both writers the argument can be fully grasped only when the textual structure has been perceived. Bruno divided his book into two parts of five dialogues each, but the thematic movement creates a sequence of 4-2-4 dialogues, where the textual center (dialogues 1:5 and 2:1) is identified as such by presenting a summary of the work as a whole (much in the manner attributed to the Psalms in relation to the Bible) and by doing so by means of emblems as well as sonnetc. The emblems, however, are merely described. This centrally placed sequence of 15 and 12 numbered emblems (*cum* sonnets *cum* explanatory dialogue) repeats, and in repeating intensifies, the message contained in the book as a whole, and it is in this sequence that we find the closest analogues to Marvell's emblematic conceits. To each side of the double center is a sequence of four dialogues, each of which has a circular structure: thus the first sequence begins and concludes with the wheel of natural objects, the last with the myth of Actaeon and the vision of the Monad. The book therefore may be said to contain three circular structures, at the same time that the ten dialogues constitute a larger circle containing these three lesser circles.[12] This arrangement recalls Cusanus' Circulus Universorum in the De coniecturis,[13] the difference being that Bruno attributes an intrinsic dynamism to his system of "wheels." As he puts it in his preface, we must try to "traverse, if not all, at least a very great number of the forms contained in the wheel of natural species" (73); we must willingly endure the sequences of descent and ascent whereby one extreme leads on to its opposite, so that in the end the heroic soul may consciously choose the higher love and ignore the vicissitude of life.

Bruno's philosophy of love—and occasionally his phrasing, too—comes very close to Augustine's De vera religione. This is not only the work where Augustine tells the artist to imitate the creative technique of the Deity by imposing unity by means of ordered arrangement; it is also the work where Augustine gives profoundly moving expression to his favorite argument that we must abandon what is mutable and mortal, fixing our hearts instead on what is changeless and immortal. We may be led to perceive the invisible reality behind the visible world (as commanded by Paul in Romans 1 : 20) by contemplating its abstract order, since the ultimate source of all order and harmony is in God, who is highest unity. The harmonious arrangement of parts which is the cause of beauty in the universe and in a work of art, reflects the unity which is God; symmetry preserves unity and makes the whole beautiful (De vera religione 30:54–56).[14] Truth is in the inward man and it is discovered when the inward man aligns himself with the highest harmony (39:72).

In Augustine, then, the antithesis is between carnal man and spiritual man as stated in 2 Corinthians 4:16–18. In a sense, therefore, the conflict between the two could be rendered as growth accompanied by decay in the manner of Marvell's lover and Bruno's. Augustine anticipates Bruno also in his description of the heroic character of the man who reaches out towards the divine, scorning to be held captive by lower things: such a man cannot be conquered and can feel no pain: "Only he is overcome who has what he loves snatched from him by his adversary. He who loves only what cannot be snatched from him is indubitably unconquerable, and is tortured by no envy" (46:86). He "is most truly and certainly an unconquered man who cleaves to God"; "Who can hurt such a man? Who can subdue him?" (cf. 46:88–47:92).

Bruno's dialogue accompanying emblem 2.1.2 comes so close to Augustine as to seem almost a paraphrase intended to be recognized: "... if a shadowy cloudy, elusive beauty painted upon the surface of corporeal matter pleases me so much and so incites my passion ... what would be the effect upon me of that which is the substantial, original and primal beauty?" The effect must be a transformation into "that most worthy and lofty light." The beauty of visible, mutable objects entices us to love beauty of an even higher kind; indeed, "it is from these base objects that he is able to have access to these higher objects in due degree" (184f.). "It is by these enticements, then, that nature's power and skill cause one to be consumed by the pleasure of what destroys him [i.e. love of the divine], bringing him content in the midst of torment and torment in the midst of every contentment ... " (187). But when Bruno adds that everything "results from contrary principles, through the triumph and conquest of one of the contraries," he is no longer within the Augustinian framework.

The context I have invoked by quotations from Bruno and Augustine goes far to explain the puzzling images of Marvell's poem. The cormorants may represent the two loves, and the lover who is all "Gules" may have had the vision which transforms. But for more precise identifications we must turn to Bruno's emblem sequence which begins with the explanation that the emblems are heraldic in character, each expressing the nature of a particular "warrior," his "affections and fortunes" (143). The emblem showing "a nude boy burning in the midst of flames" (1.5.15) perhaps comes closest to Marvell's image, but our perception of its meaning derives from all the preceding emblems, where we are told, again and again, that if the lover prove receptive to the burning arrows emanating from above he will himself "become entirely luminous in substance, may himself become all light, because his affection and his intellection have been penetrated" (205). This passage occurs in connection with the emblem showing two burning arrows upon a shield (2.1.9), representing "the war which continues in the soul of the frenzied one." Both lovers (Bruno's and Marvell's) are wounded; both become "one sole wound, in which all the affections gather to become a single affection" (212); both are menaced by raging waves "with their frightening and mortal assaults" (215), and both in the end achieve a state of indifference to the torment as "the shadows of enigmas and similitudes" are removed from "the murky sky of the human mind," making it fully illuminated (200).

Emblem 2.1.8 represents the effort to reach this state by the image of the eagle impeded in its ascent by a stone tied to one foot.[15] It is because the lover's desires at this halfway point pull him in opposite directions ("I fall to the center and am drawn up toward the sky ... " p. 201) that he is called amphibious (in Italian *ancipite*), divided, and afflicted (203). Marvell's lover is an amphibium "of Life and Death," an expression which finds its exact analogue in the preceding emblem motto, *Mors et vita* (198). When Marvell's lover is said to cuff "the Thunder with one hand," while with the other he grapples with the stubborn rock, I see a conflation of two emblems: the eagle impeded in its ascent, and the blacksmith's forge (emblem 1.5.10 presenting an anvil and a hammer). The workshop may be the lover's breast as Bruno explains, but the lover may himself become the blacksmith if he "sets to work actively exercising the intellectual powers." The intellect is "the true smith of Jove" (166f.). Marvell's lover is Prometheuslike in his stout resistance to angry heaven, and the rock, too, may recall the fate of Prometheus, but Marvell's concluding stanza suggests victory, not defeat. Dying, he "leaves a Perfume here", thus suggesting the triumphant death of the phoenix which consumes itself "on the aromatic altar" in the fire kindled by the light of the sun (155). Bruno calls his heroic lover "one and immovable, like the phoenix" (151); he is attached to one single object only, the sun (162). But the phoenix which "kindles itself in the golden sun" (187) may also represent the poet, the smoke being an apt figure for the "darkness" of poetic images. It is an apt figure also because "we can never make divine things the subject of our thought without detracting from them rather than adding any glory to them" (191). The music which resounds "within every Ear" seems to me to indicate that Marvell, too, associates his lover with a phoenix which serves as a symbol of the poet who consumes his own substance as he offers his sacrifice of praise. The solar image implicit in the myth leads on to the third and last of Marvell's images of perfection: the heraldic image of "a Lover *Gules*" merges the redness of the blood with the golden light of the sun to convey the transformation of the lover into "that most worthy and lofty light." This interpretation alone is capable of giving to the last line the climactic impact which it must have to provide a fitting conclusion.

Marvell's use of a circular structure provides strong support for my interpretation. The structure is unmistakable and undeniable, and it functions exactly like Bruno's "wheels." Although the violence is totally absent from the 97 stanzas of *Upon Appleton House*, here, too, illumination is achieved in a Bruno-like traversing of various "wheels," which concludes with the vision of perfect beauty in the person of Maria Fairfax. Bruno's theme of ascent plays a far more subordinate role in this poem, but Bruno's Augustinian advocacy of symmetrical arrangements finds its finest expression in the artful convolutions of Marvell's homage to Lord Fairfax.

III

In view of the poem's concern with chronological cycles and cycles of generation in the Fairfax family,[16] the discovery that the text pursues a pattern of interlinked circles ought not to be surprising, but surprise is inevitable in view of our inability so far to come to terms with the structure of what has seemed a fairly rambling, long country house poem. Marvell provides all the information we need to grasp his structural strategy in the ten opening stanzas on Lord Fairfax, a sequence which concludes by attributing to Nature the working of having created the estate (where the house is the first object of attention) with its "fragrant Gardens, shaddy Woods, / Deep Meadows, and transparent Floods" (10:79–80).[17] In the concluding twelve-stanza passage on Maria this list is repeated four or five times, on the last occasion in italicized form: ". . . as all *Virgins* She preceds, / So you all *Woods, Streams, Gardens, Meads*" (94:751–52). This reiterated list is the clue which should direct our attention to the fact that the 75 stanzas falling between the homage to the father and the daughter are divided into three equal parts of 25 stanzas each, the first narrating "The Progress of this Houses Fate" (11:84), the second describing the garden and the meadows, the third the woods and the river. We are told in so many words that we are taken on a conducted tour, where "with slow Eyes we these survey" (11:81), at the end of which darkness falls, and so "Let's in . . . ," and the circle is closed. The progress is logical and systematic, the transitions clearly marked, the balance exact.

But to relish Marvell's witty use of structural images we must take a second step: we must perceive that the last two 25-stanza groups are subdivided to permit each of the four named areas to possess its own circle, at the same time that all these circles and circles-within-circles are contained within the larger circle created by linking the end of the poem to its beginning. When I say "circle" this should usually be taken to mean that there is a textual center in the form of one or two stanzas (one if the sum total of stanzas is odd, two if it is even), and that stanzas equidistant from the center are linked (individually or in groups) in the manner familiar to students of Spenser and Milton.[18] In my diagram all such circles are printed in heavier ink.

(a) *The Progress of this Houses Fate*

In this first 25-stanza sequence—the only one not to be sub-divided—the closing of the circle is underlined by the repetition, in reverse order, of identical or similar words. As indicated in the juxtaposed stanzas below, the sequence is as follows: House, Nunnery, Virgin, Ruine, this dwelling, this Seat, demolishing, Virgin, Nun, House.

11

While with slow Eyes we these survey,
And on each pleasant footstep stay,
We opportunly may relate
The Progress of this Houses Fate.
A *Nunnery* first gave it birth.
For *Virgin Buildings* oft brought forth.
And all that Neighbout-Ruine shows
The Quarries whence this dwelling rose

35

At the demolishing, this Seat
To *Fairfax* fell as by Escheat.
And what both *Nuns* and *Founders* will'd
'Tis likely better thus fulfill'd.
For if the *Virgin* prov'd not theirs,
The *Cloyster* yet remained hers.
Though many a *Nun* there made her Vow,
'Twas no *Religious House* till now.

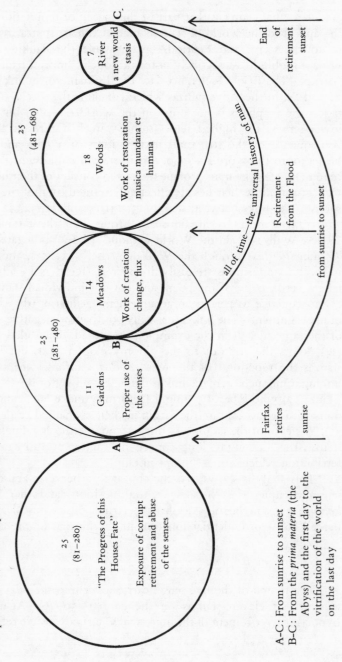

In ordine di ruota

Upon Appleton House

"fragrant Gardens, shaddy Woods, Deep Meadows, and transparent Floods" (10:79–80)

C'

7
River
a new world
stasis

25
(481–680)

18
Woods
Work of restoration
musica mundana et
humana

End
of
retirement
sunset

all of time—the universal history of man

from sunrise to sunset

Retirement
from the Flood

14
Meadows
Work of creation
change, flux

B

11
Gardens
Proper use of
the senses

25
(281–480)

A

25
(81–280)

"The Progress of this
Houses Fate"

Exposure of corrupt
retirement and abuse
of the senses

Fairfax
retires
sunrise

A–C: From sunrise to sunset
B–C: From the *prima materia* (the
Abyss) and the first day to the
vitrification of the world
on the last day

257

At the textual center is that part of the speech of temptation where the appeal to the world of sense is made explicit: stanza 23 appeals to touch, scent, and "curious tasts," while the flanking stanzas (22/24) highlight respectively taste and touch, "mortal fruit" and a corrupt "chastity." References to the human voice link stanzas 21 and 25. In these five stanzas which conclude the speech of temptation the emphasis is not only on the world of sense, but on the lower senses; the highest sense (sight) scarcely figures at all. As a consequence of the structural juxtaposition of a false and a true bridegroom the word *spouse* occurs in stanzas equidistant from the center (15/31). The nuns profane the sacred concept of their heavenly bridegroom, but their lies are effectively refuted by the true earthly spouse. The links between stanzas 13, 14, 15 and 31, 32, 33 (paired 13/33, 14/32 and 15/31) are unusually strong. Thus the statement that "These Walls restrain the World without" (13:99) is negated when "Young *Fairfax* through the Wall does rise" (33:258), and similar ironical juxtapositions are easily discovered. (Readers are advised to take a xerox copy of the poem and cut out individual stanzas in a given sequence to permit an arrangement facilitating the checking of my argument.) The links are usually positive and negative versions of the same idea as in the example just quoted. The "glad Youth" (34) points the contrast to the gloomy cloister (12), but in these stanzas the repetition of the word *cloister* reinforces the thematic linking. One such thematic link is the magic power of the fair virgin (stanza 12) whose beauty "might Deformity make fair," and of the nuns who try to capture the virgin in their enchanted castle (stanza 33). A neat antithesis appears on juxtaposing the last line in each stanza: the "Thoughts long conceiv'd" cannot prevail against the retribution which comes "in one instant."

This analysis shows that the appeal to a perverse abuse of the senses occupies the climactic central position, and that "young *Fairfax*" is cast in the role as a Christlike, true spouse whose "Offspring fierce" has a providential function in the history of the country.

(b) *Gardens and Bastions*

The theme of the five senses carries over into the next circular sequence of eleven stanzas on the garden (36–46). Against the hypocritical retirement of the nuns stands Fairfax's austere retirement where the normally sensuous appeal of the garden has been transformed by a proper use of each of the senses. A proper use is one which directs the attention to the spiritual reality behind external appearances, or to their allegorical, moral significance. At the textual center (41) is the apostrophe to Britain as "The Garden of the World" and a *"Paradise"* lost by the tasting of that "luckless Apple" which made man "Mortal." These are phrases which hark back to the centrally placed speech of temptation in the preceding sequence, with its emphasis on "mortal fruit" and "curious tasts" (22 and 23). The prominent image of the garden as a bastion neatly joins the end of the beginning (36/46); the battery of this bastion is aimed, or pointed at, the enemy which is the five senses in the first stanza (36), and in the last (46) that pride which is the root of all evil. The second stanza (37) invokes all the five senses, while its allusion to the "Morning Ray" should be related to the setting of the sun at the end of the passage on the river. A temporal cycle therefore connects the 50 stanzas within which we find the four circles of the garden, the meadows, the wood, and the river.[19]

The main theme of the garden sequence is the moral integrity of the man who cares for his conscience, "that Heaven-nursed Plant" (45:355), and his moral warfare takes in all the senses, each of which is identified by name: *ear*, *eye*, and *smell* occur in stanza 39, *taste* in 41, *touch* in 45, and *sight* in 46. The highest of the senses therefore has been placed at the very end and given a climactic function combining destruction of evil with appreciation of what is good and innocent.

Around the textual center in stanza 41 the stanzas are ranged with almost military precision. Of the several thematic or verbal echoes serving as links between stanzas equidistant from the center suffice it to mention that Fairfax himself appears at the center of each five-stanza passage leading up to, and away from, the center, and it is certainly numerically appropriate that the man who commands his five senses should be praised for so doing in sequences embodying this number in the stanza-total. According to the familiar *"holy Mathematicks"* of the period (6:47), 5 is a circular number, and when this number is squared,[20] we obtain 25—the basic structural number of Marvell's poem. If I may be permitted to adduce a little biblical number lore, 25 can signify a good or an evil tendency according to whether it is taken *in malam partem* or *in bonam*. In the one case it signifies obstinate addiction to sensual and idolatrous practices (as illustrated by the nuns), in the other a proper use of the senses and a stout resistance to sensual baits.[21] Marvell therefore would seem to have extended his witty play on mathematical concepts (as in stanzas 6–7) to the numbers embodied in the structure of his poem.

(c) The masque of the meadows

The transition to the realm of the meadows is sharp: "And now to the Abyss I pass / Of that unfathomable Grass . . ." (47:369–70). In this division (47–60) we find a Bruno-like list of items constituting the world; the list is presented as such in the poem's penultimate stanza, where the world is said to be "a rude heap" of "Gulfes, Deserts, Precipices, Stone" (96:764). Bruno's corresponding list includes mountains and valleys, rocks and trenches (fossi in Italian), stones, plains, rivers, and seas;[22] Marvell's is much shorter, but the four items figure prominently in the sequence on the meadows and with such connotative richness that they do indeed constitute a world, as Marvell says, or a wheel of natural species, to use Bruno's phrase. Although not included in Marvell's abbreviated list, the sea is very much present (as is the river) in his masquelike presentation of the "wheels." The first item, the "Gulfes," is encountered in the first line in the "Abyss" of "that unfathomable Grass"; "Precipices tall" are formed by the green spires of the grass (47:375–76), while "Desert" and "Stones" are located in stanza 55. Marvell's "wheel," then, begins with the abyss, which Augustine defines as the prima materia used by God in his work of creation,[23] and Marvell refers to the creation of the world in stanza 56 ("The World when first created . . ."). The concept was sufficiently important for Bartholomæus Anglicus to include a chapter "De abisso" in his De Proprietatibus Rerum: the abyss, so he explains, means sine base, "withoute foundement and grounde" (i.e. "unfathomable," to use Marvell's epithet), and this is why the term applies to the "primordial and first matere" undistinguished by form.[24] Augustine links the concept with the mutability of the world: it denotes a "formless fundamental, through which things are altered and changed from one form to another."[25] When form is imposed on the abyss or prima materia, change and time enter, dominating the world in the manner of Marvell's emblematic mowers with their scythes. Change is certainly a key concept: "No Scene that turns with Engines strange / Does oftner then these Meadows change" (49:385–86). Of all things that have form, "none is closer to formlessness than earth and the deep" (*Confessions* 12:19), hence the extreme mutability of the world depicted in this circular sequence on the 'Deep Meadows' (10:80) with their "unfathomable Grass" (47:370). In this sequence the double center (53–54) describes a "triumph" which seems an ironic version of the Dance of Death. Their key words are symmetrically arranged: *Mead, Hay // Hay, Mead, Hay*. (The cricles tread by the females in stanza 54 stand reflected in the circular structure of the stanza itself.) References to *Obsequies* and *Funeral* link the stanzas enclosing the double center (52/55); the *scythe* is a key image in 57 as well as 50; the theme of change links 49 and 58, drowning 48 and 59, while witty inversions dominate the introductory stanza as well as the last (47/60).

The meadows, then, show "all the wonderful variations which take place in the world" (*Confessions* 12:28), but their spiritual significance, as derived from the word *abyss*, is to serve as an image of the unregenerate soul content to remain "*amid the roar of the floods*" sent by God. Fortunately, however, the apostle Paul "calls upon those who are sunk deeper than himself in the abyss," telling them to undergo "*an inward change*," a remaking of their minds (cf. 13:13 quoting Ps. 41:8 and Rom. 12:2). Faith is symbolized by the dry land from which the living sould emerges, a soul so transformed by spiritual gifts that it can "*scrutinize everything*" (cf. 13:22 quoting 1 Cor. 2:15), and so catch "a glimpse of eternity *as it is known through your creatures*" (cf. 13:21 quoting Rom. 1:20). All the change and mutability which we see around us every day, then, should compel us to seek an inward change enabling us to ascend from the visible to the invisible world of eternity.

(d) *The masque of the "Temple green"*

It is entirely in keeping with Augustine's argument that the next passage (61–83) begins with a retreat from the flood into the safety of the Ark, that traditional symbol (or type) of rebirth and regeneration through the church. But Hugh of Saint-Victor, too, deserves quoting again to illustrate the traditional character of

Marvell's thought: "Turning, then, from the works of creation, as from a flood beneath us from which we have emerged, let us begin to treat of the works of restoration, and with them now go, as it were, into the ark."[26]

In Marvell's presentation of the works of restoration trees and birds are major concepts, air and fire being the dominant elements. The connotations of these concepts are as appropriate to the theme of restoration as grass and hay, earth and water are to the theme of the physical creation. The circular structure is indicated by letting the sequence begin and conclude with typological images of redemption (the Ark and the Exodus), and by verbal echoes: *Flood* and *Wood* (61) are repeated in the last stanza in reverse order as *Woods* and *Floods* (83). The double center (69–70) shows the bird as executor of justice (69) and the tree as an image of man (70) who dies content as he sees the triumph of the *"Traitor-worm"* cut short. As in the preceding passage the double center shows the triumph of death, but here the triumph is invalidated by the oblique allusion to Christ's redemptive death which secures eternal life for the soul. In this passage man is seen as both tree and bird, as mortal and divine; the "Labyrinths" of the woods (78:622) is the *mundus peccatus* where redemption may be found so that the forest becomes, not a labyrinth of sin, but a "Temple green" (64:510).[27]

The balancing of parts around the double center may be briefly diagrammed as follows:

Redemption (the Ark)	61–62	78–77	Redemption (Exodus and *imitatio Christi*)
Safe enclosure	63–64	76–75	Safe enclosure
The harmony of music	65–66	74–73	The harmony of Nature and divine revelation
Birds and trees	67–68	72–71	Man as bird and tree

69: bird ⎫
70: tree ⎬ Judgment and Mercy

The physical communion with the *res creatae* (74–75) is perhaps best glossed by again quoting Hugh of Saint-Victor on the Ark of Noah: when we are "spiritual in mind and body equally" we will "after our small measure understand everything through the illumination of our minds. . . . We shall perceive with our mind, and in a manner of speaking with our bodies too," since "our bodily senses are themselves converted into reason, and reason into understanding." Then our "understanding will pass over into God. . . ." (p. 69). In *The Heroic Frenzies* Bruno has a similar passage on the progress from "the lowest in nature to the highest" (224ff.); and just as Bruno (explicating the myth of Actaeon) writes about the few who "in this deserted wood" perceive "the light shining through the obscurity of matter" and so "arrive at the font of Diana" (225), Marvell takes us from the wood to the river and, finally, to a meeting with the nymph who is Maria Fairfax.

(e) *The river and the "Chrystal Mirrour"*

The last circular passage (79–85) presents a world where "all things are become new" (2 Cor. 5:17) so that the mirror of nature, like the mind which contemplates it, has achieved a new purity. As a consequence the distinction between the sun and its reflection (or the invisible world and the visible) has been virtually obliterated. This is what we learn in the first two stanzas (79–80). In the last two stanzas (84–85) the *stasis* which binds even the river—that archetypal image of flux and transience—reflects the permanence and abiding peace of the spiritual world. The very fishes seem "As *Flies* in *Chrystal* overt'ane" (85:678). The theme of being betwixt connects stanzas 80 and 84: in the former "all things" are in doubt whether they be in the mirror "or without," while in the latter the Halcyon flies "betwixt the Day and Night," calming the river and benumbing "*Admiring Nature.*" The idea of looseness prevails in the stanzas closest to the centre (81/83). In stanza 81 the speaker abandons himself to the scene (i.e. aligns himself with the harmony of nature); in the central stanza (82) he recalls that "*young Maria* walks to night" so that he must forego his "Pleasures slight," and hence in stanza 83 nature, too, "it self doth recollect," rejecting its looseness as the speaker does his. The looseness is a permissible one now that the natural state has regained its harmony, permitting the interpenetration of the visible and the invisible to be directly perceived. The "veils and shadows" have been lifted, and we see, not "in a glass darkly" but in a "*Chrystal Mirrour* slick" of such surpassing brightness that it recalls the "once and future state" of complete innocence. As a representative of this state, Maria holds the center. When Marvell in this central stanza (82) dismisses his "Pleasures slight" (referring to himself as a "trifling Youth") he does so in words which invoke the sentence preceding the famous Pauline image of the mirror: "When I was a child, I spake as a child . . . but when I became a man, I put away childish things" (1 Cor. 13:11). The various "masques" are at an end, and the more serious task remains of praising the "*Blest Nymph*" nursed in a "Domestick Heaven" (91–92).

(f) *Linking the end to the beginning*

It is satisfying to ascertain that a poem whose praise consists in attributing a seemly order and proportion to the estate and its owner (4:25–26), should itself be orderly and well proportioned. It remains to indicate how the circle of the poem as a whole is closed.

The concluding image of the fishers who have "shod their *Heads* in their *Canoos*" (97:772) so that the "dark *Hemisphere* / Does now like one of them appear" harks back to the image of the first stanza, where the architect "Did for a Model vault his Brain" (1:6). In each case the head has been used to provide a kind of house or dwelling. The linking continues through the stanzas that follow: a lack of proportion is the common denominator for stanzas 2 and 96; the denunciation of splendid palaces and gardens of stanza 95 has already been heard in stanza 3, just as the perfect order of Fairfax's house (4) connects with the perfect order of his "*Woods, Streams, Gardens, Meads*" (94). The Fairfax family is considered in stanza 5 as in the stanza which is fifth from the end (93), and so on. I must perforce be brief, and so suffice it to draw attention to the way in which Fairfax is praised by being related to his house, Maria to the "Gardens, Woods, Meads, Rivers" (87:696).

*   *   *

A more complete analysis and a discussion of its full implications must be reserved for another occasion, but I hope that I have shown the usefulness of the approach through textual structure. "The Unfortunate Lover" may still remain an enigmatical poem, but we can now make more sense of many of its obscure conceits. As far as *Upon Appleton House* is concerned, we can at long last recognize, and honor, the skill shown in the invention not only of details, but of a master plan which so arranges these details that they become parts of a fully integrated whole. It seems an almost providential act of poetic justice that we can celebrate the tercentenary by restoring to this poem the unity which it possesses to such an eminent degree.

Notes

1. *Opere Italiane*. ed. Giovanni Gentile (Bari, 1908), 2:484. Quotations in English are from P.E. Memmo, tr., *The Heroic Frenzies* (Chapel Hill: University of North Carolina Press, 1964). See also Paulina Palmer, "Marvell, Petrarchism, and 'De Gli Heroici Furori,'" *English Miscellany* 24 (1975): 19–57.

2. *Opere Italiane*. 2:427: "... quei giorni lieti / Troncommi l'efficacia d'un instante, / Che femmi a lungo infortunato amante." Memmo, p. 208: "... for me those happy days were shattered by the power of one instant, which made of me an unfortunate lover forever."

3. The book was printed in London, like the *Spaccio de la bestia trionfante*. For a brief account of Bruno's London period, see Memmo's preface pp. 15–22.

4. See the edition by D.I.B. Smith (London: Oxford University Press, 1971), p. 199. In the original edition the reference occurs in Part 2, p. 117.

5. See my essay "Ars Aeterna: Renaissance Poetics and Theories of Divine Creation," *Mosaic* 3 (1970): 40–61; reprint in *Chaos and Form*, ed. Kenneth McRobbie (Winnipeg, Canada, 1972), pp. 101–19. This argument will be more fully developed in a forthcoming book on the subject.

6. The sentence concludes Part 1.

7. *De doctrina Christiana* 2.6.7–8.

8. English quotations are from the translation by Arthur D. Imerti (New Brunswick, New Jersey: Rutjerj University Press, 1964).

9. Hugh of Saint-Victor, *Selected Spiritual Writings*, tr. by a Religious of C.S.M.V. (London, 1962), p. 143. See pp. 138–48 where these metaphors occur over and over again.

10. See dialogues 1.3 (p. 114); 2.1.7 (p. 199); 2.2 (p. 216), and 2.5 (pp. 260–62).

11. Dialogue 2.2 (p. 216).

12. As in a long poem the plenitude of themes and thematic images permits two or more structures to be embodied in the same text. To suggest the overall circular structure the following diagram may be useful:

$$1 \quad 2 \quad 3 \quad 4 \quad 5 \quad 1 \quad 2 \quad 3 \quad 4 \quad 5$$

centre
Actaeon
the role of the will
the system of contraries
the wheel of Nature, the muses,
blindness, light

When the sequence of 27 emblems in dialogues 1.5 and 2.1 is seen as a single unit, the work contains the same number of units as the circular chorus—9. Bruno's choice of 27 emblems (divided into 15 and 12) was scarcely fortuitous in view of his pronounced interest in number symbolism, nor is it difficult to see that 27 summarizes the three nines of the heavenly, celestial, and earthly spheres. Bruno's own comments on the number 9 (quoted in my opening paragraph) makes this interpretation a likely one.

13. *De coniecturis* 1.16. See Nikolaus von Kues, *Philosophisch-Theologische Schriften* 2 (Vienna, 1966), p. 74.

14. English quotations are from Augustine, *Of True Religion*, tr. J.H.S. Burleigh (Chicago: University of Chicago Press, 1964). This translation is too inaccurate to be of any great use; a Latin text with reliable French translation is available in *Oeuvres de Saint Augustin*, 8 (Paris, 1951).

15. This well-known emblem occurs in Alciati, *Emblematum liber* (Milan, 1531), pp. 12–13. See also Whitney, *A Choice of Emblemes* (Leiden, 1586), p. 152.

16. My diagram shows two temporal cycles: from sunrise to sunset and from the first day of creation to the end of the world.

17. The first number refers to the stanza, those that follow to the line numbering.

18. See particularly A. Kent Hieatt's analysis of Spenser's "Epithalamion" *Short Time's Endless Monument* (New York: Columbia University Press, 1960), Alastair Fowler's *Triumphal Forms* (Cambridge University Press, 1970), and his analyses of Milton's "Nativity Ode" in *Fair Forms*, ed. M.-S. Røstvig (Cambridge: Rowman and Littlefield, 1975), pp. 54–117.

19. Since 100 is a circular number (like 10, 1,000 and so on), 50 may be taken to represent a half-circle or a temporal "hemisphere."

20. The number 5 (like 6) is circular because it reproduces itself in the last digit when multiplied with itself. The body of man could be represented both as a square and a circle, so that the numbers 5 and 25 may be said to "equal Man" (6:48). But 25 is not only the square of 5; since 5 is circular, it becomes "spherical" when lifted to its second powers. I take the last four lines of stanza 6 as in part "self-referring" in the sense that they refer to the poem's circular form. Circles are, in a sense, "immured" in the square number 25.

21. See the chapter on the number 25 in Pietro Bongo's *Numerorum mysteria*, a handbook for students of the Bible authorized by the Roman Catholic church and published (at Bergamo, Venice, and Paris) no less than eight times in the years from 1583–84 to 1614. Bongo was a canon in the cathedral church at Bergamo. For the use, by orthodox theologians, of number symbolism, see my study of "Structure as Prophecy: the Influence of Biblical Exegesis upon Theories of Literary Structure," in *Silent Poetry*, *Essays in Numerological Analysis*, ed. Alastair Fowler (London, 1970), pp. 32–72.

22. The list begins and concludes the circular poem mentioned in my opening paragraph.

23. *Confessions* 12:3–5. English quotations are from the translation by R.S. Pine-Coffin (Harmondsworth: Penguin Books, 1964).

24. Bartholomæus Anglicus, *On the Properties of Things*, tr. John Trevisa (Oxford: Oxford University Press, 1975), 1:664f. The chapter is found in book 13

on water, since "*Abissus* is depnesse of water vnsey ... For oute of þe depnesse comen alle waters. ..."

25. Cf. 12:11 (p. 288).

26. *Selected Spiritual Writings*, pp. 146f.

27. For an exposition of the symbolic import of the labyrinth, see Wolfgang Haubrichs, *Ordo als Form. Strukturstudien zue Zahlenkomposition bei Otfrid von Weissenburg und in karolingischer Literatur* (Tübingen, 1969), pp. 285–93 ("Exkurs IV: Die christliche Interpretation des Labyrinths").

MARVELL'S SATIRES

The Artist as Puritan

WARREN L. CHERNAIK

I. FORMS OF IRONY

PERHAPS THE CENTRAL PROBLEM in Marvell criticism is how to reconcile the two Marvells. On the one hand there is Eliot's Marvell, the detached, fastidious, sophisticated ironist, the author of the Mower poems, "To his Coy Mistress," and the *Horatian Ode*; on the other, there is the radical Puritan, the political activist and moralist, serious, committed, and uncompromising in his political and religious beliefs, the author of "A Dialogue between the Resolved Soul and Created Pleasure," *The Growth of Popery*, and the millenarian prophecies of *The First Anniversary*. My thesis in this essay is that Marvell, like Milton, is centrally a Puritan, but that he differs from most other writers in the Puritan tradition by his consistent irony and wit. He himself described his most ambitious prose work, *The Rehearsal Transpros'd*, as an attempt to show "that it is not impossible to be merry and angry" at once, "without profaning and violating those things which are and ought to be most sacred."[1]

In Marvell's satires and polemical writings, the wit and irony are turned outward, in the service of a perceived truth. The satiric poet is "sworn Enemy to all that do pretend," demolishing the flattering portraits that "servil' wit, and Mercenary Pen" regularly provide, using his wit to expose the fraud implicit in the statues men erect to themselves.[2] Marvell's satires are all essentially icono-

268

clastic, directed at false ideas of heroism, dignity, and grandeur, the lies of political and artistic sycophants, intriguers, and image-makers, the impressive but specious "Pageantry" and "Chimaeras" with which men deceive others and themselves. In organizing many of his satiric poems around an address to a painter, sculptor, or architect, he makes his iconoclasm quite explicit: such poems as *Last Instructions to a Painter*, "The Statue at Charing Cross," and "Clarindon's House-Warming" seek to establish an aesthetic of realism in opposition to the idealizing tendencies characteristic of "historical" painting, statuary, grand public buildings, and heroic panegyric.[3] Marvell sees his role as the servant of truth, however unpalatable it may be in contrast with comforting illusion. Each victim, whether he be hack poet, ambitious clergyman, lord chancellor, or occupant of a throne, is left "scarce ... a rag to his breech," stripped of the false dignity with which he clothes himself, revealed in all his deformities by the harsh and ungenerous light of wit. "Where ought is extolled beyond reason ... it is necessary to depreciate it by true proportion": the satiric poet recognizes a greater obligation than that of expediency, a higher decorum in truth. Armed with his privileged vision, the poet is able to discover the imposture, reveal the culprit "in his own likeness":

> For they do but abuse themselves who shall any longer consider or reverence such an one as a Clergy-man, who as oft as he undresses degrades himself and would never have come into the Church but to take Sanctuary. Rather, wheresoever men shall find the footing of so wanton a Satyr out of his own bounds, the neighbourhood ought, notwithstanding all his pretended capering Divinity, to hunt him thorow the woods with hounds and horn home to his harbour.[4]

The satirist is thus in part militant moralist, who sees himself as a voice for truth amid liars, Abdiel surrounded by Satan's legions. Like most committed men of strong convictions, he is apt to identify truth with one particular doctrinal position to the exclusion of others, seeing his own motivation as "the strong Antipathy of Good to Bad."[5] Yet the passage from *The Rehearsal Transpros'd* just quoted suggests a further motivation for the satirist which may be called aesthetic rather than moral—the sheer joy of the chase, and the delight in manipulation of words, the marshalling of metaphors, rhythm, and such resources of language as alliteration for their own sakes. In the most effective satires, wit is an end as well as a means, and it is perhaps the aesthetic, impersonal dimension of satire to which Dryden pays impressive tribute in his remarks on the character of Zimri in "A Discourse concerning Satire," which rescues satire from mere partisanship and allows it to transcend its occasion.

> There is still a vast difference betwixt the slovenly butchering of a man, and the fineness of a stroke that separates the head from the body, and leaves it standing in its place. A man may be capable, as Jack Ketch's wife said of his servant, of a plain piece of work, a bare hanging; but to make a malefactor die sweetly was only belonging to her husband.... The character of Zimri in my *Absalom* is, in my opinion, worth the whole poem: 'tis not bloody, but 'tis ridiculous enough. And he for whom it was intended was too witty to resent it as an injury.[6]

This impersonal, detached wit is Marvell's most characteristic signature, and it is evident in his satires in verse and prose as well as in his nonsatiric verse. As with the polemical wit of satire, this second type of wit is seen as revelatory of truth, but here truth lies hidden by the opaque nature of reality, not by the venality of men who find it in their interest to conceal it. Only the poet is enabled to penetrate appearances with his imaginative vision. By metaphorical analogy, the universe is made coherent; the unexpected illuminations of the imagination light up a reality whose contours ordinarily lie obscured in the semi darkness of quotidian circumstances:

> As Lines so Loves *oblique* may well
> Themselves in every Angle greet:
> But ours so truly *Paralel*,
> Though infinite can never meet.
>
> ("The Definition of Love," ll. 25–28)

And you would do well and wisely not to stretch, Gold-beat, and Wyer-drawe Humane Laws thus to Heaven: least they grow thereby too slender to hold, and lose in strength what they gain by extension and rarefaction.

> (*RT*, 2, p. 256)

In both passages the conceits express a meaning which is inexpressible other than by the precise yet suggestive means of metaphor. Heterogeneous materials, in Johnson's famous phrase, are yoked by violence together, yet when yoked in conjunction no longer appear heterogeneous: the truth lies revealed in this particular collocation of materials, whose connection was not apparent before.

In each of these passages, moreover, the ironic tone reflects larger ironies, an awareness that, however much we may regret it, the world is fallen and that we must therefore chasten our expectations:

> And had God intended it so, it would so have succeeded, and he would have sway'd and temper'd the Minds and Affections of Mankind so that their Innocence should have expressed that of the Angels, and the Tranquility of his Dominion below should have resembled that in Heaven. But alas! that state of perfection was dissolv'd in the first Instance, and was shorter liv'd than Anarchy, scarce of one days continuance.
>
> (*RT* 2, p. 231)

Through all the variety of Marvell's poetry, he has one recurrent subject: the fall of man, reenacted and reflected in different forms in the loss of innocence of Nymph and Mower, the lamentation over England laid waste in *Upon Appleton House* and *Last Instructions to a Painter*, the many unresolved dialogues between unsatisfactory alternatives. The morality implicit in much of Marvell is that of the education of Adam and Eve in the last books of *Paradise Lost*: though we may be tempted to "give ear to proud and curious Spirits," to fall prey either to "a vast opinion of [our] own sufficiency" or to despair, ultimately we must learn "to be content with such bodies, and to inhabit such an Earth as it has pleased God to allot us."[7]

A further form of irony in Marvell, then, is irony turned inward, Christian wit. Man's lot, with the soul and the body uneasily coexisting as irreconcilable and inseparable enemies, is itself ironic; his "vain Head, and double Heart" assure both that his unresolved paradoxes will cause him pain and that he will be incapable of finding any solution or relief. Man, as Marvell sees him, is doomed to feel the anguish of parallel lines, wracked by a yearning to "joyn," yet helplessly extending side by side into infinity. Yet, as a final twist of irony, in man's weakness and frustration lies his strength. It is his consciousness, his capacity for feeling guilt, pain, and loss, his unique though sometimes unwelcome gift of retrospective awareness ("What Knowledge forces me to know; / And Memory will not foregoe"), the weight of conscience which he cannot, even if he wished to do so, "atturn and indenture" over to others, that enables man to find a path to freedom. It is by the "Opposition of the Stars" that love is defined: "Magnanimous Despair" enables the lovers of "The Definition of Love" to attain a perfection denied ordinary lovers, whose "Tinsel" joys soon fade. The lovers of "The Definition of Love" have been initiated into experience, unlike the happy innocents "with whom the Infant Love yet playes," described in stanza I of "The unfortunate Lover," secure in a vegetative pastoral contentment, unaware of their inability "to make impression upon Time." It is Marvell's version of the paradox of the Fortunate Fall: the postlapsarian lovers of "The Definition of Love," gifted with consciousness, are able to defy the "Tyrannick pow'r" of fate, which in separating them can only intensify their love.[8]

Neither earthly tyrant nor outer necessity, Marvell argues, has the absolute power their partisans claim. A belief in an essential human freedom which no outward force can touch is central to Marvell's thought, as to Milton's:

> That the Body is in the power of the mind; so that corporal punishments do never reach the offender ... That the Mind is in the hand of God. ...[9]

With characteristic irony, Marvell warns that man's gift of freedom does not enable him to remake the world according to his desires, or even to make much of a dent in his environment: "For men may spare their pains where Nature is at work, and the world will not go the faster for our driving." To Marvell as to Milton, absolute freedom is a chimera and "to dispute with God" a sign of rebellious pride:

> In the shape of Mans body, and in the frame of the world, there are many things indeed lyable to Objection, and which might have been better if we should give ear to proud and curious Spirits.[10]

But in his verse and prose satires, as in such poems as *An Horatian Ode*, "The Definition of Love," "To his Coy Mistress," and *Upon Appleton House*, Marvell consistently emphasizes the role of individual will and the exercise of human freedom in a providentially ordered universe. The conception of an iron necessity which rendered all human action futile and made all talk of moral choice superfluous, a necessity "that was pre-eternal to all things, and exercised dominion not only over all humane things, but over *Jupiter* himself and the rest of the Deities and drove the great Iron nail through the Axle-tree of Nature," was antipathetic to him. The doctrine of a "Universal Dictatorship of Necessity over God and Man," so attractive to predestinarians and apologists for earthly rulers ("I have some suspicion," he writes of his opponent in *The Rehearsal Transpros'd*, the egregious Samuel Parker, "that you would have men understand it of your self, and that you are that Necessity"), in Marvell's view robs the universe of any meaning and simply deifies power. Marvell rejected Hobbist reason of state as he rejected Calvinist predestination: to him, man is a reasonable creature and therefore free.[11] No form of outward necessity can negate man's responsibility to choose between right and wrong, to determine, with the aid of his conscience, "Humane Reason guided by the Scripture," how to behave in his daily life. The soul is given an "immortal Shield," and must "learn" to bear its weight. Marvell's polemical writings and satires are all grounded in a similar conception of freedom and experience, which one can describe, in a rather unsatisfactory shorthand, as non-Calvinist or libertarian Puritan. They are, as it were, aids to the embattled soul, in which the hard freedom of truth is contrasted with comfortable enslavement to expediency: "Where the Creator's skill is priz'd,/The rest is all but Earth disguis'd." Morality, as Milton says in *Areopagitica*, cannot flourish in a climate of prescription, "unexercis'd and unbreath'd"; through exercise, through exposure to experience, the resolved soul learns to discriminate.[12]

II. THE SAVING REMNANT

Marvell's later writings generally seek to award blame or praise—in the words of Ruth Nevo, they "present the deformed image of vice and the fair face of virtue at one and the same time." On the one hand, such works "represent, / In quick *Effigy*, others Faults, and feign, / By making them ridiculous, to restraine"; on the other, they encourage those the author considers worthy of praise in hopes of increasing their number and strengthening their resolution.[13] Most men are blinded by their folly: in their "brutish fury," their greed, their swollen self-conceit, they are sunk in a "Lethargy" or boil in "a Feaver," unable to distinguish objective reality from their diseased imaginings. Marvell's extended ironic diagnosis of Parker as incurably maddened by pride is characteristic both in its wit and in its evocation of standards of rationality, humility, and self-knowledge:

> This thing alone elevated him exceedingly in his own conceit, and raised his *Hypocondria* into the Region of the Brain: that his head swell'd like any Bladder with wind and vapour.... He was stretch'd to such an height in his own fancy, that he could not look down from top to toe but his Eyes dazled at the Precipice of his Stature.[14]

The "Addle-Brain'd Citts" who abase themselves before Charles II and the Duke of York and "in Chaines offer [their] Freedome," the ambitious statesmen maddened by "overweening Presumption and preposterous Ambition" all walk in a self-imposed darkness. The power of self-interest makes it difficult to follow the narrow path of righteousness, but man is under a moral obligation to strive to distinguish between good and evil and not be ruled by mere expediency, not blind himself to a reality higher than his own comfort, his own flattering self-image. "The world in all," Marvell says in "The Loyall Scott," contains "but two nations," namely "the good" and "the bad," capable of "worth heroick" or "heroick crimes": "Under each *Pole* place either of the two, / The bad will basely, good will bravely do."[15]

This clear-cut division of mankind into "the good" and "the bad" characterizes all of Marvell's satiric writings, and often takes the form of a contrast between the unregenerate multitude and a saving remnant. From *Last Instructions to a Painter* to *The Growth of Popery* he singles out for praise a handful of men who "stood up ... for the *English* Liberties" though "under all the disadvantages imaginable," being "overlaid by Numbers" in Parliament and at all times conscious of the weight of power exerted against them:

But notwithstanding these, there is a handfull of *Salt*, a sparkle of *Soul*, that hath hitherto preserved this grosse Body from Putre-faction, some *Gentlemen* that are constant, invariable, indeed *English*-men; such as are above *hopes*, or *fears*, or *dissimulation*, that can neither flatter, nor betray their King, or Country: But being conscious of their own Loyalty, and Integrity, proceed throw good and bad report, to acquit themselves in their Duty to God, their Prince, and their Nation; Although so small a Scant-ling in number, that men can scarce reckon of them more than a *Quorum*.[16]

In speaking of this small group of resolute patriots, Marvell frequently uses military metaphors, calling forth the traditions of unselfish heroism associated with epic poetry and with republican Rome. Thus in *Last Instructions* an outnumbered Country Party M.P., faced with a surprise attack in a thinly populated house, is described as "fighting it single till the rest might arm," holding off the foe like Horatius at the bridge: "Such *Roman Cocles* strid: before the Foe,/ The falling Bridge behind, the Stream below" (ll. 248–50). Confident because they stand up for the interest of the people of England, these brave men are able to counteract the superior force of their opponents:

> These and some more with single Valour stay
> The adverse Troops, and hold them all at Bay.
> Each thinks his Person represents the whole,
> And with that thought does multiply his Soul:
> Believes himself an Army, ...
>
> (ll. 267–71)

Marvell's consistent emphasis on the small number of true patriots and the difficulty of remaining steadfast in the face of the designs of those in power no doubt reflects his Puritan conviction that man and nature are deeply infected by original sin and that the regenerate elect are at any time few in number. A belief in the innate sinfulness of man runs through his works: "Men," he says in *Mr. Smirke*, "are all infirm and indisposed in their spiritual condition." Marvell's essential Puritanism shows itself in his consistent adherence to the doctrine of justification by faith: to assume that we can merit salvation by our own unaided virtue, that the superlative merit we see in ourselves will be recognized in heaven, is in his view mere pride:

> To render men capable of Salvation there is a more extraordinary influence of Gods Spirit required and promised.... For mine own part I have, I confess, some reason, perhaps particular to my self, to be diffident of mine own *Moral Accomplishments*, & therefore may be the more inclinable to think I have a necessity of some extraordinary assistance to sway the weakness of my belief, and to strengthen me in good duties.[17]

The truly virtuous men—those whom Marvell calls "the little invisible *Catholick Church*," a "Congregation of the Faithful" who resist the external pressures, in religion as in politics, to follow the lure of power "as nimbly as the Needle to the Load stone," but instead have "always search'd and believ'd the Scriptures" and "made a stand by their Testimonies and sufferings"—are always in a minority. Like other Puritans of the libertarian left, Marvell questioned the rigidity of the orthodox Calvinist view of predestination, but no less than Milton he held that few men are found worthy of salvation.[18]

The recurrent image of the "small ... Scantling" of honorable men also reflects the belief, particularly characteristic of Restoration satire and comedy, that the fools make up an overwhelming majority in any company and that the true wits, to whom the artist addresses himself, are no more numerous than the truly virtuous. The prose satires *The Rehearsal Transpros'd* and *Mr. Smirke* are explicitly addressed to an elite of true wits and owe much of their effectiveness to Marvell's skill in manipulating the responses of a court audience, each member of whom is eager to be enrolled in the ranks of the elect in the war against folly. Dryden, whose political allegiances were entirely opposed to those of Marvell, similarly singles out in *Absalom and Achitophel* a loyal few who "ev'n in the worst of days" remained true to their principles. In Dryden's satire, as in *Last Instructions* and *The Rehearsal Transpros'd*, literary convention is ultimately inseparable from moral, aesthetic, and political convictions.[19]

The emphasis throughout Marvell's works on the "handfull of *Salt*" within the "grosse Body," moreover, reflects political realities as the author saw them. The court had many weapons at its disposal, not the least of which was the distribution of honors and offices, and Clifford before 1674 and Danby afterwards succeeded by wholesale bribery in converting opponents to supporters of the court. As Marvell writes in a letter of 1671:

> Nevertheless such was the Number of the constant Courtiers, increased by the Apostate Patriots, who were bought off, for that Turn, some at six, others ten, one at fifteen, thousand Pounds in Mony, besides what offices, Lands, and Reversions, to others, that it is a Mercy they gave not away the whole Land, and Liberty, of *England*.[20]

For the Country Party opposition to muster a majority in Parliament on a particular issue, it was necessary for the small band of steadfast opponents of the court to gain allies. In *Last Instructions*, Marvell attributes the defeat of the court's excise bill to the votes of an "unknown Reserve" of country gentlemen, financially independent and grown critical of the abuses of the court: "A *Gross* of *English Gentry*, nobly born, / Of clear *Estates*, and to no Faction sworn" (ll. 286–88). By the time he wrote *The Growth of Popery*, ten further years of experience with the same House of Commons had made him more skeptical about the motivation of his temporary allies, and he speaks of "the assimilation of ambitious, factious, and disappointed Members, to the little, but solid, and unbyassed Party."[21]

The contrast between the "two nations," the unregenerate many and the virtuous few, helps give unity to the otherwise diffuse and anecdotal *Last Instructions to a Painter*. Though no one figure dominates the poem, the Earl of Clarendon is presented both as the leader of the court forces and as the embodiment of the principles of ambition, greed, and disorder. Here as in "Clarindon's House-Warming," the Chancellor is depicted as swollen with pride, insatiable in his craving for power: "See how he reigns in his new Palace *culminant*, / And sits in State Divine like *Jove* the *fulminant*!" (ll. 355–56). The "painter" motif serves both to provide rhetorical patterning and to call the reader's attention to the painful discrepancy between reality and ideal: look here upon this picture, and on this. The deliberately grotesque and ugly details in the extended portraits of the Earl of St. Albans, the Countess of Castlemaine, and the Duchess of York

("Paint her with Oyster Lip, and breath of Fame" [l. 61]) supplant
conventional ideas of artistic decorum with an iconoclastic aesthetic
suitable to a "race of Drunkards, Pimps, and Fools" (l. 12), while
they suggest the emptiness and futility of a life devoted solely to
the headlong pursuit of power and pleasure:

> Paint *Castlemaine* in Colours that will hold,
> Her, not her Picture, for she now grows old.
> She through her Lacquies Drawers as he ran,
> Discern'd Love's Cause, and a new Flame began.
> Her wonted joys thenceforth and *Court* she shuns,
> And still within her mind the Footman runs.
>
> (ll. 79–84)

All the courtiers in *Last Instructions* live by a Hobbesian calculus, in
which motivations are devalued to the merely physical—"Love's
Cause" is a penis, the "mind" can express itself only in bodily terms
(as with the Speaker of the House of Commons, Sir Edward Turner:
"When *Grievance* urg'd, he swells like squatted Toad" [l. 877]).

Because Clarendon's confederates are led entirely by self-interest,
there are no feelings of loyalty among them, as there is no fidelity to
principle. Thus when Clarendon loses the King's favor, his former
associates are quick to abandon him and make him a scapegoat for
the failures of the policies they had supported:

> To her own Husband, *Castlemain*, untrue.
> False to his Master *Bristol*, *Arlington*,
> And *Coventry*, falser than any one,
> Who to the Brother, Brother would betray;
> Nor therefore trusts himself to such as they.
>
> (ll. 932–36)

The lesser troops of the court party are equally ruled by the desire
for personal aggrandizement. Though a disorderly mob, "whose
Horses each with other interferes" (l. 196), each seeking his own
benefit and indifferent to any other concerns, they are united and
given a semblance of military discipline by their awareness that
their interest can best be served by selling their votes to the court:
"For always he commands that pays" (l. 172).

To them succeeds a despicable Rout,
But knew the Word and well could face about;
Expectants pale, with hopes of spoil allur'd.

(ll. 157–59)[22]

Opposed to the corrupt many in *Last Instructions* are the upright few, who maintain their principles in spite of the utter darkness that surrounds them. Though they inhabit a world "rul'd by cheating" where all values appear to be inverted, yet a few men are able somehow to persevere in a course of honor and integrity.[23] In such a world, heroic and virtuous action is necessarily its own reward, since it is not likely to meet with any earthly success. Any victories are likely to be temporary, the result of momentary good fortune, defying all ordinary expectations:

> It is lesse difficult to conceive, how Fire was first brought to light in the World then how any good thing could ever be produced out of a House of Commons so constituted, unlesse as that is imagined to have come from the rushing of Trees, or battering of Rocks together, by accident.[24]

At times, all one can do is to die bravely in defense of one's beliefs. The death of Archibald Douglas, described in an extended episode, [and discussed below by Professor Messina-ed.] is thus a paradigm of how one should behave when faced with disaster, and the gallantry of Douglas points up the inadequacy of the models of behavior provided by those around him, with no sanctions to call on other than self-interest. The "feather'd *Gallants*," hoping to find entertainment in the spectacle of a battle, run away "when first they hear the Gun" (ll. 597–99); the sailors "refuse to mount our Ships" or desert to the Dutch in anger over not having been paid (ll. 600–601). The lines on "brave *Douglas*" are immediately preceded by a complementary portrait of Sir Thomas Daniel, "Of Person tall, and big of bone," whose deceptive martial appearance hides "a vain Terrour," so that when faced by the Dutch fireships "*Daniel* then thought he was in *Lyons* Den" and deserted his ship (ll. 633, 637, 642). Douglas behaves differently:

Fix'd on his Ship, he fac'd that horrid Day,
And wondred much at those that run away
. . . .
That precious life he yet disdains to save,
Or with known Art to try the gentle Wave.
Much him the Honours of his ancient Race
Inspire, nor would he his won deeds deface.

(ll. 661–62, 671–74)

Like the outnumbered band of parliamentary warriors who are able
to "recall to mind" their "former Trophees" (l. 253) before going
into battle, secure in their knowledge that they fight not for themselves but as representatives of an honorable tradition, Douglas is
incapable of fear. He faces death with aristocratic calm, in lines
reminiscent of Marvell's account of Charles I on the scaffold; as with
Charles I, his entire life has been preparation for this climactic
moment:

Down on the Deck he laid himself, and dy'd,
With his dear Sword reposing by his Side.
And, on the flaming Plank, so rests his Head,
As one that's warm'd himself and gone to Bed.

(ll. 687–90)

The Douglas episode seems in some ways anomalous, since it is
an extended set piece, stylistically and tonally at variance with most
of the poem, and Marvell in fact used the episode a second time in
an entirely different context, as the nucleus of "The Loyall Scott"
(c. 1670). But the function of the episode in *Last Instructions* is clear:
it provides, in a manner familiar to satire, an explicit statement of
the ideal against which the deviations from that ideal can be measured.
As in Marvell's nonsatiric works, the reality of nature fallen, pressing
in on our consciousness from all sides, is contrasted with the hope
of nature redeemed. Art, like life, can provide patterns for imitation,
both positive and negative:

As Mr. *How*'s Letter may serve for a Pattern of what is to be
imitated, so *The Discourse* may remain as a Mark (the best use it
can be put to) of what ought to be avoided in all writing of Controversies, especially by Divines, in those that concern Religion.[25]

Despite the apparent helplessness of poetry before the massed forces of earthly might, the poet's power, like that of beleaguered virtue, is infinite, since he bears the gift of immortality.

> Fortunate Boy! If either Pencil's Fame,
> Or if my Verse can propagate thy Name;
> When *OEta* and *Alcides* are forgot,
> Our *English* youth shall sing the Valiant *Scot.*
>
> (ll. 693–96)

In a world where values are topsy-turvy, the poet is the voice of unchanging truth, seeking to right the balance and bring others to their senses. When other potential champions have run away or bowed down before the altar of triumphant injustice, "then is the Poets time, 'Tis then he drawes, / And single fights forsaken Vertues cause" ("Tom May's Death," ll. 65–66). Though the political circumstances of individual works differ, Marvell's political writings share the same fundamental attitude: the body politic is diseased, and the necessary first step towards a cure is to face the truth.

In the envoi concluding *Last Instructions*, Marvell attempts, as though by a surgical operation, to divide the king from the corruption of his court, exercising the right of a virtuous citizen to advise his prince.

> Blame not the *Muse* that brought those spots to sight,
> Which, in your Splendor hid, Corrode your Light;
> Kings in the Country oft have gone astray,
> Nor of a Peasant scorn'd to learn the way.
>
> (ll. 957–60)

If the medicine is harsh, his defense is that truth makes its own decorum. As Dryden writes:

> The true end of Satyre, is the amendment of Vices by correction. And he who writes Honestly, is no more an Enemy to the Offendour, than the Physician to the Patient, when he prescribes harsh Remedies to an inveterate Disease.[26]

Though the passages devoted to Charles II in *Last Instructions* and Marvell's other satires show him to be "a man, with as little mixture of the seraphic part as ever man had," nevertheless the poet treats him here as capable of recognizing the truth when it is shown him and of acting in a manner suitable to a prince.[27] The plea to Charles to remove from power the palace guard who "have strove to Isle the *Monarch* from his *Isle*" (l. 968) relies in part on an evocation of the ideal of the harmonious state, violated by the "scratching *Courtiers*" (l. 978) who would destroy everything in their blind pursuit of gain: "The *Kingdom* from the *Crown* distinct would see, / And peele the Bark to burn at last the Tree" (l. 971–72). But the appeal to the king does not assume Charles's dedication to principles of good government, warning him in vivid physical details (the "grizly Wound" of his grandfather, the "purple thread" around his father's neck [ll. 920–22]) that kings too may be called to account.

Satirists notoriously find it harder to express convincing positives directly than to adumbrate an ideal realm, often associated with an unreachable transcendent sphere or an irrecoverable past, which fitfully illuminates sordid and ludicrous reality. In the closing lines of *Last Instructions* Marvell seeks to translate the idea of a saving remnant into concrete, practical form, suggesting the kind of men the king ought to appoint as his advisers. The lines carry less poetic conviction than the previous attack on "scratching *Courtiers*," yet they hold open the hope that not all men are greedy and vicious, that there are potential counselors who seek nothing for themselves and desire only the public good, that the ideal is perhaps not entirely beyond reach:

> But they whom born to Virtue and to Wealth,
> Nor Guilt to flatt'ry binds, nor want to stealth;
> Whose gen'rous Conscience and whose Courage high
> Does with clear Counsels their large Souls supply . . .
> (Where few the number, choice is there less hard)
> Give us this *Court*, and rule without a *Guard*.
>
> (ll. 983–90)

As Marvell's satires constantly point out, the temptations of power are exceedingly difficult to resist. Such poems as "The Kings Vowes" and "Upon his Majesties being made free of the Citty" portray Charles II as a man whose love of ease inclined him toward the belief that he could rule by consulting only his immediate pleasure:

> I will have a fine Parliament allwayes to Friend,
> That shall furnish me Treasure as fast as I spend;
> But when they will not they shall be at an end.
>
> ("The Kings Vowes," ll. 10–12)

Appeals to nature, reason, and the good of the nation, as *Last Instructions* and Marvell's other satires make abundantly clear, may well fall on deaf ears. Nevertheless, the poet must speak out. Here as elsewhere in Marvell, an unblinking awareness of man's boundless capacity for vice, folly, and self-deception is balanced against the hope that truth may at last prevail.

III. THE NAKED TRUTH

Throughout his satires in verse and prose, Marvell's muse, like Swift's, is Truth. His many statements expressing scorn for hypocrites and timeservers who flee from "forsaken Vertues cause," "Apostatizing" from the "spotless" truth of the artist whenever subjected to the slightest pressure, reflect his independence of character. Considered rhetorically rather than autobiographically, such statements serve as "ethical proof," intended to show the author to be a man of integrity, whom readers can trust.[28] A great number of poets, from Skelton to Yeats, have proclaimed "walking naked" as their artistic credo, and the suspicion of rhetorical ornamentation is as common among satirists as the suspicion of worldly wealth and power.

Yet the belief that truth is naked, single, and absolute raises problems for the artist. "Tom May's Death," Marvell's most explicit statement of the responsibilities of the artist, is more or less royalist in its politics, but it is uncompromisingly, rigidly Puritan in its aesthetic attitudes. A similar attitude finds expression in his iconoclastic verse satires of the 1670s, in *The Growth of Popery*, and in such lyrics as "The Mower against Gardens": metaphors are likely to be lies, and true art is "sworn Enemy to all that do pretend," forswearing the fraudulent and corrupt inventions by which "Luxurious Man" seeks to transform "plain and pure" nature into his own "double" and fallen image.[29] The uncompromising severity of his attacks upon May, presented in "Tom May's Death" as a sycophant willing to

sell his services to the highest bidder, or upon the courtiers of
Charles II, presented in his later verse satires as bloated, greedy men
who allow the body politic to become more and more diseased as
they erect palaces and statues of a specious grandeur, reflects a suspicion of art similar to that in "The Mower against Gardens" and
"The Coronet." "Tom May's Death," like Marvell's post-Restora-
tion verse satires directed at poets, architects, and sculptors, attacks
false art, art which deliberately sets out to mislead. Yet implicit in
each of these works is the Platonic and Puritan charge that all art
lies. "The Coronet" suggests that even if the artist has not, like May,
consciously "prostituted" his art ("Tom May's Death," l. 71), he
must inevitably succumb to the pursuit of a compromising "mortal
Glory." The most subtle temptation facing the artist, according to
"The Coronet," is the belief that his own art is not contaminated
by the fall, and the hardest test for the Christian is to give up what is
most beloved to him when his master demands it:

> But thou who only could'st the Serpent tame,
> Either his slipp'ry knots at once untie,
> And disintangle all his winding Snare:
> Or shatter too with him my curious frame:
> And let these wither, so that he may die,
> Though set with Skill and chosen out with Care.

(ll. 18–24)

"The Coronet" owes much of its poignancy to the paradox it
embodies, as a plea to resolve a conflict which it knows can never
be resolved, invoking an ideal simplicity by means of a complex
and carefully woven wreath of language. Like Herbert in "Jordan"
(1) and (2), Marvell proclaims that truth must be single, in the ironic
awareness that every line of the poem shows it to be mutliple.
Marvell's satires at their best show a similar recognition of the
doubleness of truth. In them, as in effective satire generally, the
impulse toward action and the impulse toward the aesthetic are held
in equipoise. Yet in the course of Marvell's later career, we can trace
a gradual movement away from ironic equipoise, away from art.

For an artist to dedicate himself entirely to action, to reject art
as inevitably fraudulent, incompatible with the singleness of truth,
is self-defeating. In the beginning of *Last Instructions*, Marvell cites

the traditional story of the painter Protogenes, who, in a rage at being unable to draw the flecks of foam around a dog's mouth, threw his pencil at the canvas:

> The Painter so, long having vext his cloth,
> Of his Hound's Mouth to feign the raging froth,
> His desperate Pencil at the work did dart,
> His Anger reacht that rage which past his Art;
> Chance finisht that which Art could but begin,
> And he sat smiling how his Dog did grinn.
>
> (ll. 21–26)

The parable can be read as illustrating that anger and art are perhaps after all compatible, that it is possible to be "merry and angry" at once.[30] Yet in another interpretation of the parable, the implications are despairing and ultimately destructive of art. When reality is sufficiently ugly, the parable suggests, art becomes impossible; the muses are silenced. Under such circumstances the choices left for the conscientious artist are limited: he can seethe in impotent rage or he can seek to draw truthfully the ugliness of reality, to make the intolerable appear intolerable in hopes of awakening an audience who blandly accepts any ignominy as a matter of course. The danger is that the swamp of reality will engulf the artist, causing him to succumb to despair:

> For the graver's at work to reform him thus long.
> But alas! he will never arrive at his end,
> For 'tis such a king as no chisel can mend.
>
> ("The Statue in Stocks-Market," ll. 54–56)

No art, Marvell tells his painter in *Last Instructions*, can "match our Crimes": reality requires not marmoreal precision and weight, but the art of the caricaturist, who can capture the momentary appearance of ugliness. The artist must draw grotesques, forgetting about the ideals of beauty and permanence except as implicit standards of measurement by which one can measure what has been lost. An artist brought up to believe in the normal Renaissance canons of art may find reality "too slight grown, or too hard" to imitate. Paradoxically, the most suitable artist to "serve this race of Drunkards,

Pimps, and Fools" is a bad artist, like the inept sculptor who designed the statue of Charles II at Stocks-market, "a thing / That shews him a monster more like than a King."

> Canst thou paint without Colours? Then 'tis right:
> For so we too without a Fleet can fight.
> Or canst thou dawb a Sign-post, and that ill?
> 'Twill suit our great debauch and little skill.[31]

The dry factuality of *The Growth of Popery* represents a further stage in the rejection of art. It is not a satire, but an "account," a "naked Narrative." Rather than employing the art of the satiric caricaturist, who seeks to heighten reality for comic and persuasive effect, following the dictates of traditional theorists who define satire and comedy as showing men as worse than they are (where panegyric and the heroic forms show them as better than they are), here Marvell strives for unembellished truth, simple fact.[32] He aims to persuade, of course, but he no longer seeks to amuse. In the opening sentence, we find no aesthetic indirectness; he chooses his words carefully for effect, but is no longer concerned "to make a malefactor die sweetly." The artist has been submerged into the revolutionary agitator:

> There has now for diverse Years, a design been carried on, to change the Lawfull Government of *England* into an Absolute Tyranny, and to convert the established Protestant Religion into down-right Popery.[33]

The distance between such a statement and the Marvell of *Upon Appleton House* is immense. Meditative retirement, the free flow of the imagination, the life of the *"easie Philosopher"* able to "securely play" on the world, drawing on the riches of nature and the even greater riches of the mind, are no longer possible. The artist's role has been reduced to documentation, demonstration, even to providing raw factual materials, texts of speeches and bills brought before Parliament, statistics. Such a work, indeed, with its raw data, minimally selected and arranged, "which may serve as matter to some stronger Pen and to such as have more leisure and further opportunity to discover and communicate to the Publick," represents a total, desperate renunciation of art.[34]

The Growth of Popery expresses in the clearest and most un-compromising form the diminishing of aesthetic disinterestedness, of the free play of wit, which characterizes many of Marvell's later writings. As in some of the bleaker passages in *Paradise Regained*, the pressure of the ugly times impinging on the poet's consciousness has led to an increasing pessimism and a narrowing of the range of choice:

> He who receives
> Light from above, from the fountain of light,
> No other doctrine needs, though granted true;
> But these are false, or little else but dreams.
>
> (*Paradise Regained*, 4:288–91)

At the end of his life, Marvell felt that conscience required that a final choice be made between art and action; the debate between soul and body, withdrawal and involvement, whose unresolved tension had been the source of Marvell's characteristic wit and poignancy, now at last found a resolution, if at considerable cost. As with the Milton of *Paradise Regained*, the final choice of uncom-promising bareness is more satisfying doctrinally than artistically. Marvell does not share the late Milton's rejection of politics, and thus for him moral choice continues to take a specifically political form, an activist's desire to "change" the world rather than simply "inter-pret" it. For the artist of conscience living in a society he finds diseased beyond hope of immediate remedy, the only alternatives remaining, Marvell came to believe, were lonely, silent despair or the discipline of cooperative political action toward a revolutionary end.[35]

IV. MAGNANIMOUS DESPAIR

At times throughout his writings—in *Upon Appleton House* and "On a Drop of Dew" as well as intermittently in the satires—Marvell's Puritan convictions led him to suggest that "*Conscience*, that Heaven-nursed Plant," could not grow in "earthly Gardens" and that the only attainable paradise was the one within.[36] Never-theless, in the perspective of Marvell's Christian irony, man remains a rational being even in his fallen state, for all the proofs he constantly gives of his irrationality. According to the political principles to which the poet held constantly throughout his career, in *An Horatian Ode* and *The First Anniversary* as in *The Rehearsal Transpros'd*, *Last Instructions*, "The Kings Vowes," and *The Growth of Popery*, "men . . . are to be dealt with reasonably, and conscientious men by Conscience." Under a system of mixed government, in which neither executive nor Parliament holds a monopoly of power, the ruler, in harmony with the land and its inhabitants, "may without arrogance be said to remain the onely Intelligent Ruler over a Rational People."

> In short, there is nothing that comes nearer in Government to the Divine Perfection, then where the Monarch, as with us, injoys a capacity of doing all the good imaginable to mankind, under a disability to all that is evil.

Though the context in each case is secular, the terms in these descriptions of the ideal government are explicitly theological: they suggest that, though man's state is fallen, it may be possible "to repair the ruins of our first parents." [37]

The ideal in Marvell's writings is characteristically invoked in order to chart its constant violations: we are reminded of the "Divine Perfection" we threw away at our first fall to warn us of the folly of throwing it away once again. Man reenacts the fall every day. Yet the sad likelihood that he will make a desert out of a peaceful and flourishing landscape, where "the whole Land at whatsoever season of the year does yield him a plentifull Harvest," that like Eve and Satan he will succumb to the temptation of greater power and dissatisfaction with what he has, does not negate a poet's responsibility to provide a "warning voice." [38] In his satires and political writings, Marvell is a realist in recognizing the brutal cynicism with which men in power feed their insatiable wills and an idealist in urging alternative standards of conduct, in insisting that it is not yet too late:

> I will have a fine pond and a pretty Decoy
> Where the Ducks and the Drakes may their freedoms enjoy
> And quack in their language still, *Vive le Roy*.
> ("The Kings Vowes," ll. 49–51, [52–54])

It is now come to the fourth Act . . . yet men sit by, like idle Spectators, and still give money towards their own *Tragedy.*

Poetry may serve as *"Cassandra*'s Song" to warn of dangers which
may yet be avoided. The poet, with "the assistance of an heav'nly
Muse," has the courage to reveal "what Servants will conceale, and
Couns'lours spare / To tell," even though the poet's warning voice
is likely to meet the same response as Cassandra's.[39]

The extended dialogue in Marvell between hope and despair,
between the fervent belief that *"Paradice's only Map"* lies open before
us and the forlorn conviction that the world is "not, what once it
was," but a "rude heap," in which we are irreparably and irreme-
diably cut off from the good for which we long, is the dialogue at
the heart of seventeenth-century Puritanism. Both Marvell and
Milton see the situation of the blind and shorn Samson as representative, not least in his ultimate solitude. Without any certainty outside
the inner court of conscience, man can never know with any certainty
whether he has been saved. Marvell consistently emphasizes the
exposed isolation of the man who seeks to follow the imperious
demands of conscience, with its "prickling leaf" which "shrinks at
every touch": a temporary respite from the pains of existence is
possible, but essentially for Marvell the man of conscience, restless
and questioning, rejecting the voice of worldly authority in all
its forms, rejecting even the consolation of a sense of solidarity
with fellow believers, is left alone with his own unanswerable
questions.[40] The firm conviction that God directs all things does not
in itself make for serenity, since the ways of God are not only
unfathomable but often incompatible with human ideas of justice,
to say nothing of our preferences. Even those who dedicate themselves
to the service of God, "such as thou hast solemnly elected, / With
gifts and graces eminently adorn'd / To some great work," Milton
writes in *Samson Agonistes*, are often thrown down "lower then thou
didst exalt them high": "Just and unjust, alike seem miserable, / For
oft alike, both come to evil end." Even at times of prosperity, "a
thick Cloud" surrounds the workings of providence; we delude
ourselves if we think that "Heavens Choice" and our own choices
will coincide. And in moments not of promised glory but "on evil
days though fall'n, and evil tongues; / In darkness, and with dangers

compast rounds, / And solitude," the conviction that God provides for his servants is difficult indeed to sustain.[41] It is far easier to succumb to the temptation of despair, to see, as Marvell did in his later years, not a "wish'd Conjuncture" of the destined moment and the chosen people, but the actual "Conjuncture" of a tyrannous, "absolutely powerful" king, a supine parliament ("we are all venal Cowards, except some few"), and a disease seemingly spreading from the court to infect the entire nation. "In such a Conjuncture, deal *Will*," he writes to his nephew William Popple in 1670, "what Probability is there of my doing any Thing to the Purpose?"[42]

When in *Last Instructions* Marvell compares England in its state of decline to the bound Samson, there is no suggestion of a possible regeneration, no sense that the dark ways of providence will suddenly be illumined, that suffering will turn by unforeseen ways into triumph. Instead, the lines suggest only ignominy, in evoking the former greatness and potential for good which have been laid waste by man's folly and venality. The possibility is broached that the "wondrous gifts of God" will indeed be "frustrate," that God has averted his eyes from the English. In punishment for their iniquities, the English, reduced to spectators, are forced to watch the Dutch navy sail undisturbed into British waters and destroy or capture those British ships which once, "Oaken Gyants of the ancient race, / . . . rul'd all Seas."

> The Seamen search her all, within, without:
> Viewing her strength, they yet their Conquest doubt.
> Then with rude shouts, secure, the Air they vex;
> With Gamesome Joy insulting on her Decks.
> Such the fear'd *Hebrew*, captive, blinded, shorn,
> Was led about in sport, the publick scorn.

The "Black Day" of England's humiliation, so different from the "blest Day" for which Marvell had seen presages under the reign of Cromwell, is made more painful by the memory of past glories and blighted promise. The imagery of rampant disorder explicitly provides standards by which the state of England in 1667 may properly be judged, but the lines do not suggest any immediate solution, except insofar as shame may lead to a resolve to bring about change:

Thee, the Year's monster, let thy Dam devour.
And constant Time, to keep his course yet right,
Fill up thy space with a redoubled Night.
When aged *Thames* was bound with Fetters base,
And *Medway* chast ravish'd before his Face . . .
Now with vain grief their vainer hopes they rue,
Themselves dishonour'd, and the *Gods* untrue.[43]

Pain and ignominy are often the human lot, and at times no response is possible other than sterile and fruitless mourning or the recognition that all joys, all hopes are transitory: "O Thou, that dear and happy Isle . . . / What luckless Apple did we tast, / To make us Mortal, and The Wast?" Implicit in the laments for fallen England in *Upon Appleton House* and *Last Instructions*, as in those passages in *Paradise Lost*, 10, where Adam mourns his own separation from the glory, happiness, and beauty he has known, is the conviction that the "high Decrees" of God are unalterable. However much we may dislike their existence and wish them away, "seasons of Discord, War, and publick Disturbance" are inevitable consequences of the fall, along with the "Thunder, and Lightning, and Tempests" which have replaced the "standing Serenity, and perpetual Sun-shine" of the prelapsarian world:

> Ever since the first Brother Sacrificed the other to Revenge, because his Offering was better accepted, Slaughter and War had made up half the business of the World, and oftentimes upon the same quarrel, and with like success.[44]

To Marvell as to Milton, wisdom begins with the acceptance of man's fallen state: "'Tis pride that makes a Rebel. And nothing but the over-weening of our selves and our own things that raises us against divine Providence." A Samuel Parker, "swell'd like any Bladder" with pride, may feel that the earth turns round at his request, that providence has ordained all things to fit his convenience. But one major lesson the Christian learns from experience is "Humility": "A Soul that knowes not to presume / Is Heaven's and its own perfume." Only if we recognize our fallen condition and accept the limitations imposed by it, Marvell says, can we hope to transcend it.[45]

Freedom then is possible, according to Marvell, only after we
have come to learn that "the world will not go the faster for our
driving." The recognition that we can never know "where Heavens
choice may light," that all things are ruled by a providence totally
beyond our power to control, predict, or understand, that men at
all times labor in darkness, that even when we seek to serve God's
cause our efforts are likely to end in utter defeat in a world in which
injustice rules, need not lead to despair, but to a kind of exhilaration.
Freed from the distraction of false hopes, we can confront the truth
openly, without recourse to comforting evasions:

> The Grave's a fine and private place,
> But none I think do there embrace.

"The poet's time" occurs when the cause of virtue appears most
desperate, when outward fortune appears implacably hostile, when
his weaker allies have fled in dismay. It is at that time, when the
temptation to succumb to despair or to abase oneself at the altar of
success is greatest, that the poet finds courage to endure in his recognition that virtue alone is free:

> Then is the Poets time, 'tis then he drawes,
> And single fights forsaken Vertues cause.
> He, when the wheel of Empire, whirlesth back,
> And though the World's disjointed Axel crack,
> Sings still of ancient Rights and better Times,
> Seeks wretched good, arraigns successful Crimes.[46]

Notes

1. Andrew Marvell, *The Rehearsal Transpros'd and The Rehearsal Transpros'd:
The Second Part*, ed. D.I.B. Smith (Oxford: Clarendon Press, 1971), p. 145; subsequent references will be to *RT*, 1, and *RT*, 2.

2. "Tom May's Death," 30, 40, in Andrew Marvell, *Poems and Letters*, ed.
H.M. Margoliouth, rev. Pierre Legouis and E.E. Duncan-Jones, 3rd ed., 2 vols.
(Oxford: Clarendon Press, 1971). Marvell's satires have been edited by George

deF. Lord in Andrew Marvell, *Complete Poetry* (New York: Random House, 1968) and in *Poems on Affairs of State: Augustan Satirical Verse, 1660–1714*, vol. 1 (New Haven: Yale University Press, 1963). I have consulted Lord's texts for the satires, sometimes adopting his readings in preference to those of Margoliouth-Legouis.

3. Letter to William Popple, 24 July 1675, in Margoliouth, 2:341. For a useful discussion of the "political implications to different styles of art and poetry," see Earl Miner, "The 'Poetic Picture, Painted Poetry' of *The Last Instructions to a Painter*," *MP* 63 (1966): 288–94. The parallel between poetry and the visual arts is a Renaissance and neoclassical critical commonplace, deriving ultimately from the Horatian "ut pictura poesis" (*Ars Poetica*, 361); see William K. Wimsatt, Jr., and Cleanth Brooks, *Literary Criticism: A Short History* (New York: Knopf, 1957), pp. 262–67; and Jean H. Hagstrum, *The Sister Arts* (Chicago: University of Chicago Press, 1958).

4. "The Statue in Stocks-Market," l. 52; Andrew Marvell, *A Short Historical Essay touching General Councils, Creeds, and Impositions in Matters of Religion* (London, 1680), p. 19; *RT*, 2, pp. 164–65, 185. John S. Coolidge, in his interesting essay, "Martin Marprelate, Marvell, and *Decorum Personae* as a Satirical Theme," *PMLA* 74 (1959): 526–32, points out a source for Marvell's satiric strategy and concept of decorum in the Marprelate pamphlets; see also Thomas Kranidas, *The Fierce Equation* (The Hague: Mouton, 1965), pp. 49–82, for a full discussion of the contrast between "inner" and "outward" decorum in Milton's prose writings.

5. *Epilogue to the Satires: Dialogue II*, ll. 197–98, in *The Poems of Alexander Pope*, ed. John Butt (New Haven: Yale University Press, 1963).

6. John Dryden, *Of Dramatic Poesy and Other Critical Essays*, ed. George Watson, 2 vols. (London: Everyman, 1962), 2:137.

7. *RT*, 1, p. 15; 2, p. 231.

8. "A Dialogue between the Soul and Body," ll. 10, 39–40; "The Definition of Love," ll. 5, 8, 16, 23, 32; "The unfortunate Lover," ll. 2, 8; *Short Historical Essay*, p. 21. In "The unfortunate Lover," the pains and frustrations of love in the fallen realm of experience are emphasized, rather than any possible transcendence, yet here too the lover gains a form of apotheosis in resisting the forces of envious fate, "cuffing the Thunder" and dying in music (ll. 50, 63–64). The paradoxes of love are embodied in the figure of the shipwrecked lover, battling against the force of storms and waves, fed by cormorant "Hopes and Air, / Which soon digested to Despair" (ll. 33–34), yet somehow surviving even death itself; here perhaps it is the confrontation of pain which gives man his identity.

9. *RT*, 1, pp. 111–12. The parallel with "A Dialogue between the Soul and Body" hardly needs pointing out.

10. *RT*, 1, p. 135; 2, p. 231; letter to Sir John Trott, Margoliouth, 2:312.

11. *RT*, 2, p. 250. For Marvell's views on predestination, see *Remarks upon a Late Disingenuous Discourse* (London, 1678), a defense of the dissenting clergyman John Howe against attacks by more orthodox Calvinists for upholding the doctrine of free will (compatible, as in Milton, with God's "Prescience") against more rigid conceptions of "universal Predetermination" (pp. 76–77).

12. *RT*, 2, p. 243; "A Dialogue between The Resolved Soul, and Created Pleasure," ll. 1–2, 35–36; *Complete Prose Works of John Milton* (New Haven: Yale University Press, 1953–2:515.

13. Ruth Nevo, *The Dial of Virtue* (Princeton: Princeton University Press, 1963), p. 7; *Last Instructions*, ll. 390–92.

14. "First Anniversary," l. 177; *RT*, 1, p. 30; 2, p. 152.

15. *RT*, 1, p. 29; "Upon his Majesties being made free of the Citty," ll. 12–13; "The Loyall Scott," ll. 97–102 (text from Lord).

16. Andrew Marvell, *An Account of the Growth of Popery and Arbitrary Government in England* ("Amsterdam," 1677), pp. 60–61, 79.

17. Andrew Marvell, *Mr. Smirke; or, The Divine in Mode* (London, 1676), Sig. g3; *RT*, 2, pp. 267–68.

18. *Short Historical Essay*, p. 23; *Mr. Smirke*, Sig. g2ᵛ. A similar position is argued by Milton in *A Treatise of Civil Power* (1659) and by such libertarian radicals of the 1640s as Roger Williams, William Walwyn, and Henry Robinson: church membership must be entirely voluntary and the idea of a national church is an absurdity, "*God* having chosen a little *flock* out of the world, and those generally poore and meane" (Williams, *The Bloudy Tenent, of Persecution* [London, 1644], p. 134).

19. *Absalom and Achitophel*, l. 814, in *The Poems of John Dryden*, ed. James Kinsley, 4 vols. (Oxford: Clarendon Press, 1958); cf. Bernard N. Schilling, *Dryden and the Conservative Myth: A Reading of "Absalom and Achitophel"* (New Haven: Yale University Press, 1961), pp. 38–44, 256–65. The titles of *The Rehearsal Transpros'd* and *Mr. Smirke* are derived from Buckingham's *The Rehearsal* and Etherege's *The Man of Mode*. According to Burnet, "all the wits" were "on his side" in the controversy with Parker, and Marvell gained the reputation of "the liveliest droll of the age" from the two parts of *The Rehearsal Transpros'd*: even "the last king, who was not a great reader of books, read them over and over again" (quoted in Pierre Legouis, *Andrew Marvell Poet, Puritan, Patriot* [Oxford: Clarendon Press, 1965], p. 201).

20. Margoliouth, 2:324–25. On the systematic use of bribery and influence, see David Ogg, *England in the Reign of Charles II*, 2nd ed. (London: Oxford University Press, 1956), 2:529.

21. *Growth of Popery*, p. 79.

22. The lengthy mock-heroic account of the battle of the excise (*Last Instructions*, ll. 131–306), in which debtors, procurers, drinkers, martyrs to the pox, and the bloated "Troop of *Clarendon*, all full" (l. 177). pass in review, presents the institution of Parliament as having been debased by men who are ruled by physical appetite alone. A similar attack on the debasement of Parliament into a body the bulk of whose members "are onely intent how to reimburse themselves ... or how to bargine their Votes for a Place, or a Pension" may be found in *The Growth of Popery*: "All of them are received into Pension, and know their Pay-day, which they never faile of: Insomuch that a great Officer was pleased to say, *That they came about him like so many Jack daws for Cheese, at the end of every Session*" (pp. 78, 80). For an excellent account of the ideology of *The Growth of Popery*, see J.G.A. Pocock, "Machiavelli, Harrington, and English Political Ideologies in the Eighteenth Century," *William and Mary Quarterly*, 3rd ser., 22 (1965): 549–83.

23. "A Lampoon," l. 6, in *The Penguin Book of Restoration Verse*, ed. Harold Love (Harmondsworth: Penguin Books, 1968), p. 112. Cf. the vision of triumphant vice at the end of Pope's "Epilogue to the Saires: Dialogue I." The term "cheat"

and references to marked cards, loaded dice, and other methods of cheating are ubiquitous in Marvell's treatment of "the publick, game" by Charles II's ministers: see, e.g., *Last Instructions*, ll. 105–22, 179, 307–14, 367–68; *RT*, 1, p. 126; and *Growth of Popery*, pp. 6, 11, 81, 155.

24. *Growth of Popery*, p. 79.

25. *Remarks upon a Late Disingenuous Discourse*, p. 16.

26. Preface to *Absalom and Achitophel*, in *Poems*, ed. Kinsley, 1:216. Marvell has ample literary precedent in the Renaissance for urging the decorum of truthful advice to a prince. Sir Thomas Hoby, for example, writes in the "Breef Rehersall of the Chiefe Conditions and Qualities in a Courtier" appended to his translation of Castiglione's *The Courtyer* (London, 1561), Sig. Zz2^v: "The final end of a Courtier, wher to al his good condicions and honest qualities tende, is to beecome An Instructer and Teacher of his Prince or Lorde, inclininge him to vertuous practises: And to be francke and free with him ... in matters touching his honour and estimation, alwayes putting him in minde to folow vertue and to flee vice, opening unto him the commodities of the one and inconveniences of the other: And to shut his eares against flatterers, which are the first beeginninge of self seekinge and all ignorance."

27. George Savile, Marquess of Halifax, "A Character of King Charles the Second," *Complete Works*, ed. J.P. Kenyon (Harmondsworth: Penguin Books, 1969), p. 252.

28. "Tom May's Death," ll. 66, 72–73. On the "ethical proof," cf. *Mr. Smirke*, Sig. g2^v: "A great Skill of whatsoever Orator is, to perswade the Auditory first that he himself is an honest and a fair man."

29. "Tom May's Death," l. 30; "The Mower against Gardens," ll. 1, 4, 9.

30. *RT*, 1, p. 145. The source of the anecdote about Protogenes is Pliny, *Natural History*, 35:10.

31. *Last Instructions*, ll. 4–8, 12, 13; "The Statue in Stocks-Market," ll. 11–12.

32. *Growth of Popery*, p. 16. See Aristotle, *Poetics*, 1, 4, 5; and *Rhetoric*, 1.9; or, for a statement roughly contemporaneous with Marvell, Dryden, Preface to *Annus Mirabilis*, *Of Dramatic Poesy and Other Critical Essays*, 1:101.

33. "Discourse concerning Satire, ibid., 2:137; *Growth of Popery*, p. 3.

34. *Upon Appleton House*, 71:561, 76:607; *Growth of Popery*, p. 17. Much of *The Growth of Popery* consists of unedited documentary material, presented verbatim or summarized with a diarist's neutrality: e.g., "A short account of some Amunition, &c. Exported from the Port of London to France, from June, 1675. to June 1677" (p. 69). As Caroline Robbins has pointed out, the cumulative effect of this factual material, revealing what might otherwise have been kept secret, adds up to a powerful indictment: see her excellent discussion of Marvell in *The Eighteenth-Century Commonwealthsman* (Cambridge: Harvard University Press, 1959), p. 54.

35. Cf. Karl Marx, *Theses on Feuerbach*, 11. For an interesting discussion of the ideas of conscience and discipline in Puritan thought, in which Puritan ideology is seen as in some respects a precursor of Marxist ideology, see Michael Walzer, *The Revolution of the Saints* (London: Weidenfeld and Nicolson, 1966), esp. pp. 320–30. *The Growth of Popery* was written in close consultation with the Earl of Shaftesbury and other Country Party leaders, and indeed may have been in part a collaborative enterprise; see Pocock, "English Political Ideologies,"

pp. 558–67; and the Ph.D. thesis of I. Caroline Robbins, "A Critical Study of the Political Activities of Andrew Marvell" (University of London, 1926), pp. 240–41, 249–54.

36. *Upon Appleton House*, 45:355–56. A similar view of the unyielding exclusiveness of the conscience's demands is implicit in "On a Drop of Dew" and in the grim account of the history of postlapsarian man in Michael's narration, *Paradise Lost*, 11 and 12, esp. 12 ll. 82–110.

37. *RT*, 1, p. 111; *Growth of Popery*, pp. 4–5; Milton, *Of Education, Prose Works*, 2:366–67.

38. *Growth of Popery*, p. 4; *Paradise Lost*, 4:1.

39. "The Kings Vowes," ll. 49–51; *Growth of Popery*, p. 155; "Third Advice to a Painter," ll. 439–41, 447. For "The Kings Vowes" and "Third Advice to a Painter," I quote the test of Marvell, *Complete Poetry*, ed. Lord. "Third Advice" has been claimed for Marvell by Lord, "Two New Poems by Marvell?" *Bulletin of the New York Public Library* 62 (1958): 551–70, but the poem's authorship is uncertain.

40. *Upon Appleton House*, 45:357–58; 96:761–62, 768. Some of the tensions implicit in the Puritan doctrine of conscience are explored in Christopher Hill, *The World Turned Upside Down* (Harmondsworth: Penguin Books, 1975), esp. pp. 152–54, 171–73, 190–92, 370–73.

41. *Samson Agonistes*, ll. 678–80, 689, 703–704; *Paradise Lost*, 7, ll. 26–28; *The First Anniversary*, ll. 141, 147. Milton's emphasis on the temptation of despair in *Samson Agonistes* is often interpreted as a direct response to the failure of the Puritan revolution; see, e.g., M.A.N. Radzinowicz, "*Samson Agonistes* and Milton the Politician in Defeat," *Philological Quarterly* 44 (1965): 454–71, and Christopher Hill, *God's Englishman: Oliver Cromwell and the English Revolution* (Harmondsworth: Penguin Books, 1972), pp. 239–40.

42. *The First Anniversary*, l. 136; Margoliouth, 2:315, 317.

43. *Samson Agonistes*, l. 589; *First Anniversary*, l. 155; *Last Instructions*, ll. 577–78, 731–37, 740–52.

44. *Upon Appleton House*, 41:321–28; *Paradise Lost*, 10 ll. 953; *RT*, 2, pp. 231–232.

45. *RT*, 1 pp. 29–30; letter to Sir John Trott, Margoliouth, 2:312; "A Dialogue between The Resolved Soul, and Created Pleasure," ll. 29–30.

46. *RT*, 1, p. 135; *First Anniversary*, l. 147; "To his Coy Mistress," ll. 31–32; "Tom May's Death," ll. 65–70.

THE HEROIC IMAGE IN
The Last Instructions to a Painter

JOSEPH MESSINA

The Last Instructions to a Painter, which most critics consider to be Marvell's, is a poem that satirically employs the convention of a poet instructing a painter to portray an illustrious contemporary among inset portraits and narrative scenes.[1] The vogue of this convention in England was begun by Edmund Waller, who used it in a panegyric on the victory of the English forces at sea over the Dutch in June 1665. The climate of the times was such that Waller's poem occasioned several satiric replies, *Last Instructions* probably the best of them. But troubles may beset even the best in this convention, for there is not much to shape the matter of the poem in the formal devices of the dramatic relationship of the poet and the painter instructed and the discontinuous narrative, which comprises several discrete actions and is broken by portraits of various characters. Such a loose convention is prone to disunity, especially when the rowdy satirist takes it over.

Compared with some of the finest pieces of Restoration satire, *Last Instructions* is a sprawling and disjointed production.[2] But its parts are more integrated than has usually been supposed.[3] An important element of the poem is the nature of its hero, passive, childlike, and pathetic Douglas, the answer to Waller's romantic hero, the Duke of York. Though Douglas is not the central portrait on the canvas, for this is of an abstraction called "our *Lady State*," he is the superior human being against whom many other characters and their actions are measured. By means of a number of contrasting analogies, Marvell relates a good deal of his material to the idea of heroism set forth in Douglas.

Last Instructions seems deranged and disjointed because the world it mirrors is one of anarchy, animalism, and purposeless comic scurry. The crowded and bustling satiric canvas lacks guiding art, for the painter has been advised to throw it out and let the chance of anger daub this public scene worked into a raging froth by Clarendon's engineering:

> The Painter so, long having vext his cloth,
> Of his Hound's Mouth to feign the raging froth,
> His desperate Pencil at the work did dart,
> His Anger reacht that rage which past his Art;
> Chance finisht that which Art could but begin,
> And he sat smiling how his Dog did grinn.
> So may'st thou perfect, by a lucky blow,
> What all thy softest touches cannot do.

(ll. 21–28)

Of course the artist's casting out of art is a stance: Marvell himself is setting up principles of order, among them his idea of heroism. Its one intensive statement, a unified tragic action ending in death, is the gauge by which to measure the inconclusiveness of the rest of the actions depicted. And its concentrated art, culminating in the image of the hero as a work of art, is set against the painter's enraged and artless response to a world engineered to insanity.

Last Instructions is a parody, but not one concerned with ridiculing conventions. Though it resembles Waller's heroic poem and the heroic poem in general and gains by this resemblance in comic effect, the main objects of ridicule are the actual people and events of the Dutch War. Waller and others—Dryden, for example, in *Annus Mirabilis*—were treating these grandly, reverently, solemnly. Marvell's business was to debunk these supposed superheroes and their affairs; to show the stupid conduct of the war and the price of stupidity in blood and shame.

One of his means was low burlesque, a technique of degrading and pulling down the wrongly lionized by rendering them grotesquely. Usually, Marvell resorts to low burlesque when portraying the court party. Some of the portrayals naturally come as court characters are introduced into the action, but some seem simply to occur, for example the ones of St. Albans, the Duchess of York, and Lady Castlemaine, placed just after the twenty-eight lines of poet-painter frame. Of these three characters, only one, St. Albans, has a later role in any of the poem's episodes. But the early appearance of the three has a function, albeit not a narrative one.[4] These grotesques are here at the beginning as gargoyles stuck into the face of the edifice. They are gross, scabrous pictures of the party that Waller praised, here reduced to pure animalism, especially sexual animalism, as when Lady Castlemaine discerns love's cause through her lackey's drawers as he runs by her (ll. 81–82). This would be just scandal-sheet swill if it were not also a comicepiphany of debased natures whose private passions foment public disorder. Since Marvell will portray sexuality very differently in his hero, what he smears on the canvas here helps to set the court party off from the heroic, to establish his tone of amused contempt, and of course to evoke the reader's amused contempt, for "our *Lady State*" in the fits of her strange passions.

Marvell uses a gentler tactic to treat the Parliamentary opposition, his allies in purpose although not always in motive. Marvell renders the country party and its contests with the court party in Parliament mock heroically, in a style which elevates what is unheroic in itself and so which enables him to set his hero off from another kind of sham heroism. In describing those in Parliament who fought a general excise and a standing army he abandons the contempt, vulgarity, and blatant distortion of low burlesque for the counterfeit solemnity and grandeur and the good-natured comedy of the mock-heroic style. But though depicted more mercifully than his foes, Marvell's allies seem merely another aspect of the mindless chaos that England experiences. The contest in Parliament is "a Battel, from all Gun-shot free" (l. 230). Despite their appearance of vigorous activity, the heroes just talk. All the action resides in the mock-heroic machinery of war. There is in fact no war, yet the energy of tumult is transferred by the metaphor to the furious noncombatants. Consequently, their nonbattle is indistinguishable from the comic scurry and bustle of other scenes on the canvas. Moreover, to render a war of words as armed strife, the effort of minds as the heavy boom of guns and dull clank of armor, says that

mind is not at work here at all; the analogy with warfare pulls down
the mindful deciding of issues to the level of war's mindless chance:

> See sudden chance of War! To Paint or Write,
> Is longer Work, and harder than to fight.
> At the first Charge the Enemy give out;
> And the *Excise* receives a total Rout.

Thus both the unflattering portraits of the court party and this
mock-heroic narrative of clownish scurry[5] help to define the hero
of the poem by contrasting him with inferior images. The Douglas
episode of course presents the thing itself, the heroic character that
Marvell holds up for emulation. The passage on the invasion of the
Dutch Admiral de Ruyter in which it is embedded, however, is
another juxtaposing of the hero with a comic image of the heroic,
another instance of Marvell's deflation of the false to articulate the
true.

To portray any hero at all was difficult. The conception of the
age was changing: Butler had rendered a supposedly heroic order
as buffoons, and Milton had treated the conventional heroic virtues
of the warrior as humors of the devil. The stage was set for antiheroic
and antiromantic days. But Marvell, like Milton, did not simply
abandon the notion of heroism. In *An Horatian Ode* and *Upon
Appleton House* he had explored some of the ambiguities of the
political hero; here he demolishes the idea. In its stead he offers a
redefined heroism, one which, like Milton's, emphasizes virtue in
solitude rather than virtue directed outward and on public display.
The result is a hero of private self-control rather than one of the
public and political life. Such an ideal of private heroism was a
likely one to emerge from Marvell, both the lyric poet of private
contemplation and the man depressed by the spectacle of contemporary politics. And if the antiheroic age which English literature
was entering is an indication, he was part of a larger movement, one
as disillusioned by the suns of the world as he, and which was rapidly
setting about the breaking down of the mythology surrounding
them. [cf. Chernaik above-ed.]

Marvell's movement toward redefinition was probably complicated by the occasion of the poem, a war that brought on a foreign
invasion. Such circumstances would seem to call for the conventional
hero of public and martial virtue, the kind of hero that Waller had

depicted in York. But the coincidence of their heroic qualities would have made Marvell's hero seem to be akin to Waller's and so an advertisement of an inadequate ideal of heroism instead of a corrective to it.

Waller's York is a man of action, the stuff of the conventional heroic poem. Marvell's poem is also full of action, but it is far from heroic action. Marvell's method is to satirize the act and its aggressive actor. Act in *Last Instructions* is inconclusive bustling on a Breugel-like comic canvas, not the means by which heroes come to glory and good fortune. The heroism of the poem is a passive embracing of death akin to that of the *Horatian Ode*, where the royal actor Charles passively and heroically bows himself down to die while Cromwell bustles restlessly. Both Charles and Douglas are heroes of sufferance, actors only in the sense that both play tragic roles in dramas. Passive, seeming to lack the essential qualities of a hero, Douglas is, paradoxically, ripe for heroism; whereas engineering Clarendon accomplishes merely villainy, self-defeating villainy, for at last the world he has wrought turns on him to destroy him. So too Cromwell, not a villain yet one who has presumed to urge "his active Star," doomed to wield always an erect sword, is in involuntary servitude to a world of which he seems master but which in fact compels him.

The redefinition of heroism means more to Marvell than a death instead of a life of heroic action. The second face of Waller's hero York is amorous, for York, in the best romantic tradition, is a lover as well as a fighter. Marvell treats amours differently, drawing upon an older and more rigorous heroic tradition in which the exercise of sexuality often becomes a preoccupation that plucks down the aspirant to nobility of body and soul, who must use his energy for other things than the satisfaction of his instincts and appetites.[6]

Last Instructions contains many pictures of human sexuality. These range from the rustic comedy[7] of the girls kissing old Tomkins, a hero of the mock-heroic Parliamentary war:

> True *Trojan*! while this Town can Girls afford,
> And long as Cider lasts in *Hereford*;
> The Girls shall always kiss thee, though grown old,
> And in eternal Healths thy Name be trowl'd;
>
> (ll. 845–48)

to the Swiftian close-up of Lady Castlemaine at work in her massage parlor:

> Great Love, how dost thou triumph, and how reign,
> That to a Groom couldst humble her disdain!
> Stript to her Skin, see how she stooping stands,
> Nor scorns to rub him down with those fair Hands:
> And washing (lest the scent her Crime disclose)
> His sweaty Hooves, tickles him 'twixt the Toes.
>
> (ll. 91–96)

The Tomkins passage is good natured, like the treatment of the Parliamentary mock heroes in general. It is in keeping with the prevailing tones of the mock heroic; and, as a reflection on Restoration heroics, it renders comic the sexual aspect of the Cavalier hero who is both lover and warrior. Passages like the second are only partly explained as the satirist's departure from the usual point of view to focus upon the bizarre. Marvell is also presenting runaway sexuality as an image of debased human nature. The heroic nature, on the other hand, is almost preterhumanly beautiful, and of course virginal:

> ... brave *Douglas*; on whose lovely chin
> The early Down but newly did begin;
> And modest Beauty yet his Sex did Veil,
> While envious Virgins hope he is a Male.
> His yellow Locks curl back themselves to seek,
> Nor other Courtship knew but to his Cheek.
> Oft has he in chill *Eske* or *Seine*, by night,
> Harden'd and cool'd his Limbs, so soft, so white,
> Among the Reeds, to be espy'd by him,
> The *Nymphs* would rustle; he would forward swim.
> They sigh'd and said, Fond Boy, why so untame,
> That fly'st Love Fires, reserv'd for other Flame?
>
> (ll. 649–60)

Marvell departs from reality: Douglas was in fact married.[8] Ignoring this, Marvell presents the heroic character as possessing a boyish immunity to love's fires. The youth is a swimmer, not a lover, though so beautiful that the nymphs woo him in the water as Neptune wooed Leander.

The heroic character is tempered, not dissolved, by its immersion in water, but it is not so tempered as to become fit metal for the arduous combats of the warrior hero. Douglas as warrior is childishly though charmingly out of touch with the compelling realities of his circumstances. He is no warrior but a boy naively and pathetically playing at swords, holding his ground as if his clear courage were a match for the Dutch stratagem of a fire ship:

> Fixt on his Ship, he fac'd that horrid Day,
> And wondred much at those that run away:
> Nor other fear himself could comprehend,
> Then, lest Heav'n fall, e're thither he ascend.
> But entertains, the while, his time too short
> With birding at the *Dutch*, as if in sport:
> Or waves his Sword, and could he them conjure
> Within its circle, knows himself secure.
>
> (ll. 661–68)

The irony is that Douglas is inadequate only because he is artless, a primitive whose chief martial virtue is courage. This is what the echo of the primitive heroic ideal suggests: the Gauls were said to fear nothing but "lest Heav'n fall." [9] In fact it is the world in which Douglas is placed that makes him appear naive and childish. In another context he is a noble primitive. Marvell's redefinition of the hero led him to present the extinction of an old ideal, in which sleight played no part and so which could not contend with it. Notice that the only conventional heroic activity that is within Douglas's power is swimming. [10] He disdains to corrupt this art by using it o make his escape:

> That precious life he yet disdains to save,
> Or with known Art to try the gentle Wave.
>
> (ll. 671–72)

Art is the first fatality in the poem, thrown out by the painter at the beginning of the enraging task to depict the world as infernal engine driven by politic minds, whose creativity has degenerated to cunning. Poetic insight has been reduced to empiricism. The puddle-deep craft of the court party, the Dutch, the French, and others is typified in the Duchess of York, empiricist projector of the Royal Society:

> Paint then again *Her Highness* to the life,
> Philosopher beyond *Newcastle*'s Wife.
> She, nak'd, can *Archimedes* self put down,
> For an Experiment upon the *Crown*.
> She perfected that Engine, oft assay'd,
> How after Childbirth to renew a Maid.
> And found how *Royal Heirs* might be matur'd
> In fewer months than Mothers once endur'd.
> Hence *Crowder* made the rare Inventress free,
> Of's *Highnesses Royal Society*.
>
> (ll. 49–58)

When the political suns contract to such hot little globes of self-interest, their fervid and degenerate rays are soon felt by the arts of the society. Poet and painter fall to raging; idealistic depiction is abandoned; the grotesque prevails, scrupulously drawn after the image seen through telescope and microscope, tools of the artist turned to empiric demythologizing:

> Or if to score out our compendious Fame,
> With *Hook* then, through the *microscope*, take aim . . .
>
> (ll. 15–16)

> So his bold Tube, Man, to the Sun apply'd,
> And Spots unknown to the bright Star descry'd;
>
> (ll. 949–50)

In trading their humanity for fox-craft, the political engineers create the hectic element in which they are then doomed to live and move. In throwing away art, or at least in assuming the stance of enraged artlessness, the artist becomes an analogue of the debased world which has subdued him and which he has legitimized by painting in its own formless likeness. At last he breaks the circle by presenting an artful image. As he dies Douglas in his very being reestablishes poetic art. In the last lines of his drama he moves closer to artistic control with each throe of death, till finally the violence of his death is completely subdued and wrought into the serenity of art.

Just before dying Douglas ignites into aggressive sexuality, but it is a chaste mistress, heroic death, whom he embraces:

> Like a glad Lover, the fierce Flames he meets,
> And tries his first embraces in their Sheets.
>
> (ll. 677–78)

For this heroic sufferer, death is no terror but a transfiguration:

> His shape exact, which the bright flames infold,
> Like the Sun's Statue stands of burnish'd Gold.
> Round the transparent Fire about him glows,
> As the clear Amber on the Bee does close:
> And, as on Angels Heads their Glories shine,
> His burning Locks adorn his Face Divine.
>
> (ll. 679–84)

"Nothing of him that doth fade, / But doth suffer a sea-change / Into something rich and strange." The change is a glorious transformation of the human being into an incredible work of art, a passage through fantastic flames to Byzantium:

> Then, in the midst of his consummation in fire,
> . . . when in his immortal Mind he felt
> His alt'ring Form, and soder'd Limbs to melt;
> Down on the Deck he laid himself, and dy'd,
> With his dear Sword reposing by his Side.
> And, on the flaming Plank, so rests his Head,
> As one that's warm'd himself and gone to Bed.
>
> (ll. 685–90)

He is childlike again, as when he was waving his sword at the Dutch. But this time Douglas is in control, more so than when aggressive with his sword or when amorously embracing fire. His dear sword in repose, the converse of Cromwell's erect sword in the *Horatian Ode*, symbolizes his having laid aside sexual and soldierly accomplishment, those glories of the mortal state. He is apart even from the body that suffers, as from the depravity of the rest of his world; yet he is conscious that he is dying. Though he experiences his death intensely, it does not touch his deep and detached part. The prison of the mortal life is being melted down by a raging fire, yet it is as if it were being opened with the oiled key of sleep.

The poet concludes the Douglas passage by pledging to immortalize for human time him who died young and quiet (ll. 691–96). It is the one who does not act, who in his stillness suggests the serenity of art, who is lifted out of the ephemeral and mundane and placed in the gallery of history.

This remarkable passage on the Douglas is made richer by its setting amidst the idyll of de Ruyter's cruise up the Thames. Here Marvell seems to present heroism without undercutting it stylistically as he did in the passage on the Parliamentary wars, for in style the de Ruyter episode fits a hero in an idyllic world, a Calidore in a world of animate beauty and lushness. That is, the episode seems to present heroism where it should not be (at least from the English point of view), among the conquering Dutch.[11] The irony then is that this lush, nymph-haunted England is spread wide open for an unresisted foreign hero. But though the style is heroic and idyllic, several false notes suggest that de Ruyter is set up as a hero only to be taken down. In fact de Ruyter, like the court party grotesques and the Paliamentary mock heroes, is a foil to the virtues of young Douglas.

> *Ruyter* the while, that had our Ocean curb'd,
> Sail'd now among our Rivers undisturb'd:
> Survey'd their Crystal Streams, and Banks so green,
> And Beauties e're this never naked seen.
> Through the vain sedge the bashful *Nymphs* he ey'd;
> Bosomes, and all which from themselves they hide.
> The Sun much brighter, and the Skies more clear,
> He finds the Air, and all things, sweeter here.
> The sudden change, and such a tempting sight,
> Swells his old Veins with fresh Blood, fresh Delight,
> Like am'rous Victors he begins to shave,
> And his new Face looks in the *English* Wave.

(ll. 523–34)

The conquering hero has entered a pastoral haven, an oasis of renewal and refreshment.[12] But after his dip into Aeson's bath, he comes up a shaved Restoration dandy, a wanton rendition of Douglas's virtue of innocent youth. Entranced by the fleeting nymphs by whom Douglas swam, de Ruyter collapses into a heap of amorousness, an Antony in Egypt. His warlike navy, meanwhile, is transformed into a fleet of party boats with other twisted versions of Douglas festooned in the rigging:

> His sporting Navy all about him swim,
> And witness their complaisance in their trim.
> Their streaming Silks play through the weather fair,
> And with inveigling Colours Court the Air. . . .
> Among the Shrowds the Seamen sit and sing,
> And wanton Boys on every Rope do cling.
>
> (ll. 535–42)

The insult to the English is analogous to a sexual one. Worse yet, it is not even a hearty and robust sexuality that the Dutch represent but a kind of poking and probing as of a great and stately lady standing naked upon the auctioneer's block. Here they debase the British flagship:

> [The Dutch] To *Ruyter*'s Triumph lead the captive *Charles*.
> The pleasing sight he often does prolong: . . .
> And all admires, but most his easie Prey.
> The Seamen search her all, within, without:
> Viewing her strength, they yet their Conquest doubt.
> Then with rude shouts, secure, the Air they vex;
> With Gamesome Joy insulting on her Decks.
>
> (ll. 726–34)

This is what must happen to "our *Lady State*" when she starts sitting for obscene portraits, or rather when Englishmen so pose her. The failure of the English, imaged by Marvell throughout as sexual depravity, has stripped them of their heroic virtues; and English women, the partners of their men in depravity and decay, have called upon themselves this insulting searching.

Meanwhile, Douglas burns. But his alchemical sacrifice is in vain. For at the end of the poem, as the polluted king, who should be the source of heroism, sits silent in his chamber, there appears

> ... a sudden Shape with Virgins Face,
> Though ill agree her Posture, Hour, or Place;
> Naked as born, and her round Arms behind,
> With her own Tresses interwove and twin'd:
> Her mouth lockt up, a blind before her Eyes,
> Yet from beneath the Veil her blushes rise;
> And silent tears her secret anguish speak,
> Her heart throbs, and with very shame would break.
>
> (ll. 891–98)

This is of course England, presented as if she were a captive virgin brought in abject, bound, naked, to the bedchamber of some rude and randy conqueror.

> The Object strange in him no Terrour moved:
> He wonder'd first, then pity'd, then he lov'd:
> And with kind hand does the coy Vision press,
> Whose Beauty greater seem'd by her distress;
> But soon shrunk back, chill'd with her touch so cold,
> And th' airy Picture vanisht from his hold.
> In his deep thoughts the wonder did increase,
> And he Divin'd 'twas *England* or the *Peace*.
>
> (ll. 899–906)

The two figures together seem to form a marvellous emblem of a land in distress being viewed by its ruler, until the king moves within the emblem, breaking it out of sexual desire, and so forms another emblem, this one revealing what he is actually doing to the land. His responses to this emblematic figure, this vision of the shame and pain which motivate the poet, descend till they echo the obscene Dutch groping. The irony of his royal divining of the figure's meaning once its sexual presence has been removed is dismaying indeed.

Though writing a poem about a war, Marvell chose not a warrior hero but a victim whose death arouses pathos, like the death of young Siward at the hands of the grizzled veteran Macbeth. One reason why Marvell created such a hero was that he loathed the Dutch War, seeing it as the plaything of Clarendon that was sapping his country. Yet the war went on, and his beloved England was invaded. To have created as England's embodied reaction to this assault a Cavalier hero, a glamorous and charismatic fighter and lover like Waller's York, would have been to glorify the war. A hero was needed, but one of a different sort, one who would excite not admiration for his prowess and rejoicing for his fortunate event but pathos for his boyish innocence and vulnerability. For pathetic, not admirable and fortunate, was the plight of England as Marvell saw it.

At the same time that Marvell created a hero fitted to the immediate emotional tenor of his land, he also followed a broader directive, one which brought his hero into conformity with a heroism like that of the martyred Charles in his own poetry, the reexamination of heroism in Butler, and the heroism of sufferance in Milton. The result was a satirizing of certain heroic postures and an elevation of a passive, suffering hero. Like the death of Charles, which is rendered as tragic drama, the death of Douglas is art of the stage, and the hero of the piece is himself distilled into art. While the audience of Charles's death is armed bands, that of Douglas is but one man, General Monk, in the stage of whose eyes Douglas joys to die (ll. 675–76). His death is practically a private affair, not a public display of virtue. It is this private passion, this one man dying in the sight of one of his fellows, that Marvell draws into the arena of public virtue and the sight of all.

Notes

1. For an example of the pictorial representation which painter poems draw upon, see George deF. Lord, *Poems on Affairs of State* (New Haven: Yale University Press, 1963), 1, the plate facing p. 124. Earl Miner discusses the relationships of the pictorial and the poetic conventions in "The 'Poetic Picture, Painted Poetry' of *The Last Instructions to a Painter*," MP 53 (1966): 288–94, reprint ed. *Andrew Marvell: A Collection of Critical Essays*, ed. George deF. Lord (Englewood Cliffs, N.J.: Prentice-Hall, 1968), pp. 165–74. See also Miner's *The Restoration Mode from Milton to Dryden* (Princeton: Princeton University Press, 1974), pp. 400–404.

2. Alan S. Fisher, in an article on the lyric qualities of *Last Instructions*, sums up a general view: "The great problem of *Last Instructions* is described in one word: sprawl" ("The Augustan Marvell: *The Last Instructions to a Painter*," ELH 38 (1971):

224). This is essentially the view of James Sutherland in *English Literature of the Late Seventeenth Century* (Oxford: Oxford University Press, 1969), p. 163. Earl Miner ("The 'Poetic Picture, Painted Poetry' of *The Last Instructions to a Painter*") and John Wallace (*Destiny His Choice*, Cambridge: Cambridge University Press, 1968, pp. 157–63) seem to acknowledge the sprawl, but they find precedent or theoretic justification of it, Miner in the graphic genres and Wallace in the literary.

3. There are exceptions to the usual judgment. Ephim G. Fogel maintains that *Last Instructions* has "close-knit imaginative unity, fine proportioning of parts, [and] continuous drive and relevance" ("Salmons in Both, or Some Caveats for Canonical Scholars," *Bulletin of the New York Public Library* 63 [1959]: 302). Harold Toliver, though feeling that Marvell was unable to hold everything in *Last Instructions* together in one mood, shows that the pastoral theme, as a corrective formula, welds the Douglas section to the concluding admonition to the king (*Marvell's Ironic Vision*, New Haven: Yale University Press, 1965, pp. 208–11). Michael Gearin-Tosh claims that Marvell's "graphic enterprise" controls and determines a structure of "genuine distinction" ("The Structure of Marvell's *Last Instructions*," *EIC* 22 [1972]: 48–56). James Quivey examines Marvell's rhetorical technique, especially the poet-painter frame, and concludes that the poem is less a "scattershot" than appears ("Rhetoric and Frame: A Study of Method in Three Satires by Marvell," *TSL* 18 [1973]: 75–91).

4. George deF. Lord feels that "No connection is established between these figures, and only St. Albans appears later in the poem." The other two are "sketched and then abandoned" ("Comments on the Canonical Caveat," *Bulletin of the New York Public Library* 63 [1959]: 360). My point is that they are blood relatives, three of a family of grotesques, and are used as part of a group of negative analogues, or foils. Such a function, though not a narrative one, is perfectly legitimate in an artistic structure.

5. I do not discuss the meeting of Parliament toward the end of the poem (ll. 807–62), for it is essentially a comic fiasco like the first meeting.

6. I am adapting the remarks of Ernst Curtius on the goals and distinguishing marks of the heroic type. See *European Literature and the Latin Middle Ages*, trans. Willard R. Trask (Princeton: Princeton University Press, 1953), reprint ed. Bollingen Series, 36 (Princeton University Press, 1973), p. 167.

7. So characterized, aptly I think, by Fisher, "The Augustan Marvell," p. 231.

8. I draw my information from the notes in Margoliouth.

9. Margoliouth's note.

10. Swimming is a heroic exercise in many cultures and literatures. Marvell would have known of its being so considered by Horace among classical authors (*Odes* 1.8) and by Castiglione and Sir Thomas Elyot among modern. For Elyot it is "right profitable in exstreme daunger of warres." *The Boke Named The Gouernour*, ed. Foster Watson (New York: E.P. Dutton & Co., 1907), 1.17, p. 75.

11. The view of Fisher, "The Augustan Marvell," pp. 232–33. See also Gearin-Tosh, "The Structure of Marvell's *Last Instructions*," pp. 52–54.

12. The pastoralism of *Last Instructions* is more fully, and differently, treated by Toliver, pp. 204–13.

CONTRIBUTORS

MURIEL C. BRADBROOK is the Mistress of Girton College, Cambridge, where she has taught for many years. She has authored numerous books, including *Elizabethan Stage Conditions* (1933), *Themes and Conventions of Elizabethan Tragedy* (1935), *The School of Night* (1936), *Andrew Marvell* (1940, with M.G. Lloyd Thomas), and more recently, *Shakespeare and Elizabethan Poetry* (1951), *The Growth and Structure of Elizabethan Comedy* (1955), and the *Rise of the Common Player: A Study of Actor and Society in Shakespeare's England* (1962). Professor Bradbrook has also written books about T.S. Eliot and Henrik Ibsen. Her most recent book is *The Living Monument: Shakespeare and The Theatre of Her Time.* (1976).

WARREN L. CHERNAIK is Lecturer in English at Queen Mary College, University of London. He has taught previously at the University of Massachusetts-Boston, Boston University, City College of New York, the University of North Wales, Ohio State University, and Yale University. He is author of *The Poetry of Limitation: A Study of Edmund Waller* (1968) and has published articles on Restoration satire.

THOMAS CLAYTON took his doctorate at Oxford in 1960 as a Rhodes Scholar and has taught at Yale and UCLA as well as at the University of Minnesota, Minneapolis, where he has been Professor of English since 1970. He is editor of the Oxford English Text *The Non-Dramatic Works of Sir John Suckling* (1971) and the forthcoming Oxford Standard Authors edition of *Cavalier Poets,* and is author of the Center for Shakespeare Studies monograph on *The "Shakespearean" Addition to the Booke of Sir Thomas Moore.* He has also authored numerous articles on Shakespeare and on textual and literary criticism, including Marvell (*ELR,* 1972).

ELIZABETH STORY DONNO currently teaches in the Department of English and Comparative Literature at Columbia University. She has prepared scholarly editions of *Sir John Harington's Metamorphosis of Ajax* (1962), *Elizabethan Minor Epics* (1963), *The Complete Poems of Andrew Marvell* (1972), and is the editor of *Renaissance Quarterly.*

FRENCH FOGLE is William W. Clary Professor of History and English Literature at the Claremont Graduate School in Claremont, California. He taught formerly at Columbia University, where he took his doctorate, and also at Barnard College, College of the City of New York, and New York University. He has also been a Senior Research Associate at the Henry E. Huntington Library in San Marino, California, editor of the *Huntington Library Quarterly* from 1952–57. His chief publications include *An Index to the Complete Works of John Milton* (1940), which he edited with F.A. Patterson; *A Critical Study of William Drummond of Hawthornden* (1952), his edition of *The Complete Poetry of Henry Vaughan* (1964; rev. 1969), and his edition of Milton's *History of Britain* in Volume 5 of the *Complete Works of John Milton* published by the Yale University Press, (1970).

KENNETH FRIEDENREICH (editor) is Assistant Professor of English at the University of Texas at San Antonio. He taught previously at the State University of New York at Stony Brook, where he earned his doctorate. Author of a study of Henry Vaughan, forthcoming in the Twayne's English Authors Series, he has also published on a variety of Renaissance subjects, including essays on Marlowe, Nashe, Milton, and Elizabethan Drama. Professor Friedenreich is also a freelance journalist who has contributed to *Newsday* and the *New York Times*. He is currently preparing a study of nativity poems of English Renaissance, and an annotated bibliography of Marlowe scholarship since 1950.

JOHN HACKETT teaches medieval and modern literature at the University of Texas at San Antonio, where he is Director of the Composition and Humanities Program. He taught formerly at the University of Missouri at St. Louis and at Wesleyan University, where he was Master of East College and Fellow of the Center for the Humanities.

ISABEL G. MACCAFFREY teaches at Harvard University, where she is Kenan Professor of History and Literature. Her most recent work, *Spenser's Allegory*, was published in 1976 by the Princeton University Press.

JOSEPH MESSINA teaches at Quincy College in Quincy, Illinois. Previously, he has taught at Hofstra University and the State University of New York at Stony Brook. At present he is writing a study of dramatic satire in the English Renaissance.

JOSEPH PEQUIGNEY is currently Associate Professor of English at the State University of New York at Stony Brook. He has also taught at Rice University and M.I.T., and was a teaching fellow at Harvard University, where he received his doctorate. He holds other degrees from Notre Dame and the University of Minnesota. He has written articles on Milton and (with Hubert Dreyfus) on Dante.

MAREN-SOFIE RØSTVIG is Professor of English Literature at the University of Oslo. She has published widely, including *The Happy Man: Studies in the Metamorphoses of a Classical Ideal*, Vol. 1, 1600–1700; Vol. 2, 1700–1760 (1954, 1958; rev. eds. 1962, 1971). She has contributed to numerous anthologies, including "Marvell and the Caroline Poets" in *The Sphere of History of Literature in the English*

Language (1970) and "Images of Perfection" in *Seventeenth-Century Imagery* (1971). She is editor of *Fair Forms: Essays in English Literature from Spenser to Jane Austen*, published in 1975, and is currently at work on *Configurations: Conceptual Structure in Renaissance Poetry*. She earned her doctorate at UCLA.

JOSEPH H. SUMMERS is the author of *The Muse's Method: An Introduction to Paradise Lost* (1962), *George Herbert: His Religion and Art* (1968), *The Heirs of Donne and Jonson* (1970), editor of selections of Marvell's and Herbert's poems and editor of *The Lyric and Dramatic Milton*. He has taught at Bard College, The University of Connecticut, Washington University in St. Louis, University of Massachusetts-Amherst, Michigan State University, University of Kent (Canterbury), and was Fulbright Professor in the English Faculty and Visiting Fellow at All Souls, Oxford, 1966–67. He wrote his essay for this volume while on a fellowship at the Folger Shakespeare Library during the spring of 1976. He is Roswell S. Burrows Professor of English at the University of Rochester and presently is at work on Shakespeare.

HAROLD TOLIVER wrote *Marvell's Ironic Vision* (1965). He has returned to Marvell in *Pastoral Forms and Attitudes* (1971), and is doing so again in *The Past that Poets Make*, now in progress. After stints at Ohio State University and UCLA, Professor Toliver now teaches at the University of California at Irvine.